Registerir

C000142894

MANCHESTER
UNIVERSITY PRESS

Registering the difference

Reading literature through register

Lance St John Butler

Manchester University Press

Manchester and New York

distributed exclusively in the USA by St. Martin's Press

Copyright © Lance St John Butler 1999

The right of Lance St John Butler to be identified as the author of
this work has been asserted by him in accordance with the Copyright,
Designs and Patents Act 1988.

Published by Manchester University Press,
Oxford Road, Manchester M13 9NR, UK
and Room 400, 175 Fifth Avenue, New York, NY 10010, USA
http://www.man.ac.uk/mup

Distributed exclusively in the USA by
St. Martin's Press, Inc., 175 Fifth Avenue, New York,
NY 10010, USA

Distributed exclusively in Canada by
UBC Press, University of British Columbia, 6344 Memorial Road,
Vancouver, BC, Canada V6T 1Z2

British Library Cataloguing-in-Publication Data
A catalogue record for this book is available from the British Library

Library of Congress Cataloging-in-Publication Data applied for

ISBN   0 7190 5613 6 *hardback*
       0 7190 5614 4 *paperback*

First published 1999

06 05 04 03 02 01 00 99   10 9 8 7 6 5 4 3 2 1

Typeset by Lucy Morton & Robin Gable, Grosmont
Printed in Great Britain by Bell & Bain Ltd, Glasgow

For Debbie, Alice and Miranda,
not forgetting Holly, Clashie, Humbug and Freddie

Contents

Acknowledgements   viii

Introduction   1

part I   **Reading for register**

chapter 1   Noticing a difference   5

chapter 2   The history (and the hijacking) of register   24

chapter 3   Two big distinctions: written/spoken
and formal/informal   49

part II   **The ways register works**

chapter 4   Registers of culture and power   75

chapter 5   Literary register   95

chapter 6   Register and genre   121

chapter 7   Translating register   132

part III   **Case studies**

chapter 8   'Pestling the unalterable whey of words':
Samuel Beckett's attempt at unstyle   149

chapter 9   Register and dialect: Thomas Hardy's voices   170

chapter 10   'Singing, each to each': sounding like poetry   190

Select bibliography   212

Index   214

Acknowledgements

I would like to thank the following people, associated with English Department at the University of Stirling in Scotland, for their help with this book: Bethan Benwell, Judy Delin, Nicholas Royle, Robin Sowerby and Pauline Morgan. Also Alastair Weir of Kippen.

Introduction

There are two dominant strands of thinking among people working on literature at the close of the twentieth century – theory and stylistics. In this book I try to borrow a concept from linguistics (the concept is register) to help readers of literary texts, so I am 'doing' stylistics, and I have tried to make it a humane stylistics. Translated into a more up-to-date register, 'humane' would become 'user-friendly', which is acceptable, but the main burden of 'humane' in this context is that it is respectfully separated from 'scientific'. Linguistics is surely a science of sorts; my point is that literary reading may not be scientific, but that it can none the less benefit from work done in linguistics.

While I come from the direction of linguistics, however, I have also tried to keep the windows open towards theory, itself the offspring of structuralist linguistics, which, in its post-structuralist manifestation, has had such enormous power. I nearly wrote 'enormous explanatory power' there, but decided not to. The point is that theory has had, famously, a deconstructive rather than an *explanatory* effect. Of course, one could claim that observing the undecidabilities in a text is also a way of 'explaining' it, but most readers will understand what I mean: post-structuralist thinking has deliberately and very effectively muddied the waters, multiplied meaning, given us the freedom of the text, historicised both writing and reading ('production' and 'consumption'), upset all applecarts. This is healthy and hard to fault (can one not always deconstruct the position from which the objector to deconstruction is objecting?), but it is not exactly the same as 'explaining' texts in the way that common sense used to do this.

Thus a tension arises where one might have hoped to effect a marriage. Theory is centrifugal and suspicious of fixable meaning (witness Derrida's attack on origins and the mythology of the centre, and his theories of *'dissémination'* and *'différance'*), while stylistics is inclined to seek 'rigorous' and scientific ways of seeing what a text means. It can thus be put in the service of a centripetal project. Many stylisticians now try to avoid being this definite, and increasingly Anglo-American stylistics is aware of Franco-American theory. But the structural problem remains: stylistics wants meaning; theory wants undecidability.

The 'solution' – if that is not too strongly charged a word – is that *meanings*, those plural entities available even in the most heady theory, are a burgeoning, rioting Brazilian jungle to be tamed (though they can never be *tamed*), or at least made sense of, with the aid of the jungle-viewing equipment provided by stylistics; while *meaning* – the big one, the Truth, the Explanation – forever eludes us. In that last phrase I suppose I have slipped into a cliché, a rather misty-eyed romanticism of things that 'forever elude' humanity – it is mythological, this 'meaning', and the wistful search for it is just another game; stylistics tells us of the cliché, theory of the mythology from which it comes, and which it supports.

This is not exactly a marriage, then, but it does suggest some sort of partnership, which seems fashionable enough for a period in which all spouses seem to have become partners.

Workpoints

At the end of each of the chapters of this book you will find a short section entitled 'Workpoints'. These are intended to supply material for use in the further consideration of register by general readers, lecturers and students. They are, I hope, a less awkward version of the 'exercises' that one sometimes finds in books of this kind.

Part I

Reading for register

I

Noticing a difference

Introducing a useful term

There is a joke, doubtless apocryphal, that I have heard once or twice in recent years. It is the one about the Cavalry officer who returns from Dunkirk in 1940 and is asked about his experiences in that dreadful rout; he replies, 'My dear, the noise! And the *people!*' Well-told this can be quite funny, though it doesn't come across as all that hilarious on the printed page; but why is it funny? What is the 'point' of this joke?

I suggest that the humour stems from the obvious mismatch between the event being talked about and the *way* it is being talked about; there is something wrong with a reaction to the chaos and slaughter of the Dunkirk beaches that concentrates on how loud the bangs were, and on the social and other shortcomings of the speaker's fellow-soldiers. The joke has the same structure of humour, perhaps, as the post-1963 familiar one-liner 'And apart from that, how did you like Dallas, Mrs Kennedy?' Murder, tragedy, horror on the one side, and shallow tourist questioning on the other: a mismatch.

But there is something else too. If we recast these jokes in a less carefully crafted form, they lose almost all of their humour. If the man returning from Dunkirk is made to say, 'It was a bit noisy, and I met some awful people', a lot of the edge goes out of the story; similarly, if the question to Mrs Kennedy goes 'Although your husband was murdered there, did you like Dallas?', it seems a very weak effort. So there is something more than a mismatch of 'content' here; there is also a mismatch of tone or *style* or *language used*. The image created by the words 'My dear' is of a rather camp individual speaking in a fairly artificial social environment, sound-ing like a character in a play, 'putting it on' in some way; his style of speech is 'wrong' in the situation, quite apart from what he is saying. There is an implicit meaning in this deliberate wrongness.

His emphatic noun phrases (The noise! The *people!*) belong to a recognisable mode of speech that reminds us of Lady Bracknell in *The Importance of Being Earnest* and they are, surely, coded as (upper-class) elderly-female rather than as youngish-male which, again, is 'wrong' coming from the mouth of a soldier just back from the France of 1940.[1]

What we are facing in these jokes is something very common in humour – mismatch, the unexpected, a misunderstanding of the situation – but we need a term with which to get hold of the precise shift in tone, style and language here. The term we need is to be found in linguistics, and it is 'register'. A register is a way of speaking or writing that suits a given situation, that has identi-fiable features which will immediately stand out if the situation is wrong. As we shall see later in this book, various linguists – prime among them Michael Halliday – have developed a sophisticated system of definitions around the term register, a system so complex that they would immediately object to my term 'way of speaking or writing'. 'Register cannot be summarised as simply as that', they would say – and we shall have to deal with this problem in due course. But for the moment, the important thing is to see that this book is an appeal for a relatively simple and user-friendly notion of register, a term I wish to rescue from the clutches of an often impenetrable linguistics.

The jokes quoted show a mismatch, something wrong in what is said. This 'something wrong' is not a mismatch in *language* in the sense that the speaker has switched from English to Dutch or Mongolian (as in the old *Punch* cartoon of two men meeting; one says 'Robinson, or I'm a Dutchman!'; the other, looking puzzled, '*Goeden morgen mijnher*'), nor is it a mismatch in *dialect* (as in the joke about there being a moose/mouse loose, which depends on the different meaning of 'moose', when the word is pronounced by someone with a Scots accent). It is a mismatch in *register*.

We do not speak 'language', we speak English or French or Swahili. Then we do not just 'speak English', we speak our dialect of English: Australian, Yorkshire, Canadian or Scots. But then –

adding the crucial third level – we do not just speak a dialect, we always, at every point in our discourse, speak in a particular register. The reaction to Dunkirk that we expect, especially from someone who has been through it, has certain qualities of seriousness about it, an attention to deeper and more desperate issues than those around noise abatement (now noise pollution – language never stays still) or the class system ('the *people*' here are, if nothing else, of a lower class than the speaker). And it would have to be couched in appropriate tones, in an appropriate style ('It was truly terrible'), with suitable narrative interludes ('One of my friends was shot in the water…'), with the right vocabulary ('The Luftwaffe machine-gunned whole regiments as they stood there'). I do not think this has much to do with 'English' *as a language* (in contrast, say, to Chinese), nor does it have much to do with dialect. It amounts, rather, to a suitable register for the discussion of warfare. Of course, as the joke demonstrates, we don't have to stick to the 'right' register all the time, but it is none the less in some sense inescapable, because if we choose to ignore the register that our culture regards as appropriate we are unavoidably making a point, or making a joke, or cocking a snook at something; all register choice involves choosing an option for a purpose. And register, like language and dialect, is universal.

My purpose here is to promote register, to show how useful it is as a concept and to suggest how readers of literary texts, in particular, can benefit from it as a tool for understanding what they read. I would hope to raise the consciousness of readers so that the enormous benefits from noticing register and pondering its significance become more or less an automatic part of the reading process. The concept itself is not new, as I have indicated, but it has been rather swamped by Hallidayan linguistics, and thus lost to view. This is especially likely in the case of students of literature who may not be fully conversant with work in systemic-functional linguistics, and even if they are may find that the treatment of register in those and other kinds of linguistics to be more a hindrance than a help to them.

When register first came on the scene as a concept in the 1950s and 1960s (a short history of it is given in Chapter 2), the definitions used were adequate for literary reading. If we had stuck to those we could have got full value from the term, and although

I am not objecting to the further use made of the concept by linguisticians *for their own purposes*, since those days, I would prefer for literary purposes to use the term in the old, straightforward way. Here are Jean Ure and Jeffrey Ellis writing in 1972; this is the opening of their article on 'Register in descriptive linguistics and linguistic sociology': 'Register is a certain kind of language patterning regularly used in a certain kind of situation. It is a social convention.'[2] That may be enough to start with, and it is certainly a good basic idea to hold on to. The words 'patterning' and 'regularly' indicate that we do not have to make do with the vaguenesses of 'style' or 'tone', but can say fairly precisely how this 'convention' works.

I started with jokes, and my aim is to discuss literary uses of register (a joke is a small piece of oral literature, a mini-text), but it is worth taking some examples from non-literary everyday life to establish how registers work; after all, we are always using language in 'a certain kind of situation', and we all know – or at our peril ignore – the 'social conventions' that govern our speech and writing.

You go to your doctor with a pain in your arm; she feels your muscles and joints for a while and asks some questions, then she says, 'I think you've got a nasty case of tennis elbow'. She next picks up her dictaphone and says into it something like 'Acute bursitis of right upper limb'. What has happened is that, although she is saying the same thing twice, she has switched from one register to another, and the reasons are pretty obvious: speaking to the patient, the doctor wants to use the most commonly understood name of the complaint so as to avoid misunderstanding; she also wants to seem a little tentative ('I think') so as to avoid the impression of excessive certainty or arrogance, and she wants to indicate a little sympathy ('nasty'). Equally, she is concerned to use a form, the second person 'you', that directly addresses the patient, and a verb ('got') that is highly typical of spoken rather than written English. All this makes her comment colloquial, friendly, comprehensible to the patient. None of this is required, of course, when she dictates a note to herself. Now she needs to specify the medical condition in the formal terms required by her profession, and she has no need to soften the information with colloquial or soothing language features; no verb appears, and the vocabulary employed is barely comprehensible to the layperson, although another doctor, coming in as locum (have I gone into too technical a register using that word?), will be able to understand the patient's problem perfectly. In my experience the doctor would be more likely to *write* the note about acute bursitis, on a file; indeed, the point of a dictaphone is to facilitate the creation of written text, so there seems to be a spoken/written distinction in play here.

Try writing in the way you speak or speaking in the way you write, and you will find it surprisingly hard; you may also lose a few friends.

Sociologists would recognise the point being made here as an example of 'code-switching', which is something that happens in all cultures. In some cases it might involve changing from one language to another – Russian aristocrats spoke French among themselves, at least on some occasions, but Russian to their servants; Catholics, or at least Catholic clergy, used to address God in Latin but each other in their vernacular; in other cases code-switching could be across dialects – as when, as we shall see, Thomas Hardy used both the Standard English and Wessex dialects in the course of the same novel (and in his own life). But most code-switching in the English-speaking world today involves changes of register.

Thus we expect one kind of English in a letter from the bank and another in a romantic love scene in a film; one English is suitable for talking to small children, another for lecturing on astrophysics. The differences are endless.

A register that most of us have had to come to terms with in recent years is computerese. It is fairly clear that at a given date sometime after the 1960s a 'whole new language' (as one might say in colloquial English) developed to cope with the rise in importance and complexity of computers. Here is a small dose of this register from a computer manual aimed at the non-technical 'lay' user of the most popular program of the 1990s:

> To create a new document, click the Start A New Document button on the Office Shortcut Bar. The New dialog box appears, containing templates for all office applications. When you use a template to create a document, the new document is a copy of the template and has no name. When you save it, the Save As dialog box appears so you can give the new document a unique name. The original template remains unchanged.[3]

Most computer-users of the end of the twentieth century will be able to make some sense of this, but it is worth pondering the implications of the fact that at the end of the nineteenth century nobody at all would have been able to make head or tail of it. The capitals ('Save As', for instance) signal a technical register being used, but other terms, not so signalled, carry special meanings too: 'create', 'button', 'applications', and so on. Typically of a new register, these terms have meanings already, meanings that were perfectly familiar to our grandparents, but they have different meanings here which require a knowledge of the register of computer-speak to make any useful sense at all in the new context.

There's nothing very sinister in this sort of development, though it will undoubtedly irritate outsiders, those who haven't, precisely, learnt the language. It is noticeable, incidentally, that the main difference between computerese and 'normal English' is at the level of lexis – that is, vocabulary. The grammar and syntax and other stylistic features of the passage are not very different from those of 'normal English', but the lexis is at once impenetrable to a non-initiate. One could not say that the passage was not in *English*, nor could one complain that it was in a difficult *dialect*. The word needed is *register*.

Hearing with a public ear

Here is an example from the satirical magazine *Private Eye*, which bases a large part of its humorous appeal on creating mismatches between form and content or between disparate pieces of news and pseudo-news. Dealing with the mid-1990s negotiations between Israel and Palestine aimed at securing peace in the Middle East, *Private Eye* ran a series of spoof articles such as the following; this one deals with a scandal that beset Benjamin Netenyahu, the Prime Minister of Israel elected in 1996, in connection with the behaviour of his current wife:

THE BOOK OF BENJAMIN WHO IS CALLED NETENYAHU

1. And lo, it came to pass that Benjamin ruled over the land of Israel.
2. And the wife of Benjamin was called Sarah.
3. And she was the third of his wives and fair to look upon as the rose that bloometh in the Gardens of Hebron.

4. Now Sarah was a handmaiden of El-Al and she cometh among the businessmen of the Land of Israel who flieth through the air.

5. And she telleth them that the emergency exodus are to the fore and aft of the air ship of the desert. And they taketh no notice.

6. And when the businessmen are sore weary of the journey Sarah handeth them a hot towel. (*That's enough in-flight stuff. Ed.*)

7. And Benjamin spoke unto the children of Israel, seeking to gain popularity like unto the leader of the Land of Am-erica, that is to the one whom is called Clintstone.

8. And he sayeth: 'Look upon my comely wife, men of Israel. Doth she not remind you a bit of Barbra Streisand? Vote for me.'

9. And the children of Israel did rejoice and did cast their votes in favour of Benjamin.

10. But the Mediaites waxed wroth for they discovered that Sarah, the wife of Benjamin, had driven from her house a handmaiden that had burnt the soup prepared for the children of Benjamin....[4]

and so it goes on. The joke depends on our recognising that there is a very specific text being brought into play: the King James Bible of 1611, the Authorised Version. From the register established in that text, and in particular from the Old Testament as it appears there, we get such features as: sentences starting repeatedly with 'And'; numbered verses; the archaic 'th' ending for the third-person singular ('bloometh'); such locutions as 'it came to pass', 'sore weary' and 'waxed wroth'; 'that' for 'which'; and other direct quotations. The 1611 Bible is so widely known, and has affected the cadences and lexical choices of so much of the English language, that it is not too much to claim that there is such a thing as 'biblical register' . It certainly isn't hard to spot, nor is it hard to spot the other register that is set against it in this pastiche: a flying ('in-flight', indeed) register is sketched in with 'El-Al', 'flieth', 'air', 'emergency exodus' and 'hot towel'. The editor (reduced, as in journalese or publishing register to 'Ed.') is conscious of this 'in-flight stuff', and obviously feels that it is not well enough integrated into the 'biblical', narrative in spite of its light disguise ('exodus' for 'exits', 'flieth' for 'fly').

The trick here is to mix registers as thoroughly as possible, so that the anachronistic 'America' is rendered biblical by having one of its syllables separated off in the manner of some Bibles that are printed this way to help with pronunciation. And Netenyahu's appeal to the voters is bathetically colloquial and vote-grabbing ('remind you a bit of Barbra Streisand. Vote for me') while trying to stick to the proper register ('And he sayeth', 'look upon', 'comely', 'does she not').

In this example, as in all others, one way of establishing register would be to 'translate' the passage into a different register. Thus, for instance, the first three sentences from the *Private Eye* article could be recast something like this: 'Sarah Netenyahu, attractive third wife of Israel's newly elected Prime Minister Benjamin Netenyahu...'. Most readers would have little difficulty in concluding that this is a version of the story in journalese, the beginning of a newspaper article that will give us the scandalous story in easily digestible form. Some features of this register are apparent even from so short an example: three sentences in 'biblical' have become less than one in journalese; the information is packaged so that we know at once what the 'angle' is – it's Sarah we are going to read about here, not her husband as in the *Private Eye* version; and of course Netenyahu is 'elected' rather than ruling, because of changed political conditions in Israel since biblical times. Above all there is a sense of haste, of packing in as much information as possible, which implies a busy readership quite different from the more stately or leisurely register suitable for religious contemplation or descriptions of the acts of God. In fact what has happened in the spoof article is that the original news story has been partially and imperfectly translated into pastiche-biblical register. We shall return to this matter of translatability, but in the meantime it is worth pointing out that understanding the *Private Eye* article now seems to depend on knowledge of several registers: biblical, 'in-flight', editorial, journalistic and even some others that are only briefly hinted at, such as naval ('fore and aft'), clichéd geographical ('the ship of the desert'), and so on.

You might ask: Why use 'register' to cover all these things? The answer is to think of the alternative: if we avoid a term like register, we narrow the field of meaning unacceptably because then we are committed to saying something like 'There's a pun here on exit/exodus' or that 'Clintstone' is a portmanteau word that brings together the name of President Clinton and the cartoon characters The Flintstones. Such points are undoubtedly *true*, but they are surely not enough by way of explanation of what is going on here. It must be subtler, broader and more in keeping with the way the mind moves rapidly across a wide range of meanings to stress that 'exit' isn't a stand-alone word that just happens to mean 'Way Out', and that 'Exodus' isn't merely the name of a major event in the early books of the Old Testament. 'Exit' comes complete with several sets of associations, one of them to do with air travel; while 'Exodus' comes with a whole baggage of stories, impressions, biblical developments, even films, from which it cannot be detached. We are not robots speaking words one at a time as little discrete lumps; we understand that there is something semantically special about the general discourse or genre or style or language game that we are in. Meaning is a matter of recognising large stretches of familiar territory even if only a small part of the territory is showing; one name for these stretches is register.

Register, if it has been thought of at all by readers and critics, has probably been thought of as 'small' – that is to say a marginal or perhaps optional feature of language. Like the cognate term 'style', register could seem to be a supplement to 'ordinary' language, an extra, something added to improve the value of writing, but not essential. But register is big – it is, indeed, coterminous with language itself, just as dialect is. One cannot speak 'English', one has to speak a dialect of English, be it only the 'Standard' variety; similarly one cannot just speak 'Standard English', one has to speak in a register, be it only the most 'neutral' variety.

The size of register

Here are the next four points from the Ellis and Ure article cited above, now discussing the importance of register in sociolinguistics in 1972; they establish fairly comprehensively that register is a 'big' concept.

> Register offers a means of social control. By choosing a register – that is, a type of language pattern – language users seek to impose a pattern of social behaviour....

> The range of registers mastered by the individual member of the community reflects his language experience. Together they form his idiolect.

> The range of registers available in any one language community ... reflects the experience of the community; the range of registers corresponds to the range of situations of language use....

> esponds to social and cultural change more directly than
> aspects of language.... Indeed it is by their register range,
> y their linguistic features, that 'developed' languages are rec-
> and distinguished from 'undeveloped' ones....[5]

The implications of these large claims have not been sufficiently explored, and this is the more surprising in that a good deal of the most energetic recent work in literary study has concerned political, gender and 'post-colonial' issues, where there seems to be a crying need for an attention to the different registers in which classes, genders and other social and racial groups express themselves. Perhaps recent work on, or with, Bakhtin has to some extent filled this need; I shall consider this promising connection in a later chapter.

Register can be observed at any level of delicacy, and in this it differs from language, and dialect. If one catches a few words of Estonian on the lips of a passer-by, then one concludes that he or she is (or at least is talking) Estonian, and that is about all there is to be said. It either *is* the language or it isn't. If one notices some rich Geordie phraseology in a friend's speech, and asks, 'Do you come from Newcastle?', and thus gets into the conventional – though always fascinating – conversation about origins, accents and dialect, one cannot *disagree* very fruitfully or interestingly – or at least, any disagreement about 'whether such-and-such a phrase is Geordie or not' can easily be settled, and that is that.

Register, on the other hand, isn't either–or, it isn't just a matter of having a command of one or two languages or, like Tess of the D'Urbervilles, being 'bilingual' in two dialects ('Wessex' and 'educated' or, say, Standard English and North-Eastern English); it involves a far greater number of possibilities, to the point that one might employ dozens of different registers in a day. The possibilities for disagreement – that is, for fruitful and interesting dispute – are far higher than in the cases of language and dialect; a simple example would be the question of how to address small children: is baby-talk demeaning and non-educational, or is it comforting and suitable, and educational in a different way? There is something ethical about register.

For different purposes it is possible to distinguish with different finenesses of discrimination ('delicacy'). Most linguistic interactions in the workplace may fall into a single category – say, 'colloquial banking register' if you work in a bank – but within that general category, for another purpose, it would be equally fair to discriminate between the sentences involving more technical banking register ('The rate for the Deutschmark has tightened again this morning', or 'We've started imposing a new penalty on unauthorised overdrafts') and those involving a more casual social register ('How did you get on with that chap this morning?'). This might depend on whether you are discussing a problem with a senior colleague or making friendly noises to an equal colleague. At an even finer level of discrimination, you might want to distinguish between what would be an appropriate announcement to a meeting ('We have started to *impose* a new penalty...') and the more colloquial version ('We've started imposing...'). Even the more social-colloquial register of 'How did you get on with that chap?' can easily be shifted to another register: 'Did that geezer piss you off a bit this morning?' If these levels of register discrimination are available in the relatively uncomplicated interactions of branch banking, they may be of considerable importance when we are analysing the infinite subtleties of literary discourse.

There are, after all, no limits to register analysis. Register, like language and dialect, is coextensive with text. We can stop and consider the register implications, at any level of delicacy, of any piece of text, oral or written, that we come across, and this will form an ideal jumping-off point for almost all further analysis, whether of 'the words on the page' beloved of New Criticism, the power structures in the text (Foucault) or the slippery and undecidable nature of language and meaning (Derrida). Register is the place where stylistics and 'theory' can come together most effectively. If that makes you think of Bakhtin, whose work is stylistic but who has been hailed as something of a solution to the mysteries of theory, then perhaps a marriage can be effected, as we shall see.

Reading the black prints

My main aim is to rescue and promote register as a tool for the reading of literary texts. Looking for a reasonably clear literary example to end with I have found Iris Murdoch's *The Black Prince* (1973). Murdoch was a somewhat self-conscious novelist whose work shows signs of her reading; she was also extremely good at assembling a cast of clearly defined characters, each of whom represents an intersection of points on various intellectual and moral scales. If there is anything in reading for register, it should be fairly apparent in her work.

The Black Prince is narrated in the main by a retired tax inspector called Bradley Pearson. Although he is fifty-eight, it is a love story, a tale of the powerful passion which he and the young daughter of an old friend conceive for one another. There are moments when it is easy to forget that the style of narration is not simply that of 'Iris Murdoch herself' – for it has some of 'her' wit, perception and command of language; the novel is, moreover, writing written by a writer (Pearson the narrator/hero is a blocked novelist). But close attention to the register employed by Pearson quickly opens a gap between him and his 'creator'. Here is an early bit of Pearson's self-presentation:

> When this story starts – and I will not much longer delay its inception – I had already retired, at an earlier age than is usual, from the tax office. I worked as an Inspector of Taxes because I had to earn a living which I knew I should never earn as a writer. I retired when I had at last saved enough money to assure myself of a modest annuity. I have lived, as I say, until latterly, without drama, but with unfailing purpose. I looked forward to and I toiled for my freedom to devote all my time to writing. Yet on the other hand, I did manage to write, and without more than occasional repining, during my years of bondage, and I would not, as some unsatisfied writers do, blame my lack of productivity upon my lack of time. I have been on the whole a lucky man. And I would say that even now.[6]

This, of course, in spite of being writing about writing, is not 'Iris Murdoch herself'. Who it 'is', insofar as we can determine this, depends on the information given (this is a retired tax-inspector) but also on the register it is given in; the latter provides at least as much information as the former.

Thus: here is someone who has read Henry James! That is clear enough from the vocabulary and clause structure of some of the sentences, with their embeddings and subordination. It is also someone educated, thoughtful, 'literary'. But 'Bradley Pearson' is not a real person (there are some grounds for questioning whether Iris Murdoch, or you, or I, or anyone else, is a 'real person' in quite the sense we unthinkingly use that term, but it is useful to maintain some sort of distinction between fictional and non-fictional 'people', and Pearson is undoubtedly a fiction). When we are reading a paragraph like the one just quoted we are in the presence of language, not just imparted information, and language that *means* in various ways; one of these ways concerns the register characteristics apparent. So one of the least dubious things we can say on reading this bit of Iris Murdoch is that we have here a particular register of English.

It is largely a written register, though it is set up to sound somewhat like the spoken voice of the character; it is his interior monologue, his way of thinking about himself, how he would like to sound; what he wants, in a revealing phrase, to *sound like* is chaste, careful, worldly, sophisticated, elegant perhaps, honest, and so on. These are what the chosen register creates the impression of.

The register is set by some of the lexical (vocabulary) choices – 'delay its inception' is a rather grand and formal way of saying 'keep you waiting' or 'beat about the bush' – and also by grammatical and syntactical features: 'I will not' for 'I won't', (like 'upon' for 'on') and the placing of the adverbial 'much longer' in the middle of the verb rather than at the end of the clause. These are formality features. It is easy to translate the passage into another less formal register: 'to assure myself of a modest annuity', for instance, tells us a good deal about Bradley Pearson partly because he does *not* say 'to make sure I had enough to live on for the rest of my life'; 'latterly' gives a different impression, means something different at the level of register, if not at the level of the dictionary, from 'recently'. 'Occasional repining' has an entirely different effect on our understanding of the character from, say, 'getting cheesed off from time to time'. It is the register that gives us most of the information here.

There is no such thing as a 'natural' or 'neutral' language from whose unsullied eminence we can survey the messy languages of the workaday world. Similarly there is no such thing as a 'natural' dialect; most of us may think that the way *we* speak and write is *the* way of doing so, but there are simple historical, political and geographical reasons for the way we all perform linguistically; there is no gold standard for English, or for Standard English, or for any other language or dialect (though, as Bakhtin pointed out, we have to keep a notional 'centre' in play, or we would end up back at the Tower of Babel). By the same token, there is no such thing as a 'natural' register – a way of speaking and writing that is some- how pure, or guaranteed from outside history and geography as Normal in the strictest sense.

This becomes very evident as we watch Bradley Pearson *presenting* or *representing* himself. His slightly arch, Jamesian style is transparently 'artificial', as are all styles and all registers (as, in- deed, is language 'itself'), only here the artificiality is foregrounded. The trick of the novelist is to make it *seem as if* there is a real or non-artificial or natural style against which his or her particular style is set. In this novel we get it only in odd pieces of dialogue when, of course, characters other than Pearson have to speak English in the more or less conventional colloquial way to seem convincing. But Pearson himself seems to be acutely aware of the artificiality of all language, and the way he shows it is by hinting at registers he has heard but which are not his own; he does this by the judicious but unusual use of inverted commas (much, I realise, as I have done in putting them round expressions such as 'Iris Murdoch herself' above). The result sounds like the following passage; it occurs when Pearson is talking about his protégé, the novelist Arnold Baffin, father of his young love:

> I 'discovered' Arnold, a considerably younger man, when I was already modestly established as a writer, and he, recently out of college, was just finishing his first novel. I had by then 'got rid of' my wife and was experiencing one of those 'fresh starts' which I have so often hoped would lead on to achievement.[7]

The scare quotes here (or perhaps I should call them 'scare quotes' in order to signal that I'm trying for a more serious register than *journalese*) – anyway, the scare quotes immediately establish a whole world of assumptions and clichés and conventional expressions, perhaps even conventional thoughts and behaviour, that exist around Pearson (the narrator) in the society, the culture, in which he lives. The metaphorical nature of the expressions so highlighted becomes more obvious, as does the fact that they are conventional and belong to a certain sort of discourse. What is being indicated is that there are *registers* available to Pearson that he does not want to be trapped by or make full use of – he prefers to operate in another, less hackneyed register, and has an amused but also slightly anxious relationship with the banal world to which the quoted words point. *He* can do better than 'got rid of' when he is talking about his ex-wife, and he obviously doesn't really believe in the 'fresh starts' of which a certain rather bracing kind of moral thinking is full. This technique is rather like putting inverted commas round 'Born-Again' (as in 'born-again Christian'; I've added capitals to make the point even clearer) or 'mid-life crisis' (or 'Mid-Life Crisis'), and it specifically distances the writer from the register world in which 'Fresh Starts' or being 'Born Again' are accepted, obviously meaningful or credible.

Pearson uses this trick frequently in the earlier part of the novel, and we get plenty of opportunity to consider registers which, as it were, we *might* have been offered. Thus he talks of Arnold Baffin 'devot[ing] himself to "writing"', and as a result that we are then not surprised to read that '[Baffin] wrote easily, producing every year a book which pleased the public taste. Wealth, fame followed.' Evidently the chaste, fastidious, controlled Pearson so clearly indicated by the register of these very sentences is at odds with the sort of writing, or 'writing' (or the result of 'being a writer'), that goes with prolificness, popularity, wealth and fame.[8]

Interestingly, if Pearson felt more enthusiastic about Baffin's style of work he would himself employ a more Baffinesque register here and expand on the merits of his friend with more *gush*. This is what he says about the matter when he finally lets us have his opinion explicitly:

> Arnold Baffin's work was a congeries of amusing anecdotes loosely garbled into 'racy stories' with the help of half-baked unmediated symbolism. The dark powers of the imagination were conspicuous by their absence. Arnold Baffin wrote too much, too fast. Arnold Baffin was just a talented journalist.[9]

We can read this best if we pay attention to the registers involved. First there is the superior tone of the intellectual reviewer who can manage such difficult locutions as 'congeries' and 'unmediated', and knows that in some quarters, my dear, perhaps in the old days, Baffin's tales would have been considered 'racy'. This superior reviewer knows about the 'dark powers of the imagination', and is clearly conversant with the poetic or spiritual sides of literature (or should it be 'Letters'?). He also knows exactly how the word 'garbled' works, and can manage a little assonance ('amusing anecdotes').

Second, there is the tone of genuine venom, the points where Pearson's feelings overwhelm his urbane tone and something like jealousy seems to be showing through. 'Half-baked' hardly fits with the register of the rest of this short passage, and the cliché 'conspicuous by their absence', banal for Pearson, feels like a deliberate piece of bathos after the dark powers have been mentioned, a calculated register shift for the sake of effect.

Third, there is a summarising structure here, a tone of finality and accusation, in the repetition of Baffin's name. A Greek Sophist, teaching rhetoric to the young men of Athens, would have been proud of the rhythm and balance of this structure; the name appears at the beginning of the first sentence of the passage, in full, and then again in full at the start of the third and fourth sentences. The summaries of Baffin's failure become quicker and more damning at each stage of the three-pronged attack. This trick of repetition is one that can be heard in the mouths of sarcastic schoolmasters and schoolmistresses, on the lips of barristers, and in Parliament. And, of course, we remember from Antony's speech in *Julius Caesar* how often Brutus was an honourable man.

Fourth, we begin to see that the inverted commas could be spread around more freely. If 'racy stories' gets them, why not 'dark powers' or 'amusing anecdotes'? Isn't the whole passage 'set up' in some way to *represent* or *give the impression of* a particular voice, tone, style, register? In *A Dance to the Music of Time*, Anthony Powell even has his narrator, Nick Jenkins, talk at one point about being 'in love' (with inverted commas): 'It was at the time that I was "in love" with Jean Duport...'. The inverted commas create a doubt in the reader's mind that makes him or her ask not so much the banal question 'Ah! Was he *really* in love with her then?' as a much wider question about the whole cultural business of 'being-in-love', a question that brings to mind the discourses and registers in which being-in-love usually occurs. The effect is to make the text more textual and intertextual, and less of a naively transparent window on to reality.

What appears to be happening in a passage like this one from *The Black Prince* is that a number of roles are being adopted in quick succession. When characters are described in fiction we try to 'read' them according to roles, to recognise personae we are familiar with; but all the time we are 'reading' the narrator through the registers he or she employs and, of course, there is an interaction between the two. Iris Murdoch is just slightly more open about this process than some other novelists. Thus, when we meet the minor character Roger in *The Black Prince*, we find this:

> I will not attempt a lengthy description of Roger.... He always referred to himself as a 'public school boy', which I suppose he had been. He had a little education, and a great deal of 'air', a 'plummy' voice and a misleadingly distinguished appearance.[10]

The openness here consists in the self-conscious note of *description* with which the paragraph starts, and the obvious adoption of culturally and socially prefabricated expressions. Roger *calls himself* 'a public school boy', but everyone in the culture around him talks about his 'air' and knows what a 'plummy voice' is when they hear one; they also probably have a cliché about a 'distinguished appearance' such that those words, too, could have gone into inverted commas. Pearson's description is prepacked, fitted into a register, just as Roger's persona is and just as all our opinions of each other, it is implied, tend to be. Simultaneously Pearson is revealing his own smartness of observation, his own cynicism about these social personae, and his command of but distance from the registers involved. And as the novel progresses this sort of thing becomes his own register, so that he can even put inverted commas round such innocent expressions as 'dinner parties' and 'costume jewellery'. For Roger and his wife, living beyond their means, 'There were "dinner parties" and a big car'. One begins to wonder what words would *not* be candidates for this sort of treatment. Why not 'a big car' too? It is a well-known phrase and, like 'dinner parties', it carries a charge of meaning beyond its immediate reference (a 'big car' is more than just a larger-than-average motor vehicle). This habit in Pearson's writing comes to represent the curse that is on all writing, perhaps on all use of language: namely, that it is condemned to a sort of radical insincerity. As Pearson himself says, 'Of course men play roles ... women play roles too...'. The point about the registers that Pearson echoes in his narrative is that they are themselves roles, social and cultural constructs, and the writer can no more do without them than he can do without language itself. Murdoch – wryly, I suspect – puts into Pearson's mouth, or pen, the predicament in which she too finds herself. Every word is 'registered', borrowed from the mouths and pens of others, someone else's marked property, so it is no wonder that Pearson writes little and systematically destroys most of what he does write. (The point of Murdoch's novel seems to be that True Art and True Love, the gifts of the gods, can somehow, for a while at least, transcend this limitation.) Bradley Pearson, surely standing in for Iris Murdoch, makes the point:

> How can one describe a human being 'justly'? How can one describe oneself? With what an air of false coy humility, with what an assumed confiding simplicity one sets about it! 'I am a puritan' and so on.... Faugh! How can these statements not be false? Even 'I am tall' has a context. How the angels must laugh and sigh.[11]

Perhaps we should write permanently in inverted commas, to signal that our voices are not 'our own' – they come to us preregistered.

Workpoints

What is a horse? Sometimes it is a horse, sometimes it is a nag, a gee-gee, Dobbin. Sometimes it is a

graminivorous quadruped.

Why? What does it tell us about Mr Gradgrind in Dickens's *Hard Times* that he so sternly prefers the last of these terms?

Register. 1. A set of features of speech or writing characteristic of a particular type of linguistic activity or a particular group when engaging in it. E.g. journalese is a register different from that in which sermons are delivered, or in which smutty stories are told.
Oxford Concise Dictionary of Linguistics, 1997

Register is 'a fixed pattern of vocabulary and grammar which regularly co-occurs with and is conventionally associated with a specific context.'
Paul Simpson, *Language through Literature*, 1997, p. 10

Notes

1 There was a version of this joke, clearly intertextually related to it, in a cartoon in an undergraduate publication in Cambridge in the 1950s. A young man, identified as belonging to the supposedly effete King's College, emerges from the back of a rugby scrum, saying 'My dear, the noise. And the dirt! And the *people*!' I am indebted for this version to Lord Cecil Parkinson.

2 Jean Ure and Jeffrey Ellis, 'Register in descriptive linguistics and linguistic sociology', in Oscar Uribe-Villegas, *Issues in Sociolinguistics* (Mouton, 1977).

3 *Getting Results With Microsoft Office for Windows 95* (Microsoft Corporation, 1995–6), p. 47.

4 *Private Eye*, 902, 12 July 1996.

5 Ure and Ellis, 'Register in descriptive linguistics'.

6 Iris Murdoch, *The Black Prince* (1973) (Penguin Books, 1975), p. 17.

7 *Ibid.*, p. 29

8 Inverted commas imply cynicism or sarcasm – a way of elevating oneself and setting oneself apart, but at the same time a frustration: 'I'm stuck – I can't find another way of saying this.' The self-consciousness preyed on and played with by postmodernism is a curse of inarticulacy or inauthenticity, and is clearly operating here.

9 Murdoch, *The Black Prince*, p. 31.

10 *Ibid.*, p. 51.

11 *Ibid.*, p. 71.

2

The history (and the hijacking)
of register

A short prehistory of the term

The term 'register' was first used by T. B. W. Reid in 1956:

> The linguistic behaviour of a given individual is by no means uniform;
> placed in what appear to be linguistically identical conditions he will on
> different occasions speak (or write) differently according to what may
> roughly be described as different social situations: he will use a number
> of different registers. [1]

Reid perhaps chose this word (an earlier suggestion had been 'gears') because of an analogy with music. The *Oxford English Dictionary* defines 'register', under definition 8b, as 'the compass of a voice or instrument; the particular range of tones which can be produced by certain voices'. This is connected to the use of the word in organ-playing, where it refers to a 'slider' that controls a set of pipes, and hence is used for the set of pipes itself and its characteristic tone. Halliday was to pick up this musical analogy in 1964: 'All speakers have at their disposal a continuous scale of patterns and items, from which they select for each situation type the appropriate stock of available harmonies in the appropriate key. They speak, in other words, many registers.' [2]

The point is that a register is not a single note; the word refers to a range of related sounds. Just as the whole of this text that you are reading is in a consistent language (English) and in a consistent dialect (Standard British English), so it is also in a largely consistent register. I've pulled out one particular slider, as it were, activated one particular set of pipes, and I'm playing away happily on them for you. Or perhaps not. Is 'playing away happily' in quite the same formal register as the rest of this section? When I started the chapter with the words 'The term register was first used...' I was in academic-expository register, while 'playing away happily' sounds more colloquial. One speaks more registers than one does languages or dialects.

One difference between registers on the one hand, and languages and dialects on the other, is that it seems possible to make a shift in register a good deal faster, more usefully and more often than in the others.

Many paragraphs in many types of text contain more than one register, while there are very few changes of *language*. Sometimes people slip in a Latin quotation or a German word when they are writing in English, but it would normally be of the semi-domesticated variety, such as *mutatis mutandis*, which is on its way to being in the loanword category which includes such items as *paterfamilias*. Or it could be a term such as *Weltschmerz* or *Schaden-freude*, which aren't quite English yet but are also semi-absorbed. Equally, there are few changes of *dialect* in most English texts (Scott, Hardy and George Eliot give different characters different dialects, but there is precious little narrative or expository prose that shifts about dialectally).

Register is the only slippery one, and thus the one most charged with possibility for literary meaning, since the reader is always aware that a particular point *could have been put differently*. While there isn't much to be gained from speculating that 'this text' might have been in Polish or Lancastrian, there is a lot to be learned from the fact (to take an example from Halliday) that on a toothpaste carton you might read 'Ideal for Cleansing Artificial Dentures' but you would be less likely to read 'Just Right for Cleaning False Teeth'. In this case your ability to identify the special advertising-speak is the first step towards understanding how you are being manipulated.

Reid's crucial point is that register depends on 'conditions' or 'social situation'; knowing a language means having a command of its socially acceptable varieties as much as of its grammar and lexis; this is obvious even for those who have never heard the term 'register'. Thus in many languages, certainly in most European languages, notions such as literary language, 'bad language', 'baby-talk', 'elevated language' or 'slang' have long been recognised.

Sociolinguists employ the term *codes* (as in 'code-switching') to indicate the different 'languages' employed by individuals in different situations. So the idea of register should not seem too unfamiliar.

Although Reid invented the term, he did not quite invent the idea of register. Similar notions have been canvassed throughout the history of Western thought about writing. We can find this sort of comment in Aristotle's *Poetics* (*c.* 330 BC):

> Epic and tragic poetry, comedy too, dithyrambic poetry, and most music composed for the flute and the lyre can all be described in general terms as forms of imitation or representation. However, they differ from one another in three respects: either in using different media for the representation, or in representing different things, or in representing them in entirely different ways.[3]

This seems quite promising in that it specifically concentrates on artistic productions, and is thus on the literary side of the division between register-in-general and register-in-literature; and it provokes thoughts about *genre*, but also about the 'different ways' of doing art, which sounds like a step towards the notion of register. Throughout the early sections of the *Poetics*, Aristotle is concerned with differences and diversities in the arts, especially as these concern the language used for the representation of different events and qualities.

Following Aristotle there developed a classical tradition of 'levels of language', part of the notion of 'decorum' whereby certain styles were deemed by classical authorities and their Renaissance followers to be suitable for certain subjects. Horace, Cicero, most Latin authors and, following them, Sidney, Boileau and other classicists simply assumed that there were, naturally, styles to suit subjects.

Johnson and Swift, among many others, were concerned in the eighteenth century to polish up the English language so that it could become as fit a vehicle for high thoughts as Latin. Johnson claimed that he had 'laboured to refine our language to grammatical purity, and to clear it from colloquial barbarisms, licentious idioms and irregular combinations' (*Rambler*, 14 March 1752). Swift, developing Aristophanes' pronouncement that 'High thoughts must have high language' (*Frogs*, line 1058; note that this is the play in which the 'lowest' creatures are also given their own appropriate voice), told a friend: 'Proper words, in proper places, make the true definition of a style' (*Letter to a Young Clergyman*, 9 January 1720). The very persistence of this sort of advice indicates the ubiquity of indecorous or improper English alongside the recommended variety; as Bakhtin might say, there is always a Rabelaisian carnivalising at work alongside correct usage.

Throughout the history of the English language there have been register disputes. A kind of ground bass of commentary on the language has always been audible, generally concerning the proportion of Old English words to French, Latin or other, learned, expressions being used at any given time. In the Renaissance for instance, when people again became conscious of style ('It is most true, *stylus virum arguit*, – our style bewrays us', says Burton in *The Anatomy of Melancholy* [1621–51]), the very classicism to which a later generation would aspire was sometimes regarded with suspicion, as in the sixteenth-century debate over 'inkhorn terms' imported from Greek and Latin, some of which seem quite outlandish and some of which we now use daily. Ben Jonson thought 'conscious', 'inflate', 'strenuous' and 'spurious' were 'terrible, windy words'. The most accessible example of this debate can be found in the speeches of Don Armado in *Love's Labour's Lost*, from the very end of the century.

A lot of this sort of discussion can be reassigned to the category of register. What else, for instance, is Wordsworth talking about when, in the Preface to the 1798 *Lyrical Ballads*, he appeals for a poetry written in 'the language men do use'? And what else is Gerard Manley Hopkins referring to when he tells Robert Bridges that 'The poetical language of an age should be the current language heightened, to any degree heightened and unlike itself, but not… an obsolete one' (Letter of 15 February 1879)? Spenser, who sought Chaucerian archaisms for his *Faerie Queene*, would not have agreed.

Debate and dispute among these prescriptive critics and writers frequently concerned 'what kind of English' was to be used in a way that implies an interest in something very like register. As early as Caxton efforts were made to standardise the language on a dialectal or regional basis (London won), but even then there was an implication in the debate that metropolitan English was somehow better, more educated and generally more useful than its country (or academic) cousins. Here is George Puttenham writing in 1589 in his *Arte of English Poesie*:

> The [English of] our maker or poet must be heedyly looked unto, that it be naturall, pure, and the most usuall of all his countrey: and for the same purpose rather that which is spoken in the kings Court, or in the good townes and cities within the land, then in the marches and frontiers, or in port townes, where straungers haunt for traffike sake, or yet in Universities where schollers use much peevish affectation of words out of the primative languages, or finally, in any uplandish village or corner of a Realme, where is no resort but of poore rusticall or uncivill people.

This reflects the state of educated aspiration at the point when English was becoming the modern language we know. Its earlier history had been something of an improbable muddle, although one has to presume the existence of register consciousness in Middle English, perhaps in Old English too.

The development of the concept of register

Before Reid's work, J. R. Firth, writing in 1948, developed the notion of what he called the 'context of situation' in a way that we can see as another possible precursor to 'register'. He is not concerned with the *level* of English employed, nor with the prescriptive aesthetic considerations that exercised writers in the eighteenth century, but he is aware that different Englishes suit different situations. He had already developed the idea of a 're-stricted language', which he defined as 'serving a circumscribed field of experience or action' with its 'own grammar and diction-ary'. He posits the example of a 'language manual' in which there is 'a picture of a railway station and the operative words for trav-elling by train' and sees this as a parallel 'with grammatical rules'. That is, there is a language for travelling by train, known to 'ini-tiated persons in the society under description', and this language can be learned according to schemes and categories similar to those of grammar. Just as we can form viable sentences in English only if we know English grammar, so similarly we can engage in 'lan-guage events' involving train travel only if we have learned the appropriate words and their organisation from a study of the railway system. The context more or less determines the language. This 'parallel' of Firth's is highly appropriate for our study of register, because register, too, is as it were a parallel grammar, determining what can be said and how it can be said, at another level. Furthermore, Firth is also – most encouragingly – concerned that his notion should be anchored in the social. He calls his 'context of situation' a 'schematic construct' which 'makes sure of the sociological component'.[4]

In their *Encyclopaedia of Linguistics* (1969) Jeffrey Ellis and Jean Ure trace the development of more modern thinking about register and cognate terms.[5] They start with a German linguist, one Wegener, who tried in 1885 to differentiate fields of context in language by pointing out, for instance, that in the context of hunting the German word *Löffel* (usually 'spoon') would suggest specifically 'hare's ear', because that is how the word is – or was – used among the German shooting fraternity. Under 'normal' or neutral circumstances *Löffel* would be collocated not with *Hase* (hare) but with *Gabel* (fork). Firth picked this up in the 1930s in his concept of restricted languages: 'effective action and good manners require appropriateness of language in situational context. This leads to ... the notion of *restricted languages*.'[6] Ellis and Ure mention a handful of international linguists, but focus on a number of British linguists working in the 1950s and 1960s before arriving at Michael Halliday.

In the forty years since Reid wrote, and in the thirty years since the Ellis and Ure Encyclopaedia entry, register has been developed as a concept, notably by Halliday and those working with him in, for instance, *The Linguistic Sciences and Language Teaching* (1964) and many other publications. Perhaps we should pause at this point and consider where register had got to when Halliday took it over.

When we read the material available, it seems that the idea of register was pretty much established during the 1960s; it was definitely something that was orientated towards the social and was part of a move towards linguistics-in-action. Firth's 'situational context' (as his 'context of situation' had become by 1957) had been specifically recommended, as we have seen, because 'it makes sure of the sociological component'. It is not surprising, therefore, that it was in Halliday's *functional* linguistics that register made its strongest mark. Typically, in *The Linguistic Sciences and Language Teaching*, Halliday stresses this in such propositions as:

> Language is not realised in the abstract: it is realised as the activity of people in situations, as linguistic events which are manifested in a particular dialect and register.
>
> Language varies as its function varies; it differs in different situations. The name given to a variety of language distinguished according to its use is 'register'.
>
> The category of 'register' is needed when we want to account for what people do with their language.[7]

And, most simply and trenchantly of all, here is Halliday in *Language as Social Semiotic* (1978): 'Language is as it is because of what it has to do.'

This emphasis on function, use and the social is what should have made a marriage possible between contemporary theory – that is, the work of the (largely French) theorists who have become fashionable since the mid 1960s – and contemporary stylistics. Modern 'critical theory' or 'literary theory' has a powerful strand of homogenisation running through it: it discourages us from separating literary texts from texts of other kinds (Barthes, Derrida); it regards all text as issuing equally from the unconscious (Lacan); it sees all language and discourse as inextricably bound up with social power relations (Foucault); and it hears in all texts the voices of the social reality from which they come (Bakhtin). In Britain, the best-selling title in 'theory' has, since publication in 1983, been Terry Eagleton's *Literary Theory: An Introduction*, which concentrates on the universally political basis of literary and critical activity. This homogeneity, this unanimous orientation towards *integrating* text and psyche, text and context, text and situation, text and society, text and culture, fits exactly with the deeper tendencies of functional linguistics or sociolinguistics as they relate text to its social and psychological matrix through the concept of register. There were no banns called in the 1960s (you will look in vain for cross-references between Derrida and Halliday), but that marriage is no less on the cards for being overdue. One of my purposes here is to explore this possibility.

'Register' could have been adopted by literary critics and theorists at any time from the 1960s onwards, but it seems to have got stuck in the place made for it in contemporary linguistics, as part of general (rather than specifically literary) stylistics; this in spite of the fact that it can be worked easily into the Bakhtinian mould and used for literary purposes. Equally it is not *contradictory* as far as the post-structuralist mainstream is concerned. For alongside 'homogenisation' goes deconstruction, and what better tool could there be for the recognition of the deconstructive properties of a text than an analysis of the voices out of whose unharmonious babble it is made? What is more convincingly intertextual than the suggestion that Barthes's 'tissue of quotations' (one of his definitions of 'text') is in fact a tissue of registers? For a register is, among other things, a quotation from an anonymous source.

Yet literature study at all levels has been frightened off using concepts such as register, because the linguistics with which they are surrounded is too technical and complicated. This isn't the fault of the linguisticians: it is up to us 'lettrists' to boldly go into stylistics, even though we know full well that there are monsters of complexity and 'scientific rigour' waiting over the border who will not part willingly with the conceptual prey they have captured. But this can be a humane undertaking, and there is no need to slay the dragon; why should we not be allowed to *share* the intellectual helpings available?

Field, tenor and mode

I do not propose to spend much more time on the history of the concept of register, as the important thing must be to rescue it as a useful idea from its exclusive use by linguists rather than to contest with them endlessly on their own ground. Let me repeat that I have no objection to the special use made of the term by Halliday and others for their own general purposes – indeed, let a thousand flowers bloom – but it seems essential not to allow so handy a tool to remain wrapped in a series of distinctions and technicalities so impenetrable as to encourage the reader of literature to turn his or her back on stylistics and go back to 'common sense'. If the hijackers have taken your means of transport, you normally have to go back to walking, but I think it might now be possible to get the car back from them and, for our purposes, to scrape off the (linguistic) paint with which they have coated the vehicle.

We need a linguistically informed literary reading – literature is obviously made up of material that can be analysed, and to some degree explained, by linguistics – but we may not need a whole box-set of sledgehammers to open some of the more delicate nuts of literary discourse. We do need register, but we may not need the entire apparatus with which it is currently weighed down. As William of Ockham put it, sharpening his razor, 'A plurality must not be asserted without necessity.'

Let me take, as an example of this overweightedness, the well-known division – made by various writers on register and finally formulated by Halliday in 1964 – whereby register is dealt with under three aspects: field, tenor and mode.

Field concerns subject matter, and generally what the text is about. If we establish that the text is, for instance, a recipe – in the field of culinary arts, so to speak – then we have made the first point about its register; at the very least we will recognise food lexis in the text.

Tenor concerns the interaction involved. Who is saying or writing this text to whom? What are their relative positions socially or culturally in the power structure? Let us say that I am being taken through the recipe *viva voce* by a famous chef in person; this is quite a treat, and I feel lucky. Here is a second register point: the chef may well use imperatives and exhortation, tell jokes, while I do more listening, initiate fewer exchanges and generally act respectfully.

Mode concerns the medium employed in the utterance of the text. Is it a telephone call? A written poem? A public speech? A private letter? Let us say that I have received the recipe by word of mouth, I have written it down, and now I am passing it on to you orally. Here is a third register point: the written form will use all sorts of abbreviations and precise measurements, while probably avoiding the jokes and hesitations of the spoken forms.

These three categories are useful for the purposes of linguistics in general, no doubt, and have a small part to play in the study of literature, but we should remember that they were developed to cover any linguistic interaction whatsoever, texts of all kinds in all situations, and they are consequently far too complicated to apply constantly to literary texts. I shall deal with them in the order: tenor – mode – field.

First, the 'tenor' of a *literary* text could be considered as an invariant and thus uninteresting. The 'communication' in literature (to adopt a crude model of what goes on in writing and reading for the sake of clarity) is between author and reader. We are not talking here of the 'real' author or the 'real', actually present reader; at most we are describing an interaction between implied author and implied reader, and these two entities remain in a fairly fixed position with regard to one another.

Shakespeare, then – at least on this first level of analysis – does not fulfil a definable social role *vis-à-vis* his readers; he is not their fellow-team-member or employee or relation, he is just 'Shakespeare', an imaginary being with the same logical status as any other author; his tenor is unchanging. (Is there a joke here about 'keeping the even tenor of his way', which would be suitable in this sort of book, being a reference to Thomas Gray's 'Elegy in a Country Churchyard', or another joke about tenors and basses which would be less suitable?) The tenor involved in a reading of *Hamlet* is simply: 'Implied-Author-of-literary-text / Implied-Reader-of-literary-text', and that is a structure that never varies with any reading of any such text.

Similarly, 'mode' is virtually an invariant in literature, too. Once one has said 'literary', one has confined oneself to a particular written – indeed, printed – 'channel' or mode of communication. The differences generated by such variations as poetry readings or performances of plays do not have much effect on the register features of a text; a poem read aloud, even in an auditorium, is identifiably in the same register as that poem read in a book, and although it is true that certain genres of lyric poetry do betray their origins in oral performance, this is only as much as to say that *part of the register* of lyric poetry is a certain declamatory style complete with imperatives and exclamation marks ('Awake!', 'Hark!'). 'Mode' is useful for discriminating between the styles to be found in such texts as telegrams, radio commentaries, newspaper articles, lectures and technical manuals; these are truly separate modes of communication and one can translate between them to make the point. The telegram brings news which will sound very different when it has been 'written up' for the newspaper, and different again when I try to retell it orally to friends at home. But when one has made the point that much early poetry was delivered *viva voce*, and that plays are performed as well as read, one has said most of what is necessary about 'mode' in literature.

Before considering field, an excursus on the other two categories seems necessary. It has to be admitted that *within the context of fiction* there are characters who may have interesting power relations with one another (tenor), and – in novels, for instance – one may come across phone calls, telegrams, love letters, speeches, and so on (mode). There may even be moments when it is worth pointing this out by using these two terms, but on the whole the best thing is simply to talk about register *tout court*. When Mr Jaggers, in *Great Expectations*, speaks in his special way to Pip, it is unnecessarily analytical and rather plodding to insist that because this is a powerful middle-aged lawyer talking to a small lower-class boy, we have here an example of the importance of tenor; for what would the demonstration of the point be except to say that the tenor is that of a powerful middle-aged lawyer talking to a small boy? The point is otiose. What we need to say is that there are legal and authoritarian features in Mr Jaggers's speech, register elements which can be identified and which mark him for what he is.

These elements may be slightly modified when he is talking to Pip (this would be where the tenor would *show*), but that isn't much helped by bringing in the term 'tenor'. Jaggers uses imperatives and short, unsoftened sentences, he also talks about *boys* (he 'knows them' and they're 'a bad lot') but such grammatical and lexical points do not need to be subjected to an extra level of analysis whereby we have to point out that these are his tenor towards Pip, for that would require, in support, a mere repetition of the same points: imperatives, short sentences, 'boy', and so on. Jaggers can be shown to speak in a recognisable register because of a raft of sociologically-determinable reasons; that will usually be enough.

Then, similarly, in the matter of 'mode', taking the example of a telegram presented as such in a novel, one can simply say that the relevant section of the text shows a switch into 'telegraphese', which is, of course, a register. I see no advantage in *adding* the term 'mode'.

Here is a concrete example. Chapter 3 of P. G. Wodehouse's *Right Ho, Jeeves* opens with Bertie Wooster demonstrating a mastery of telegraphese and builds up to a series of brilliant register shifts which, not surprisingly, generate a good deal of humour.

Aunt Dahlia cables her nephew from the country: 'Come at once. Travers.' Telegrams, when they existed, were expensive, and the prudent chap (am I slipping into Wodehousean register?) kept the words to a minimum (it was fascinating, when sending telegrams, to see how much of English is inessential for the bare transmission of information). It isn't hard to imagine how a well-bred lady like Aunt Dahlia would have conveyed the same point ('Come at once') in a letter. However urgent, the letter would at least have had 'Dear Bertie' at the top and 'Love from your Aunt Dahlia' or some such formula at the bottom. And there would have been an avoidance of the imperative mood ('Come'), with a preference for polite declaratives and conditionals ('I'd be most grateful if you'd...'); Dahlia would also have avoided using her surname.

Bertie replies: 'Perplexed. Explain. Bertie.' Here again we find compression (no 'I am perplexed') and the imperative. But Aunt Dahlia responds, for she is not unduly patient, even for an aunt: 'What on earth is there to be perplexed about, ass? Come at once. Travers.' We can feel her trying to keep her temper here; her question and the name-calling ('ass') are in non-telegraphic register; in fact they are pretty well standard 1920s colloquial, and they enable us to hear something of the tone of Aunt Dahlia's (famously loud) voice. But her explosion is contained and limited, and this is signalled by a return to that most contained of all registers, telegraphese. 'Come at once' is repeated verbatim.

Bertie doesn't want to go and stay with his aunt at this point, and it takes him the space of three cigarettes to think out the right reply. Like his aunt, he feels the need to break out of the confining register imposed by the telegram, and he finds the shortest non-telegraphic formula for procrastination: 'How do you mean come at once? Regards. Bertie.' The joke is that the almost painful succinctness of telegraphic register was developed in such a way as to make misunderstanding highly unlikely – it is hard to find much ambiguity in Aunt Dahlia's command. Not surprisingly, she cables back:

> I mean come at once, you maddening half-wit. What did you think I
> meant? Come at once or expect an aunt's curse first post tomorrow.
> Love. Travers.

Once again we find a mixture of registers. The first two sentences
are colloquial non-telegraphic. The third sentence starts with the
telegraphic 'Come at once' again, but then shifts into written-
literate: 'expect' has a special, perhaps Gothic, meaning here, something like a Gothic novelist's equivalent of 'Watch out for' which
goes well with 'an aunt's curse' (though that is humorous, because
the Romantic formula 'a someone's curse' does not normally collocate with aunts but, rather, with mothers or fathers). Then Aunt
Dahlia switches to banal business-speak with her mention of the
first post tomorrow, before reverting to telegraphese by using her
bare surname.

Bertie then takes a line that would be worthy of analytic philosophy at its most sceptical and painstaking:

> When you say 'Come' do you mean 'Come to Brinkley Court'? And
> when you say 'At once' do you mean 'At once'? Fogged. At a loss. All
> the best. Bertie.

The cheekiness of this lies not only in its refusal to play the normal
conversational game (Grice's Maxims seem relevant here: Bertie is
breaking the maxim of co-operation) or its refusal to operate
according to the laws of common sense; it also stems from Bertie's
deliberate mishandling of register. Absolutely the last thing you
did when you sent a telegram was to question the terms being
used; at most you might quote back a garbled word and add
'Clarify' to it (as in 'Clarify Squerx'), but entering into quasi-philo-
sophical discussion of the contents of the telegram you were
replying to was quite against the spirit of breathless economy that
the medium engendered. Clarity was, anyway, almost certain. Bertie
is being cheeky by breaking register rules.

When Bertie gets home from an afternoon at his club (the
Drones, where he has 'spent a restful afternoon throwing cards
into a top-hat with some of the better element'), he finds this
waiting for him:

> Yes, yes, yes, yes, yes, yes. It doesn't matter whether you understand or
> not. You just come at once, as I tell you, and for heaven's sake stop this

backchat. Do you think I am made of money that I can afford to send you telegrams every ten minutes. Stop being a fathead and come immediately. Love. Travers.

The register features of this are fascinating. First, in the string of 'yeses' Aunt Dahlia is almost managing to shout on paper; it is colloquial-impatient, as is the colloquial idiom 'You just' which follows; this latter is even a vulgarism, rather beneath Aunt Dahlia's class norm. Then there are the fillers, the padding that makes conversation so different from discursive prose and, *a fortiori*, different from telegraphese: 'as I tell you' and 'for heaven's sake', which add indexical information but no other kind; they tell us that this is being said impatiently, but add nothing to the 'content' of the point being made. The clichéd hyperboles, too, belong far away from the register of the telegram – it is in the sloppy, linguistically comfortable disputes of everyday colloquial encounters that we hear 'Do you think I'm made of money?' and 'every ten minutes'. So this is Aunt Dahlia sounding sometimes like a telegram, sometimes like an angry parent addressing an erring child, sometimes like a woman shouting, sometimes like a piece of rather banal conversation; she shifts about among her registers even though she 'should' be confined to a single rigid style. Later in the exchange Aunt Dahlia's (deliberately rather synthetic) anger boils over again: 'Oh, so it's like that, is it? You and your engagement book indeed.' And she continues in this spoken colloquial vein for several lines, but she ends this telegram with: 'Deeply regret Brinkley Court hundred miles from London as unable hit you with a brick.' This may seem like a sudden, ludicrous attempt to save money as she suppresses pronouns, the verb 'to be' and some other features ('*I* deeply regret *that* Brinkley Court *is* a hundred miles from London as *I am* unable *to* hit you'). But what has happened is simply that the pull of the register (telegraphese) has become too strong for her, and at the end of her piece she has reverted to type.

It is notable that in all that I have said about this passage in P. G. Wodehouse I have not had to mention the word 'mode' once. 'Register' has served us perfectly well. In fact I did feel the need of 'mode' at one point: when Aunt Dahlia threatened to send an aunt's curse by 'first post tomorrow', I would have liked to point out that she evidently found telegrams the wrong mode

in which to deliver curses. That seems to me to be entirely legitimate as a use of *mode*, but it shows that the term needs only a
marginal place in literary reading. It's worth having it in the armoury, but only just.

Meanwhile, we have left field still awaiting attention. If we have
marginalised tenor and mode, and are thus left with field alone,
there is a good logical reason for suggesting that we also
marginalise this term. After all, if a category (register) is largely
coterminous with one single subcategory (field), then presumably
one of the two can be jettisoned. In a paper delivered in 1966,
Michael Gregory, considering the different candidates then available for the differentiation of varieties of language, mentions register as a term being employed by the linguist J. C. Catford; for
Catford, 'social role' is the 'situational correlate' of register which,
in its turn, 'closely corresponds to Field of Discourse'.[8] In general
I would suggest that we approach literature with this correspondence in mind; the simplest way to cut through the complexities is
to suggest that, for the most part, register *is* field. The first question we need to ask, in order to enter into any discussion of a text,
is: 'What are the fields or registers in play here?' In which case we
may as well just ask: 'What are the registers involved in this?' Only
much later, if and when necessary, might we need to distinguish
between field, tenor and mode.

So I propose that for 'field' we simply use the term 'register'
itself, and bring tenor, mode and field into play only where the
distinctions those terms make are really needed. The important
thing is to be able to ask the question: 'What register is this text
in?' Or, more likely: 'What registers are present here?'

The question should be a natural third after the first two obvious
ones, namely 'What language is this text in?' (answer: 'English')
and 'What dialect is this text in?' (answer: 'Lowland Scots of the
nineteenth century', or 'Deep South USA of the early twentieth
century' or 'Standard British'). The third question, 'What register
is this?', is just as important for the establishment of literary
meaning as the other two.

Interestingly, in literary reading, the question about register will
normally render the other two superfluous. For, after all, reading
hardly takes place in ignorance of the language being employed;
you aren't going to sit up with a start halfway through a book and

say, 'Good heavens! I hadn't realised that this novel was in *German*.'
And equally, when you become aware of dialect in a novel, you
don't treat it *as dialect*, something to be considered for its own
sake, or for its linguistic interest; dialect in literature becomes a
register feature. Country folk in British English fiction speak a
sort of Wessex dialect according to the curious convention that
the English West Country is somehow more agricultural than the
rest of the United Kingdom; but when a Hardy peasant slips in
some good Dorset expressions the reader understands that this
character is of a particular social class and education. This is
precisely the information that we would normally associate with
register, not dialect. The dialect spoken *is* dialect (though it may
not be at all accurately represented, and then again, where does
one geographical or temporal dialect stop and another start?), but
the significance of its being dialect is a significance of register. In
literature, dialect tells us what register tells us, and anchors the
speaker in a social reality that has only marginally to do with those
classic parameters of normal dialect study: geography and period.[9]

The more recent history of the term

The 1960s saw a good deal of promising work in the field of
register but, as I have suggested, the *literary* potential of the concept
was not and has not been taken advantage of; indeed, linguists
have more or less hijacked the term and, by wrapping it in an
impenetrable apparatus of distinctions, have rendered it too fear-
some an object for literary use.

A good example of where the possibilities of register were
missed was in Crystal and Davy's *Investigating English Style* (1969).
Early in the 'Theoretical Preliminaries' of this book the authors
criticise certain stylisticians for adopting terminology that is not
used rigorously or consistently (this is the usual linguistician's
objection to the imprecise art of literary stylistics):

> The criticism of inconsistency can best be illustrated from the use of
> the term *register* (which is a fundamental notion in 'Neo-Firthian'
> stylistics). This term has been applied to varieties of language in an
> almost indiscriminate manner, as if it could be usefully applied to
> situationally distinctive pieces of language of any kind. The language of

newspaper headlines, church services, sports commentaries, popular songs, advertising, and football, amongst others have all been referred to as registers in one work.[10]

This 'one work' turns out to be Michael Gregory's article 'Aspects of varieties differentiation', referred to above, and Crystal and Davy's objection is expanded thus:

> There are very great differences in the nature of the situational variables involved in these uses of English, and... it is inconsistent, unrealistic and confusing to obscure these differences by grouping everything under the same heading, as well as an unnecessary trivialisation of what is a potentially useful concept.[11]

The reason for this surprising strength of animus against Gregory's mild, inoffensive and effective article becomes apparent ten pages later, when the authors, protesting that they do not wish to develop their notion of 'province' in texts into a 'theory of province', add, gratuitously, that they will not expand such a theory 'in the same way that some scholars have done with a "theory of register" (thus, to all intents and purposes, equating "register" with "stylistics"!)'. Their fear, apparent in the unusual exclamation mark (the only one I have found in their book), is clearly that reading-for-register, conceived in a broad and dynamic way, will put them out of business. It is they, after all, who, earlier in their study, declare that 'the end the stylistician is seeking' is 'to compose a single linguistic picture of the text as a whole', after which 'the descriptive aspect of the linguist's role is complete. The tasks which then follow – critical interpretation and evaluation – are not his concern.'[12] This defensiveness is typical of the problems that have bedevilled the application of linguistics to literature. Crystal and Davy are made nervous by the prospect of someone who, with feet still planted firmly in their linguistic soil, wants to operate with larger concepts than those of linguistics itself, and they see that 'register' can be used for such large-scale operations, so they don't like it. Thus the chance of a linguistically informed literary criticism, using register, is missed.

The alternative to this sort of dismissal is hijacking. I use this word because although the term 'register' was developed in a linguistic context, as we have seen, the literary potential was clearly there from the start and could have been made much more of. Take these points from Halliday's 1964 book, for instance:

> It is not the event or state of affairs being talked about that determines the choice [of language], but the convention that a certain kind of language is appropriate to a certain use....
>
> Linguistic humour often depends on the inappropriate choice and mixing of registers: P. G. Wodehouse [as we have seen] exploits this device very effectively. Fifty years ago the late George Robey used to recite a version of 'The House that Jack built' which ended as follows: '...that disturbed the equanimity of the domesticated feline mammal that exterminated the noxious rodent that masticated the farinaceous product deposited in the domiciliary edifice erected by Master John'.[13]

This is not exactly a discussion of register in Jane Austen, but it should excite the student of literature; what is literature, after all, other than a series of conventions about appropriate language? And what better method for starting to pin down that elusive concept 'style' than this sort of translation from one register into another?

Since the flowering of interest in register and related concepts in the 1960s, there has been a steady but not copious stream of books and articles which consider these topics. On some rare occasions, writers in the field have mentioned literature, but more typical would be an article such as Ruqaiya Hasan's 'Code, register and social dialect' (1973),[14] a fascinating approach to the topic in general, but not one that seems immediately applicable to literary analysis. It is true that Hasan has also written extensively on literary topics, for instance in her 'The place of stylistics in the study of verbal art' (1975), to which we shall return in Chapter 4, below,[15] but she imports large sections of Hallidayan functional linguistics into her analyses under the weight of which the literary insights gradually sink.

Halliday's *Language as Social Semiotic* (1978)[16] is perhaps the high-water mark of recent thinking about register. Certainly much of what I have to say in this book is a response to this study of Halliday's, and perhaps a development in more literary directions of the ideas contained in it. To be fair to Halliday, he does try to include literature in his grand scheme of things. He has a category of 'language as art', for instance, and refers to the inseparability of language and literature (p. 11), even going so far as to say that '*all* language is literature' (p. 147). The importance of his work, however, is in its establishment of the category of *text*; this is not always or necessarily literary text, of course, but it is still a great improvement on the subsentential notions of a more formalist linguistics. Texts have a life of their own, a status and a meaning-generating power that earlier linguists had not accorded to them, and this is a great advance for the student of literature; the *textuality* of a piece of writing, leading out into notions of genre and literary convention, is a most fruitful concept. The 'text-in-situation' is 'the basic unit of semantic structure' (p. 60); surely this is a useful way of approaching literature. A good summary of Hallidayan thinking on the topic can be found in his *Language, Context and Text* (with Ruqaiya Hasan, 1985), which contains much of the same material as is to be found in his *Introduction to Functional Grammar* of the same year.

So far so good, but for the literature student there are problems with Halliday's excellent work. Since this is, in a sense, the crux of what I have to argue in this book, I will concentrate for a moment on three of the main problems. They are not errors by Halliday, nor are they illogicalities or misunderstandings; we are not talking about a revision of his work here. Rather they are problems for the specific task of analysing the registers of literature and should be set alongside my earlier questioning of the triad 'Field–tenor–mode', above, where I was not concerned to 'explode' those notions but merely asking to be allowed to set them aside, for the purposes of literary analysis, without thereby being obliged to drop the notion of register altogether.

Problem one. Halliday's scheme is far too complicated to be of immediate use to a reader of a literary text. His 'schematic representation' of language as social semiotic (see p. 69 of *Language as Social Semiotic*) requires extensive sociological, philosophical and linguistic thought before it can even be understood. No reader of Wordsworth, Eliot or Iain Banks is going to be able to retain such a diagram even sketchily in his or her mind while trying to read *The Prelude, The Waste Land* or *The Wasp Factory*; the explanatory value would be small for any given moment in any of those texts, or in any other. We need register, but we do not need a full apparatus of almost Hegelian complexity for our purposes.[17]

Problem two. Halliday makes the crucial distinction that register is to be defined in semantic, not formal, terms: 'registers are different semantic configurations'. He seems to suggest the philosophical existence of some sort of objective meaning, dependent on register, which exists 'semantically' before being 'realised' in the formalities of actual language.[18] This goes against the whole thrust of the post-structuralist thinking that has done so much to loosen up literary reading in the last thirty or forty years of the twentieth century. We cannot, at this time of the day, be expected to go back to searching for a non-linguistic or pre-linguistic truth 'behind' the formal signs of which literature is composed.

Problem three. Halliday's interest in register goes the wrong way for us (see his pp. 32–3). He explicitly dismisses the sort of register analysis which asks 'which features of language are determined by register?' or – saying the same thing in another way – 'what peculiarities of vocabulary, or grammar or pronunciation, can be directly accounted for by reference to the situation?', and offers examples of this such as 'instances of near-synonymy where one word differs from another in level of formality, rhetoric or technicality, like "chips" and "French-fried potatoes", or "deciduous dentition" and "milk teeth" … these are commonplaces which lie at the fringe of register variation'. In place of this question, he says, we should instead be asking the question: 'Which kinds of situational factor determine which kind of selection in the linguistic system?' Now it will already be obvious, and it will become more obvious as this book progresses, that it is precisely the stylistic choice between 'chips' and 'fries' that we are interested in as literary readers; it is the 'peculiarities of grammar', and so on, that will teach us what we need to know about literary texts. Putting things the other way round, as Halliday suggests we should, is impossible in literary analysis; we *have* to start with 'the words on the page' because, in literature, that is all there is; there are *no* 'situational factors' of the kind he is thinking of pre-existing the text in our case; one may be able to predict that a context in which doctors discuss a patient in 'real life' will generate medicalese, but one can predict nothing from the situation in which one picks up a novel.[19] So Halliday may very well be right about the orientation of these matters a far as register in general is concerned (and he is clearly thinking of the classic register situation in which *under certain given circumstances* people use certain kinds of language), but in the matter of literature, the 'kinds of language' are not secondary and predictable; they come first, and themselves create or constitute the world of the text.

Since Halliday, a number of linguists have worked with register. Mohsen Ghadessy, for instance, has edited *Registers of Written English*,[20] which contains Halliday's essay on 'The language of physical science', in which he gives some basic and useful definitions, such as: 'A register is a cluster of associated features having a greater-than-random ... tendency to co-occur; and, like a dialect, it can be identified at any delicacy of focus' (p. 162). But there is surprisingly little on literary register in this otherwise admirable collection; indeed, the literary is not canvassed directly at all as a separate category. Ghadessy's subsequent collection (*Register Analysis: Theory and Practice*[21]) rather supports my thesis, against Crystal and Davy, that register can operate as a wide and unified theory, containing, as it does, articles on a very wide variety of register-related topics. The first essay in the collection, by Robert de Beaugrande, gives a good history of the concept which, significantly, doesn't mention literature.

Helen Leckie-Tarry's *Language and Context: A Functional Linguistic Theory of Register* (1995) is typical of the Hallidayan school of register studies.[22] It focuses only briefly on literature, and in general is short on examples of language use; intensely theoretical, and in places quite abstract, it cannot offer much very directly to the student of literature. Also from the Australian headquarters of functional grammar, Christie and Martin's *Genre and Institutions: Social Processes in the Workplace and School* (1997) contains some material promising for literary analysis – for instance the essay on 'Entertaining and instructing: exploring experience through story' by Joan Rothery and Maree Stenglin – but on the whole the focus is on typically Hallidayan concerns: school education, news reporting, technical media, and so on.[23]

Of more interest to literary students has been Michael Toolan's collection *Language, Text and Context: Essays in Stylistics* (1992), where half of the essays concern literary texts, and one even employs the concept of register. Brian McHales's 'Making (non)sense of postmodernist poetry' sees the highly difficult texts of poets such as J. H. Prynne, Charles Bernstein and John Ashberry as resisting register ascription (the 'assimilation' of their poems to 'any voice or register or speaker-position whatsoever' seems impossible), yet he can still use the term effectively, commenting on the 'juxtaposed and competing registers' of much of their verse which is often 'saturated with specific registers' such as the medical.[24]

Of considerable interest is Paul Simpson's *Language through Literature: An Introduction* (1997).[25] This study of English *through* analysis of literary texts (an unusual and brave approach) opens, after a brief section entitled 'Why stylistics?', with a longer section specifically on 'Register and literary language'. This is most promising. Simpson, who denies that there is any ontologically definable 'literary language', defends this denial by insisting that his 'real intention' in doing so is 'to emphasise the full panoply of linguistic resources that are available to writers': 'Literary discourse… derives its effectiveness from its exploitation of the entire linguistic repertoire.' This excellently Bakhtinian point is precisely the one that leads me to employ 'register' so vigorously. Far from being a marginal or 'small' term, register is the conceptual place where we can bring together all the voices of a culture, also known as the full panoply of linguistic resources of that culture. *That* is the place at which literary reading should start.

Workpoints

Decorum: 'appropriateness', 'fittingness', which is according to Milton 'the grand masterpiece to observe' (*Of Education*, 1642), was a central tenet of rhetorical theory and of literary criticism in classical antiquity. The matching of style to subject and to speaker was a major preoccupation of the sophists who taught rhetoric in fourth-century Greece. With the development of formal criticism at Alexandria in the next century and the categorisation of literature into genres, each of which was deemed to have its appropriate style and register, decorum (Greek, *to prepon*) became central. So confident were critics such as Aristarchus in the notion that they censured even Homer for violations of epic decorum. Alexandrian attitudes were taken over wholesale

> by the Romans and decorum forms the implicit basis of all that Horace has to say about style in the *Ars Poetica*, and the explicit basis of the poetics of Cicero and Quintilian. In the Renaissance the Roman inheritance is everywhere apparent. In England it is a central commonplace of such writers as Puttenham, Sidney, Johnson, Dryden and Pope.
>
> For Halliday the difference between registers and dialects is that in dialects we say the same thing in different ways while in registers we say different things in different ways.
>
> But here are Leech and Short in their *Style in Fiction* (1981):
>
> [Style is dependent on finding] 'alternative ways of rendering the same subject matter' (p. 39)
>
> I don't think there ever is such a thing as the *same* subject matter (how would we know, anyway?) but Leech and Short, who use 'style' in a way that is very closely equivalent to my notion of register, are surely nearer the mark than Halliday.

Notes

1 T. B. W. Reid, 'Linguistics, structuralism and philology', *Archivum Linguisticum*, vol. 8, Fascicle 1, 1956, pp. 28–37.

2 M. A. K. Halliday, A. MacIntosh and P. Strevens, *The Linguistic Sciences and Language Teaching* (Longman, 1964), pp. 93–4.

3 Aristotle, *Poetics*, in T. S. Dorsch (ed.), *Classical Literary Criticism* (Penguin, 1965), p. 31.

4 J. R. Firth, 'Personality in language and society', in *Papers in Linguistics 1934–1951* (Oxford University Press, 1957), p. 182.

5 Cf. the entry LANGUAGE VARIETIES: REGISTER by Ellis and Ure in A. R. Meetham (ed.), *The Encyclopaedia of Linguistics, Information and Control* (Pergamon Press, 1969), pp. 251–9.

6 J. R. Firth, *The Treatment of Language in General Linguistics* (The Medical Press, 1959).

7 Halliday, MacIntosh and Strevens, *The Linguistic Sciences*.

8 Michael Gregory, 'Aspects of varieties differentiation', *Journal of Linguistics*, 3, 1967.

9 Halliday comes close to making this point but seems to think that it is a special feature of British English:

In Britain, the choice of dialect is bound up with choice of register in a way that is unique among language communities of the world: it is a linguistic error to give a radio commentary on cricket in cockney or sing popular songs in the Queen's English. Many of the languages of older nations show some such mutual dependence between dialect and register. (Halliday, MacIntosh and Strevens, *The Linguistic Sciences*, p. 94)

Apart from the fact that the second of these sentences more or less contradicts the first, this is based on a pretty dubious assumption. Reading the news in Andalusian dialect would have quite a strong register effect in Spanish (for being Andalusian is not only a geographical matter, it carries further cultural and social implications, including those of a certain romantic, rustic and even earthy character). My point, anyway, is limited to the claim that *in literature* dialect is tantamount to register; see my chapter on dialect, Chapter 9 below. See Halliday, MacIntosh and Strevens, *The Linguistic Sciences*, pp. 87 ff.

10 David Crystal and Derek Davy, *Investigating English Style* (Longman, 1969), p. 61.

11 *Ibid.*

12 *Ibid.*, p. 22.

13 Halliday, MacIntosh and Strevens, *The Linguistic Sciences*, p. 19.

14 In Basil Bernstein (ed.), *Class, Codes and Control* (Routledge, 1973), vol. 2.

15 Ruqaiya Hasan, 'The place of stylistics in the study of verbal art', in H. Ringborn (ed.), *Style and Text* (Skriptor, 1975).

16 M. A. K. Halliday, *Language as Social Semiotic: The Social Interpretation of Language and Meaning* (Edward Arnold, 1978). See also Halliday's *Functional Grammar* (Edward Arnold, 1985).

17 See Halliday, *Language as Social Semiotic*, p. 69.

18 See, for instance, Halliday and Hasan's *Language, Context and Text: Aspects of Language in Social-Semiotic Perspective* (Deakin University Press, 1985), where the oddity of seeing register in semantic terms is apparent in the phrase 'of course' as it appears in the following sentences: 'A register is a semantic concept…. Since it is a configuration of meanings a register must …, of course, include the expressions, the lexico-grammatical and phonological features, that typically accompany or REALISE these meanings' (p. 39).

19 Of course, as we shall see in Chapter 4, one knows a great deal about a text called 'a novel' even before one has started to read it, but that is not the sort of situation that Halliday has in mind. All one knows in advance about 'a novel' is that it exists in a *literary* context of novelness; this is not the same sort of animal as the context in which

any other kind of text comes to one.

20 Mohsen Ghadessy, *Registers of Written English* (Pinter, 1988).

21 Mohsen Ghadessy, ed., *Register Analysis: Theory and Practice* (Pinter, 1993).

22 Helen Leckie-Tarry, *Language and Context: A Functional Linguistic Theory of Register* (Pinter, 1995).

23 Frances Christie and J. R. Martin (eds), *Genre and Institutions: Social Processes in the Workplace and School* (Cassell, 1997).

24 Michael Toolan (ed.), *Language, Text and Context: Essays in Stylistics* (Routledge, 1992).

25 Paul Simpson, *Language through Literature: An Introduction* (Routledge, 1997).

3

Two big distinctions: written/spoken and formal/informal

Delicacy

Most things in both nature and culture can be observed at different levels of delicacy. As usual, it is the *differences* that are brought into play which determine the available meanings. 'Japan is an industrial country', for instance, is 'true' in so far as Japan could not be put in a category alongside countries with a predominantly rural economy if the question being asked were 'Which are the industrial countries?' But walking through an agricultural area of rural Hokkaido, it would be inadequate to insist on the statement about industrialisation; now other things would need to be said: 'This is a non-industrial part of Japan' (different from the industrial part), at least. Similarly, the moon is 'a planet' if we are trying to distinguish it from a star, but the sentence 'This is all dust and rock' is a reasonable one to utter if we are standing on the moon and noticing that its surface is different from the surface of the Earth. The question is always the Wittgensteinian one of the distinction that is being made, and the point here is that even opposites (industrial/agricultural) can both be 'true' if the delicacy of focus is altered.

It is worth bearing this delicacy argument in mind when we are deciding what counts as a register. The distinction being made depends on the delicacy of focus: 'American' is a useful category to distinguish a wide variety of things from their European or African counterparts, but it seems far too general for most purposes when it is used inside America itself; the term starts to lose meaning as a whole congeries of disparate peoples, cultures, climates, and so on, come into view. Perhaps registers also work in large-scale and small-scale ways, and the term can be used in a very general way but also broken down into smaller subsections.

What follows is an attempt to sketch out two of the larger distinctions that are useful in trying to distinguish the register of any given text: written/spoken and formal/informal

Written versus spoken

A good deal of work has been done by linguisticians on the difference between written and spoken language and, in general, the differences seem to be large.[1] Halliday, for instance, comes to the conclusion – certainly surprising to amateurs in the field – that the grammar of spoken texts is much more complex than the grammar of written texts. Normally, though, the honours go the other way: in writing we employ a wider range of vocabulary than we do in speaking, and we can experiment more freely with what are called – misleadingly, therefore – 'figures of speech'; also with syntactical arrangements, word order, clause structure, and other things. So in most senses, though not in all, spoken English is 'simpler' than written English.

This is an excellent example of where we need to rescue literary study from the high anxiety engendered by looking too deeply into linguistics. For the fact is that in the huge complexity of the comparison between written and spoken language, there is much that is of little or no relevance to the reading of literary texts. The approach which presumes that the full panoply of conversation analysis is suitable for application to a piece of text that happens to contain conversation may be mistaken. *Some* of the terms from conversation analysis may be useful in describing the style of a text, but there is little to be gained from attempting a complete dissection with these tools.

First of all, let us be clear: literary texts bear little, if any, resemblance to natural speech as recorded and transcribed. One can find almost nothing in any literary text that remotely resembles a real conversation. Here is a transcript of spontaneous speech from Benson and Greaves's *The Language People Really Use*;[2] as they point out, it has 'lost many markers' which would show the spontaneities, interruptions, loudness, and so on; none the less, it hardly 'reads well':

B. Well speed reading um... you... to be perfect you have to read sixteen pages... in one minute...

G. Oooh boy...

G. That's hard...

B. (*overlapping*) about um thousands of words I don't know. They're real thin... letters... an... you're... they're... I don't know... how many thousands of words... you read... huh...

G. I...

B. Well I was watching this show and em there was this lady and he kept on flipping the pages like this...

Even in the plays of Harold Pinter, the characters sound a good deal more organised than this. Despite being tidied up, as they obviously have been in this transcription, 'B' and 'G' appear superficially to be talking without any grammatical structure at all. In fact, of course, there is a grammar operating here that is a good deal more complex than that of more 'written' English, but it is a grammar with which readers of literature almost never have to do.

In literature there is none the less much represented speech, as we have seen, including dialogue in drama and fiction; free indirect speech and indirect speech in fiction; and some limited versions of these in verse. All these representations of speech are *registered*; since they are made of language, there is no choice, and it might be expected that they would conform to some general rule whereby they represent spoken English by employing the registers that real speech employs. But this may be looking at things the wrong way round, and I would suggest that we try something else. Instead of: 'Represented speech in literature "should" or may show signs of ("real") spoken register' let us try: 'Various spoken registers are among the possibilities open to literature and may be used in any context, whether that of represented speech or not.' The fact is that literature always comes to us 'voiced', and voicing can, at any point, borrow the register clothes of *either* written *or* spoken English for its different purposes. Characters can at times speak in absolutely written English, and the narrator in fiction can operate in a conventional version of spoken English. I suspect that it might even be impossible to establish that the majority of represented speech in literature is in spoken register. Indeed, as we have said, very little literature is written in *truly* spoken mode; even Harold Pinter, colloquial as much of his dialogue undoubtedly is, can be shown to have balanced and organised his exchanges in a way that scarcely qualifies as truly spoken. Compare the real recorded conversation, as given above, with the following colloquial exchange from *The Caretaker*:

DAVIES   What's this?

ASTON   It's a smoking-jacket.

DAVIES   A smoking-jacket. (*He feels it.*) This ain't a bad piece of cloth. I'll see how it fits. (*He tries it on.*) You ain't got a mirror here, have you?

ASTON   I don't think I have.

DAVIES   Well, it don't fit too bad. How do you think it looks?

ASTON   Looks all right.

DAVIES   Well, I won't say no to this, then.[3]

The difference is immediately obvious. Pinter's conversation seems a good deal more coherent (there are far more 'cohesive ties' than there are in the spontaneous speech), and even in a play which is getting nowhere, this local piece of dialogue seems to be getting somewhere, and understanding is occurring. None the less, this clearly counts as spoken register in contrast to many other more formal or written styles.

Perhaps it is a question not of 'How close has this playwright managed to get to truly spoken English?' but rather, more simply, of whether or not the writer, whether of mimetic or diegetic material, introduces *some* elements of what is conventionally considered to be the spoken. Very often, in dialogue, spoken register is *not* used – the verse sections of Shakespeare seem a good enough example but one could add the plays of Wilde and substantial parts of Shaw, Beckett, even O'Neil. On the other hand, fictional narrators (who often present us with dialogue and other forms of represented speech) can easily work in something approximating to spoken mode themselves when they are simply narrating. Here is the opening of a short American novel that had a good deal of success in the early 1970s, Erich Segal's *Love Story*:

What can you say about a twenty-five-year-old girl who died?
    That she was beautiful. And brilliant. That she loved Mozart and Bach. And the Beatles. And me.[4]

This, I submit, is in spoken. Perhaps I should write 'spoken' since it does not quite have the messiness of truly spoken English, and the words sit too neatly on the page for us to be entirely convinced, but this is a fair attempt to represent somebody talking – talking in this case to an implied reader. We can imagine a close friend to whom we have put a sympathetic question about the recent death of the woman he loves. He either gazes unseeing into the distance or, possibly, fixes us with a serious or ironically smiling gaze, shrugs his shoulders and launches into his heartfelt lines: 'What can you say about a twenty-five-year-old…'.

Because conversational turn-taking is quite strictly controlled, it would be surprising if this voicing were able to continue unchanged for long. How long a monologue can you stand, even from the closest friend? And so it is here; the implied reader can't butt in, but a character can and when she does intervene the narrator, by contrast, begins to sound a lot less spoken himself. Segal's narrator continues:

> Once, when she specifically lumped me with those musical types, I asked her what the order was, and she replied, smiling, 'Alphabetical.'

Instantly the game is given away, and the tyranny of the written (this is literature, after all) reasserts itself. The earlier 'spoken' mode ('What can you say…'), with its grammatical incompletions, its short words and short sentences, its rhetorical question, its simple declaratives followed by strings of noun-phrase objects (she loved Mozart *and* Bach *and* the Beatles *and* me) is replaced with a longer sentence of at least four clauses involving both subordination and co-ordination, more polysyllabic words and, most telling of all, the embedding of elements such as 'smiling'. This is no longer spoken, this is creeping up on written even though the narrator will make another bid for spoken voicing at the end of this first paragraph when, having discussed the question of where he came in the list of his love's loves, he says he always had to be 'number one', and concludes, 'Family heritage, don't you know?' This brings us back to the rhetorical question and the grammatically incomplete sentence of spoken register.

Here is an example of the opposite phenomenon – not now of the narrator writing in 'spoken' but of characters whose speech is represented in written register. In Johnson's *Rasselas* (1759) the characters 'speak' in very much the same register as the narrator, and almost no concession is made to spoken register at all. The narrator opens Chapter 3, for instance, with this two-part sentence; for convenience I have italicised the direct speech:

> On the next day his old instructor, imagining that he had now made himself acquainted with [Rasselas's] disease of mind, was in hope of curing it by counsel, and officiously sought an opportunity of conference, which the prince, having long considered him as one whose intellects were exhausted, was not very willing to afford: '*Why, said he, does this man thus intrude upon me; shall I never be suffered to forget those lectures which pleased only while they were new, and to become new again must be forgotten?*'[5]

Of course the italicised 'spoken' part of this carries some of the characteristic signs of direct speech including a verb in the present tense and the use of the first person, but those things aside I see little difference between the register of Rasselas 'speaking' and that of the narrator narrating; both are in written register. Rasselas when speaking, for example, can manage a neat chiasmus –'Lectures *interesting* – when *new*: to be *new* again – must lose all *interest* (be forgotten)' – and he indulges in subordination ('which pleased…'), just as the narrator seems to subordinate instinctively; indeed, more than half of the narrator's section is subordinated, and there is subordination-within-subordination in the 'which the prince' clause.

The proof of the monologic quality of this prose, where register does not shift from spoken to written when the narrator takes over from a character but instead barely changes under any circumstances, can be found in the interchangeability of the two sections. Without any radical register changes, much of the first part could be put into some form of represented speech:

> On the next day his old instructor officiously sought an opportunity of conference [with Rasselas]: 'I presume, he reflected, that I have now become acquainted with the prince's disease of mind and I am in hope of curing it by counsel.' The prince was not very willing to afford this encounter: 'I have long, said he, considered this old man as one whose intellects are exhausted.'

The match cannot be made perfect, nor can we quite achieve the converse perfection in rendering the 'spoken' section into narrative, but the overall impression of a single register remains. The lexis of the non-italicised section is approximately equal, in register value, to that of the italicised, spoken section, which could start something like this: 'Rasselas asked of himself the reason for the intrusions of this man: he would never be suffered to forget those lectures...' One cannot quite keep the full Johnsonian tone in making transpositions such as this, but it is clear, at least, that the register can be made largely consistent whether the material is presented by the narrator or through the speech of a character.

Here is a passage from Chapter 26 of *Rasselas* which, in a bare excerpted state as presented here, seems to be impossible to assign to either a character or the narrator:

> In families, whether there is or is not poverty, there is commonly discord: if a kingdom be, as Imlac tells us, a great family, a family likewise is a little kingdom, torn with factions and exposed to revolutions. An unpractised observer expects the love of parents and children to be constant and equal; but this kindness seldom continues beyond the years of infancy: in a short time the children become rivals to their parents.[6]

This could be Rasselas himself, or one of the other wise voices of the novel, asserting the usual Johnsonian pessimism about human nature; or it could perfectly well be the narrator, more directly, doing the same thing. It includes some of the usual markers of Johnson's formal style: embedding, subordination, chiasmus, parallelism, Latinate vocabulary, and so on. I have left in a clause that I was tempted to omit – the fourth clause, 'as Imlac tells us'. At first I thought that this would too obviously reveal that this passage is in fact direct speech by Princess Nekayah, Rasselas's sister, explaining things to her brother as she does several times in the novel; 'Imlac' is another character in the novel – wise, Rasselas' mentor, and a poet. But for someone who has not read the novel, the clause 'as Imlac tells us' could be equivalent to 'as Plato tells us', where Plato is not a fictional character and where, of course, 'us' means 'everyone' rather than 'you-and-I who are talking together'. So, I submit, this piece of dialogue, as it stands, is indistinguishable in register terms from the narrative in which it is embedded. So far from being marked as speech, it is utterly written in nature, and Princess Nekayah is to be admired for her astonishing rhetorical powers (though I wouldn't necessarily want her to talk to me like that for a whole evening).

Does one need to go much further than this? A small number of stylistic tools can be employed to demonstrate the spoken or written quality of any piece of text. In the case of a literary text, there is little need to go on into the largely separate topic of the vast differences between spoken and written language in general, since *truly* spoken register, language 'as she is spoke' in most situations in the everyday world, is almost entirely foreign to the literary text. For most purposes it is sufficient simply to establish whether the register of the text in question is on one or the other side of the conventional divide spoken versus written. It need not be the first point to observe about a text, but I suspect that in practice it will play a large part in any assessment of the 'tone' (and therefore the meaning) of the text.

Formal versus informal

Most people are aware of levels in their own language: slang is appropriate in one context but not in another; a certain form of words is expected from someone writing a letter of condolence, another from someone telling a joke; these are the staple elements of the notion of register, as we have seen. One metaphor often employed to make a basic distinction among these elements is that of formality. Some examples of language are more formal than others

Literary texts play along the fault-lines of the formal/informal distinction endlessly. Often there is an overlap, a congruence, between it and the spoken versus written distinction discussed above. In general the formal equates to the written and the informal to the spoken, but it is worth retaining a distinction between them since there are examples of formal spoken English and, conversely, examples of informal written English. The sermons of Lancelot Andrewes or John Donne in the seventeenth century are highly formal but they have rhetorical elements that mark them as being designed to be spoken; conversely, there are children's stories written in very informal registers that none the less sound highly written.

Here is a fairly formal opening from a generally informal novelist, Evelyn Waugh. It is the start of *Put Out More Flags* (1942), the first volume in the *Sword of Honour* trilogy:

> In the week which preceded the outbreak of the Second World War –
> days of surmise and apprehension which cannot, without irony, be
> called the last days of peace – and on the Sunday morning when all
> doubts were finally resolved and misconceptions corrected, three rich
> women thought first and mainly of Basil Seal. They were his sister, his
> mother and his mistress.[7]

The formality features here include:

1. The length of the first sentence.
2. The presence of subordination and embedding ('without irony'
   embedded in a parenthesis).
3. The 'elevated' lexis ('apprehension' for 'fear'; 'which preceded'
   for 'before').
4. Parallelism ('doubts … resolved / misconceptions … corrected').

Here these formal features are also signs of written register, but
this next passage, from a few pages later in the novel, though also
definitely written, has few of the four features listed, and is not
very formal:

> Freddy was in uniform, acutely uncomfortable in ten-year-old trousers.
> He had been to report at the yeomanry headquarters the day before,
> and was home for two nights collecting his kit, which, in the two years
> since he was last at camp, had been misused in charades and picnics
> and dispersed about the house in a dozen improbable places.[8]

The written aspects of this include omissions of elements that
would probably be included in an oral delivery (examples of
ellipsis): the first sentence, in spoken mode, would be more likely
to read 'Freddy was in uniform, *and he felt* acutely uncomfortable
in ten-year-old trousers.' The second sentence, in spoken, would
have repeated the 'he' so that it would read 'and *he* was home for
two nights'. Equally, only in written would one be likely to find
the multiplication of levels involved in the embedding of 'in the
two years since he had been at camp' inside the subordinate clause
'which … had been misused'.

So this is written, but it is hardly very formal; the lexis rises
to 'misused' and 'dispersed' (in place, perhaps, of 'messed around
with' and 'scattered') but the style is generally clichéd ('acutely
uncomfortable'), comfortably sloppy ('collecting his kit') and makes
intensive use of that most banal of English verbs – 'to be' ('Freddy

was', 'He *had been*', '[he] *was* home for two nights', 'he *was* last at camp'). These comments are not adverse criticism of Waugh. There is no reason to suppose that the register of this passage is any less carefully calculated than that of his most formal or 'poetic' paragraphs.

Thus, although there is an overlap between the formal and written categories, sometimes a perfect congruence between them so that it does not matter which we use, there are also cases where it seems more useful to stress the written nature of the text in question and others where the formality is what is important. Let us, at all events, keep both words in our critical armoury.

It would be out of place to allow oneself too much anxiety in the handling of these distinctions concerning formality and writtenness and their opposites....

No, that's too formal and defensive a tone to adopt; I'll try instead: There's no point in getting too worried about using these terms, formal, written, and so on. Literary reading cannot operate on a fully systematic basis, and it may simply not be useful or possible to categorise every element in a text as written–formal or spoken–informal, or some hybrid of these categories. Sometimes it is better to use one term; sometimes it is better to use another. Here is a passage from early in Robert Louis Stevenson's *Travels with a Donkey* (1879).

> It was already hard upon October before I was ready to set forth, and at the high altitudes over which my road lay there was no Indian summer to be looked for. I was determined, if not to camp out, at least to have the means of camping out in my possession; for there is nothing more harassing to an easy mind than the necessity of reaching shelter by dusk, and the hospitality of a village inn is not always to be reckoned sure by those who trudge on foot. A tent, above all for a solitary traveller, is troublesome to pitch, and troublesome to strike again; and even on the march it forms a conspicuous feature in your baggage. A sleeping-sack, on the other hand, is always ready – you have only to get into it; it serves a double purpose – a bed by night, a portmanteau by day; and it does not advertise your intention of camping out to every curious passer-by. This is a huge point. If the camp is not secret it is but a troubled resting-place; you become a public character; the convivial rustic visits your bedside after an early supper; and you must sleep with one eye open and be up before the day. I decided on a sleeping-sack; and after repeated visits to Le Puy, and a deal of high

living for myself and my advisers, a sleeping-sack was designed, constructed, and triumphantly brought home.[9]

Before we comment on the formality or writtenness of this, there is a preliminary point that needs to be made. Reading other texts of the mid-Victorian period will demonstrate that some of the old-fashioned lexis involved in this passage is typical of its time – here is a crucial point untouched by the Hallidayan analysis in terms of field, tenor and mode. Stevenson writes an English some parts of which have disappeared, and we have to identify them and think about their implications before we can be accurate in our register analysis of this or any other non-contemporary text. Thus, 'a sleeping-sack', 'a portmanteau' and 'an easy mind' all seem to require comment. The first two are simply obsolete versions of 'sleeping-bag' and 'suitcase', and perhaps fairly register-neutral (though that is never strictly possible; sleeping-sacks and portmanteaux presumably formed part of Victorian 'camping-speak' and 'traveller-speak' respectively.) 'An easy mind' still makes sense because of such expressions as 'I wasn't easy in my mind about it...', which has a definitely colloquial air; but here I think that 'easy' is almost synonymous with 'lazy', or 'concerned for creature comforts' or (to shift register and come right up to date) 'not wanting hassle'. This makes 'easy' hard to place on the written/spoken or formal/informal scales.

After we have thought about the date of the text, then, we can read it for the formality or otherwise of its registers. Stevenson's tone carries a great deal of his meaning, and the tone is generated by these registers; his semi-serious, late-Romantic, British-humorous persona in the *Travels* in itself tells us of a particular view of the world, and constitutes a self-presentation of a clearly definable kind. This tone is brought about by a special mixing of register features. Thus on the one hand there is little in the paragraph quoted above that could be said to be seriously formal, although there is a flavour of something heavyweight in the phrases 'hard upon October' and 'high altitudes', and perhaps in the constructions 'I was determined, if not to camp out, at least to have...' and 'it is but a troubled resting-place'. On the other hand, it seems appropriate here to identify a good deal of written register. Nobody, even in 1879, ever *spoke* such clauses as 'A tent, above all for

a solitary traveller, is troublesome to pitch', or 'it forms a conspicuous feature in your baggage'. Typical *written* features here
include nominalisation (noun forms instead of verb forms, as in
'a solitary traveller' instead of 'someone who is travelling alone'),
embedding ('A tent, above all…') and slightly 'elevated' journalistic cliché ('forms a conspicuous feature').

But within the written register that Stevenson indulges in there
is a good deal of 'talk'. The second person gives a strong flavour
of the spoken: '*you* only have to get into it', '*you* become a public
character'; this dialogic strain is in contrast to the 'I' of the first
sentences and of the circumlocutions 'those who trudge on foot'
and 'a solitary traveller'. In fact, all three persons are thus deployed
in one paragraph, 'I', 'you' and 'those who'. This tends to involve
the reader but also to keep the overall register slightly unstable: a
sort of freewheeling tone develops, whereby sometimes we are
looking at the narrator 'from the outside' ('I was ready to set forth'),
sometimes from the inside ('I decided on'); sometimes we are asked
to check our own memories for parallel experiences ('you', but this
'you' is also an 'I' and a 'one', of course); and sometimes we are
being asked to look at the narrator looking at others while including both himself and ourselves among them ('those who'). This is
a long way from high seriousness and also some distance from low
comedy; the monolithic nature of some kinds of written English
is absent; instead, the lighter and more shifting tone of the conversational is presented not directly (little conversation ever sounds
truly like this) but through the shifting registers.

The rhetorical, emphatic nature of the short sentence 'This is
a huge point', sandwiched between much longer and more complex sentences, comes straight from the urgent insistence of the
lecturer, public speaker or pub bore explaining his meanings only
too clearly. Other spoken or conversational elements include 'on
the other hand' (which can be either colloquial or written, but
sounds spoken here) and the phrasal verb 'get into'. But these
form a contrast with such locutions as 'the hospitality of a village
inn is not always to be reckoned sure by those who trudge on
foot', which introduces a very *written* passive ('is not to be reckoned
sure by…') in contrast to the bright actives of 'This is a huge
point', 'a sleeping-sack is always ready', or 'you become a public
character'. Of course, the usual humour is generated by this shifting

about in register; thus at the end of the quoted paragraph the register seems to rise with the three fairly formal words 'designed', 'constructed', and 'triumphantly', while the topic under discussion, the thing that is being 'brought home' like some trophy, is just a sleeping-bag, an object that hardly needs the architectural-engineering reality (or register) of design and construction.

In the next chapter I shall be discussing the relationship between register and genre. For the moment I will just signal that this style of Stevenson's is interestingly reproduced in a number of travel writings. Here is a passage from Sir John Murray's *Sketches of Persia* (1861):

> Muscat is governed by a prince whose title is Imam, and whose author-ity, like that of many chiefs in Arabia, is more of a patriarchal than despotic character. Though he has large fleets, including some fine frigates, and a considerable army to garrison his possessions on the coast of Africa, the shores of Arabia and the islands of the Persian Gulf, he must attend to the summons of any inhabitant of Muscat who calls him to a court of justice. Your sceptics who deny the existence of any just administration of power, except in the commonwealth of Europe, may call this a mere form. Be it so: yet the knowledge that such a form was observed went far, in my mind, to mark the character of this petty government.[10]

Superficially, this bears no great resemblance to the passage from Stevenson, yet their relationship becomes clearer from a register analysis. Here, again, we have the freewheeling play with three persons: after describing the (third-person) Imam of Muscat, Murray introduces at least the ghost of the second person with 'Your sceptics', where the 'your', although not a true possessive, refers to the European addressee of this discourse, and thus to 'me'; it is the equivalent of the public speaker's 'You may think'. Then he moves on to mention the first person, himself: 'in my mind'. There is something less formal about this mixture of per-sons than there would be about an equivalent discourse couched only in one. This sort of passage, incidentally, is also reminiscent of Swift in *Gulliver's Travels*, a fact which demonstrates the intertextual or 'borrowed' nature of registers and styles in general.

Then again, Murray goes on to become mildly facetious, some-thing in the Stevenson manner, unnecessarily 'elevated' in a way that makes one suspect him of lacking full seriousness; and, just as Stevenson ends his paragraph with some rather overblown lexis in which he describes simply bringing home a sleeping-bag he has ordered and bought, so Murray ends up on a pseudo-serious note:

> But it is the eye, the disposition and the judgement of the observer, more than what is actually seen, that stamps the condition of distant nations with those who have to form their opinions at second-hand; and the generality of readers, who have their happiness grounded on a natural prejudice in favour of their own ways and usages, lean towards such as minister to their pride and patriotism, by throwing a dark shade on all they meet different from Old England, or some of those countries in its vicinity, for which their good climate, cheap viands, and well-flavoured wines have created a predilection.[11]

Here we can see that a humorous tone – sarcastic even – is taking the reader in one direction, while a certain orotundity of phrasing is taking him or her in exactly the opposite direction. The sheer length of this final sentence, with its multiple clauses, subordination and use of words such as 'predilection', indicates an almost Johnsonian tone and intent, while the lexis of the later part of it laughs good-humouredly at a certain sort of compatriot of Murray's, a man (probably, indeed, a *man*) who refers from time to time to 'Old England' and, when challenged, admits that some of the countries near home aren't too bad either … the, er, *viands* are good (any more immediately comprehensible term might show up my greediness more clearly), and the wine (I'd better not use too technical a term) is *well-flavoured*. I'm sure you get the point I'm making…

Romance versus Germanic

Formal – and to a slightly lesser extent written – registers show a preference for Latinate vocabulary, while informal and spoken registers prefer Anglo-Saxon vocabulary. This useful pattern is rather too simple, because the 'core vocabulary' of English, the most spoken and everyday part, is only partly Old English (in late-twentieth-century register, Anglo-Saxon has become Old English) and partly the early Norman French 'loans' (impositions?) from the years following the 1066 Conquest. By using simple words from 'OE' and 'NF' we manage to sound basic, ordinary, not highfalutin; while Latin words brought directly into the language at or since the Renaissance tend to get a bit posh and make us sound serious, grand, and so on. So it is not so much a choice between Germanic and Romance as a choice between a mainly Germanic core and a mainly Latin post-Renaissance English, with the former doing the more down-to-earth jobs and the latter performing the more elegant and less mundane operations.

Nobody is more Latinate than Gibbon (unless it be Dr Johnson). Here is a bit of Volume II Chapter XIV (what register effect do Roman numerals have?) of Gibbon's *Decline and Fall of the Roman Empire* (1776–88):

> The reconciliation of Constantine and Licinius, though it was embittered by resentment and jealousy, by the remembrance of recent injuries, and by the apprehension of future dangers, maintained, however, above eight years the tranquillity of the Roman world.[12]

This sentence contains eighteen lexical words (that is, nouns, verbs, adjectives and adverbs, words with a semantic 'content', not merely 'grammatical' words such as prepositions). Of these, only two ('embittered' and 'world') have discernibly Germanic origins. The others come either from Latin directly or from Latin via French – except for 'eight' which can be traced back to a common Aryan root and appears both to be related to Latin *octo* and French *huit* on the one hand, and to German *acht* on the other. In other words, there is a high proportion of Latinate vocabulary here. Even if we discount 'eight' and the two proper names, we have thirteen Romance words against two Germanic.

But here is the notoriously laconic Ernest Hemingway, writing in 1950:

> After a while Jackson drove the car down the ditch and willow lined road with the car's big headlights on, looking for a place to turn. He found one, finally, and turned carefully. When he was on the[13]

I have stopped at that point, with 'the', because that is the thirty-eighth word and the Gibbon sentence above is also thirty-eight words long . Some similarity is thus established, but if we do the same count for Hemingway as we did for Gibbon, we get very different results. In the Hemingway there are seventeen lexical words (counting the unhyphenated 'willow lined' as two words), of which only six ('car', 'lined', 'place', 'turn', 'finally' and 'turned') are of Romance origin, while eleven are Germanic. What is more, three of the Romance words ('lined', 'turn' and 'turned'), although derived ultimately from Latin, in fact came into English not via French after 1066 but in the Anglo-Saxon period and so have a Germanic flavour to them. One might then say that Gibbon's coefficient of formality is Romance 13; Germanic 2, so say 6.5; while Hemingway's is Romance 6 (or fewer); Germanic 11 (or more), or say 0.5.

Nobody would accuse Gibbon of being laconic. There are several aspects of his neoclassical language that make him seem quite the opposite (including his clause structure and punctuation), but the origins of his preferred vocabulary (his 'lexical choices', if you want to sound more technical) also explain a good deal of the register effect he creates. Similarly, going in the opposite direction, Hemingway, when he wants to simplify, focus and reduce his writing, chooses a particular range of vocabulary. Here, at the end of *Across the River and into the Trees*, a novel about war, *machismo* and death (as it says on the blurb of the Penguin edition of 1966, it's about 'the great Hemingway themes – youth and age, love and war, and above all, what makes a man'), there is no place for the cool rationalised distance imposed by Latinate polysyllabic lexis [= long words]; instead Hemingway wants to create an effect of almost arid directness, an illusion of disillusionment. So he goes as Anglo-Saxon as is reasonable.

Here's a bit of Lawrence of Arabia. It's from *Seven Pillars of Wisdom* (1926), the tale of Lawrence's exploits in World War I, in Arabia against the Turks. Lawrence was a good classical scholar, but he is telling a gripping first-person narrative, wants to depict the astonishing chastity of the desert, and cannot afford always to rely on his Latin education to get his effects. So he goes quite Germanic at times:

> It was very dark; a pure night enough, but the black stone underfoot swallowed the light of the stars, and at seven o'clock, when at last we halted, only four of our party were with us.[14]

Here only 'pure' and 'party', out of some sixteen lexical words, have a classical origin; the rest have Old English roots and are, typically, inclined to be monosyllables ('dark', 'night', 'light', 'stars', 'last'). On the other hand, Lawrence can also manage this sort of thing, describing the food shortage that beset his army (and their prisoners) after the capture of Akaba:

> Green dates loaded the palms overhead. Their taste, raw, was nearly as nasty as the want they were to allay. Cooking left them still deplorable; so we and our prisoners sadly faced a dilemma of constant hunger, or of violent diurnal pains more proper to gluttony than to our expedient eating. The assiduous food-habit of a lifetime had trained the English body to the pitch of producing a punctual nervous excitation in the upper belly at the fixed hour of each meal: and we sometimes gave the honoured name of hunger to this sign that our gut had cubic space for more stuff. Arab hunger was the cry of a long-empty labouring body fainting with weakness. They lived on a fraction of our bulk-food, and their systems made exhaustive use of what they got. A nomad army did not dung the earth richly with by-products.[15]

I think most readers would agree that Lawrence isn't taking hunger very seriously here – even sneering at its trivialised English version. He stays detached from the undoubtedly difficult business of feeding an army in the desert – thereby giving himself extra status, of course, since he managed to bring off this feat while not panicking or getting too upset. This peculiar and perhaps very English mind-set is generated for us in large part by the register choices Lawrence makes. Especially, he shifts between a Germanic and a Romance-based style.

Thus this passage begins with little Latin and no Greek; the first two sentences are all Germanic, and only 'taste' has a Latin origin, but I think it is clear that the register begins to change with the first important Romance word, which is 'deplorable' in the third sentence. As soon as we meet this word we are in a different world – a moment's thought is required to consider the etymology and exact meaning of 'deplorable', and the impression it gives is of a certain insouciant objectivity in the face of this horrible food. This impression is reinforced by the string of 'high', highly educated and, therefore, Latinate words that follow 'deplorable': 'dilemma' (we think of this word as Greek, which it is, but it came into English, like a lot of Greek words, via its Latin version), 'diurnal', 'expedient', 'assiduous', 'punctual', 'cubic'. These clash with the down-to-earth and, therefore, mostly Old English vocabulary that shares the honours of this passage: 'cooking', 'hunger', 'eating', 'gut', 'dung'. The effect of this is to take some of the seriousness out of the narrative. A more monologic register would appear more serious; this chopping about among registers signals a less than total commitment to the awfulness of the Lawrence undertaking, consonant with his apparent aim of rising above the merely physical and local, and seeing things in a broader philosophical (and highly British) context. Lawrence's sensitivity to register, and his broader designs, are apparent from the very title of his work: *Seven Pillars of Wisdom*. Why didn't he choose something like the title given to the abridged version, *Revolt in the Desert*? In a marvellous demonstration of how genre, intertext and register coalesce, the phrase comes from the Book of Proverbs: 'Wisdom hath builded a house: she hath hewn out her seven pillars.' So Lawrence is making the claim, at a biblical level of seriousness, that he is engaged with the construction of a divinely inspired historical temple, and is in the hands of a female deity of immense power. The arrogance is stunning, though not altogether repellent.

Lexical sets: words and their friends

We left the word *cliché* hanging and unattended to early on in this chapter; and we have used the word '*collocation*'. [Why *we*? What nervousness impels me back into the formal-academic plural? Register reveals anxiety – or confidence. I'll try to stop it.] These two are crucial when we are reading for register. They have some big brothers and sisters, too:

Lexical sets
in lexical fields
in semantic fields;
also:
descriptive systems.

All of these are useful terms when we are thinking about the vocabulary of a register. They all refer to slightly different aspects of the same thing, as it happens, and can generally be used interchangeably, although sometimes their different emphases need to be brought out. It depends on the angle from which you are looking at the text. These terms refer to groups of words which go together. The high-register, formal word for 'going together' is 'collocation' (note how the informal 'going together' sounds more *verbal*, while the formal 'collocation' sounds more *nominal*; *collocare* is the one-word, polysyllabic, Latin equivalent of a Germanic phrasal verb which, in core English, becomes two monosyllables). Things which go together or collocate a lot, which we find virtually always together, become so closely associated that we call them clichés. Here are a few:

readily available; heartily sick of; absolutely useless
the din of battle; an unavoidable delay
for what seemed like an eternity
the body was found in a pool of blood
in black and white
raining cats and dogs.

By the time we have got up to set expressions ('raining cats and dogs', 'as drunk as a lord', 'I blew my top') it is better to use the word 'idiom'; but these are clichés too, and there are no strict dividing lines here.

A cliché is simply what we *expect* to find next – the body is less likely to be found in a pool of gin. Similarly, in lexical sets and the others it is just a matter of what has regularly been collocated; the usual is then what we expect. Linguists sometimes use what are called 'cloze tests' to find out what people expect at various levels of language analysis; in these, subjects are invited to complete sentences or other stretches of text by filling in missing words. I don't think many English speakers, at least in Britain, would have much difficulty in completing 'raining cats and ——' or 'as sick as a ——'. This latter example might have several answers ('dog', 'parrot'), but these would not include 'armadillo', 'camel' or 'lord').

Another form of test that would make the same point about cliché, idiom and collocation would be one which offered alternatives. Thus: which of the following are you more likely to be, when you are 'distraught' or 'frozen' or 'silent' or 'confused'?

completely
totally
absolutely
utterly

Each of the epithets ('distraught', and so on) could be preceded by any of the words listed, but some seem more likely than others. I'd go for:

utterly distraught
totally or completely frozen
absolutely silent
utterly confused

These might be called 'open clichés', because they are not compulsory in the way that some idiomatic expressions are.

Moving up further we come to whole sets of words that go together – lexical sets making up lexical fields. The key point here is that the introduction into a text of any term from a lexical set is liable to bring with it the register implications of that set. Indeed, the words 'lexical field' are themselves often collocated with the related notion of 'semantic fields' – the lexical aspect being the words employed, and the semantics referring to the meanings or concepts involved. The 'semantic field' is not the *same* as a register, but it is worth pointing out that 'register' covers the same ground as both lexical field and semantic field; sensitivity to both of these is a requirement for sensitivity to register. All three notions, furthermore, flow into one another seamlessly.

Thus, for instance, if you are presented with the expression 'pieces of eight', a number of things can (perhaps *should*) occur. Some lexical sets of a fairly banal kind seem available such as that of numbers (six, seven, eight, nine) and coinage (doubloons, piastres, thalers, louis d'or, pieces of eight…), and there is a broader lexical field in which we might expect to find the Spanish Main and several elements concerned with parts of Europe and the New World in the seventeenth century. But the semantic field is highly likely to be that of piracy. Inside this field, lexical collocations of a well-known kind can be expected. Pieces of eight will figure among such words as

skull and crossbones (Jolly Roger)
wooden legs and eye patches
the Caribbean; privateers, buccaneers
treasure; cutlasses; cannon; rum
walking the plank

The list could be extended. As a lexical field, it has a certain coherence which can be roughly subsumed under the term 'piracy', but then we are involved in the broader meanings of that term under which the other terms can be grouped as 'hyponyms' ('undernames'). These broader meanings are the semantic field of piracy, and may involve considerations such as legality, adventure, *machismo*, rebellion or the history of the English, French and Spanish at a certain date in a certain area of the world.

A neat way to organise one's thoughts about all this is simply to bring in the term 'the register of piracy'. As usual intertextuality comes to our aid; we can find the register displayed in Robert Louis Stevenson's *Treasure Island* (both the words of that title belong to the lexical set of piracy). But if we think of this whole complex as a register then we have a term which covers both the lexis and the semantics – everything, indeed, from the smallest element to the broadest consideration. For 'register', as I have insisted so often, immediately implies the full social implications of who-is-speaking-like-this, and how and where and why.

Workpoints

Here is a rule-of-thumb list of distinctions for a first effort at register-analysis: Is the text in question:

- Latinate or Germanic?
- inclined to long or short sentences?
- hypotactic or paratactic?
- inclined to use figures of speech or not?

There is a continuum of collocations, from clichés and idioms up through lexical sets and fields to complete discursive structures (genres), which generate expectations of various kinds. 'Cloze tests' would reveal remarkable uniformities of expectation among readers. We 'know where we are', when reading, far more than we realise we do.

We **register** post, objections, births, deaths.
　　At school we take the **register**.
　　It seems to mean a **list**. From Latin *regestrum*, from Latin *Regesta*, a plural implying things (*res*) done, carried or carried

out; see *Gesta Romanorum* – the deeds of the Romans. From *gerere*, originally 'to carry' but thus 'to manage' or 'to rule'. You need a ruler for a register.

> First introduced in the 1950s, the term [register] retains some of the connotations of the musical sense ... in that it suggests a scale of differences, of degrees of formality, appropriate to different social usages of language. It is part of the communicative competence of every speaker that he or she will constantly switch usages, select certain features of sound, grammar, lexis, etc., in the different situations of everyday life...
>
> Katie Wales, *A Dictionary of Stylistics*, 1989

The same word can belong to different registers at different dates in its history:

Undertaker (according to the *OED*):

1586	one who undertook to hold crown lands in Ireland
1697	godparent, 'baptismal sponsor'
1740	impresario or dramatic producer
1819	one of those who colonised the island of Lewis
1823	a publisher
1960s	USA, one overtaking in the show lane
1698→	*one who carries out the business of funerals* (note the near-coincidence in time of the *opposite* ideas of birth and death – in 1697 and 1698).

I am not only changing topic when I quote what I am about to quote. Notice that, as it is a dictionary entry, it is in a different register, too:

> **'Caretaker speech'**: motherese but with recognition that not only mothers use it. Also 'caregiver speech'.
>
> *Concise Oxford Dictionary of Linguistics*

Dialect and register combine to provide a range of possible descriptions for the English employed on any particular occasion. Here is a list from a popular book by David Crystal:

English
British English
Twentieth-Century British English
Twentieth-Century British Standard English
Twentieth-Century British Standard religious English
Twentieth-Century British Standard religious English as heard in sermons
Twentieth-Century British Standard religious English as heard in sermons given by the Referend Fred Smith
The English Language, 1988

A literary version to cover a 'metaphysical' sonnet might end up with:

Seventeenth-Century English Standard Poetic English as found in the shorter poems of John Donne

Notes

1 See, for example, Halliday's chapter 'Spoken and written modes of meaning', in D. Graddol and O. Boyd-Barrett, *Multilingual Matters* (Open University, 1994). Here is one of his examples of the difference between written and spoken:

More written	*More spoken*
Every previous visit had left me with a sense of the risk to others in further attempts at action on my own part.	Whenever I'd visited there before I'd end up feeling that other people might get hurt if I tried to do anything more.

The difference (for me a difference in register) is to be found in such things as number of clauses (one against four) and lexical density (lower in the spoken text). See also Halliday's monograph *Spoken and Written Language* (Deakin University Press, 1985).

2 James D. Benson and William S. Greaves, *The Language People Really Use* (Book Society of Canada, 1973).

3 Harold Pinter, *The Caretaker* (Methuen, 1960).

4 Erich Segal, *Love Story* (Hodder, 1970).

5 Samuel Johnson, *The History of Rasselas, Prince of Abyssinia* (1759) (Penguin, 1976), p. 44.

6 *Ibid.*, p. 93.

7 Evelyn Waugh, *Put Out More Flags* (1942) (Penguin, 1943), p. 9.

8 *Ibid.*, p. 10.

9 R. L. Stevenson, *Travels with a Donkey in the Cévennes*, (1879) (Folio Society, 1967), p. 12.

10 Sir John Murray, *Sketches of Persia* (John Murray [no relation, I believe, though Sir John was an ancestor of the present writer – 'the present writer': is that too pompous a tone? What's wrong with 'mine'?], 1861), p. 6.

11 *Ibid.*, p. 7. If we are talking intertextuality, it might be intriguing to set this passage alongside the following paragraph from Waugh's *Put Out More Flags*, a novel quoted earlier in a different context:

> The history Lady Seal had learned in the schoolroom had been a simple tale of the maintenance of right against the superior forces of evil and the battle honours of her country rang musically in her ears – Crécy, Agincourt, Cádiz, Blenheim, Gibraltar, Inkerman, Ypres. England had fought many and various enemies with many and various allies, often on quite recondite pretexts, but always justly, chivalrously and with ultimate success. (p. 19)

The point of register-connection here is the word 'England' (compare 'Old England'), which means something like 'the part of Britain about which I feel patriotic in a historical-romantic kind of way, and which involves certain moral and other qualities of a fundamentally decent and therefore victorious sort'. This definition can be dated fairly precisely, say to the time bracket 1700–1960. The touch of sarcastic humour is also present here, as in Murray – 'recondite pretexts' doesn't quite square with the moral glory of English success in arms.

12 Edward Gibbon, *Decline and Fall of the Roman Empire* (John Murray, 1887), vol. 2, p. 142.

13 Ernest Hemingway, *Across the River and into the Trees* (Penguin, 1966), p. 237.

14 T. E. Lawrence, *Seven Pillars of Wisdom* (Penguin, 1962), p. 247.

15 *Ibid.*, pp. 322–3.

Part II

The ways register works

4

Registers of culture and power

What is needed is a profound understanding of each language's socio-ideological meaning and an exact knowledge of the social distribution and ordering of all the other ideological voices of the era.

Mikhail Bakhtin

Power and the word

One of the big advantages of reading for register is that a register automatically belongs to a certain time and place – in other words, has a position – in the society or culture (or 'real world') in which the text is produced. It also has a history leading all the way up to the present moment in which the text is being read, and the register thus has a specific contemporary status for the reader. Far from being some dry formal category with its roots in the empty air, register is firmly planted in the world, and belongs to a place and time that can be clearly established. It would be hard to make the same claim for such concepts as 'tone', or even 'style', but paying attention to register more or less obliges the reader to anchor his or her reading in the social, economic and cultural conditions of the text's production, and to consider the social structures of his or her own times.

It is none the less the case that literature itself (a social construct too, after all) has generated a 'literary register' which is recognisable and perhaps even essential to an understanding of a literary text. To operate a *reductio ad absurdum* for a moment, it is worth trying to imagine what reading, say, a verse epic would be like in the absence of any knowledge whatever of the registers and conventions of poetry. For one thing, the epic would presumably appear to be historically accurate, while the language would seem bizarrely formal and excessively metaphorical.

In Chapter 5 below we will consider this phenomenon of literary register (together with its ineluctable partners, genre and intertextuality), but in the meantime we will dwell for a while on the *power* implications of register, and trace some of the ways in which it brings the world (society, culture, power relations) into the most unpromising texts. We are here in the 'real world' as much as in the 'fictional' world of literature (though the use of the same registers in these two suspect categories may hint that there is not as much difference between them as is generally assumed), and a good person to help us get into this arena is Roland Barthes. Barthes's structuralist and post-structuralist work – from *Mythologies* (1956), essays demonstrating the culturally constructed nature of what is known as 'French bourgeois life', to his death in 1980 – spanned the literary and the non-literary virtually as though they were woven together in a seamless web. He it was, for instance, who created the 'mythology' of his own life by writing a book about himself in a series of studies of French authors generally entitled '*X Par Lui-même*.' The volume on Barthes is, indeed, *par lui-même*; but it is not therefore 'more true' than other volumes in the series, written by specialists in the work of the relevant author. *Roland Barthes par Roland Barthes* is also, in its way, a work of fiction.

When Barthes gave his inaugural lecture at the Collège de France in 1977 (thereby encouragingly initiating his academic career at the age of sixty-two) in the presence of his friend and sponsor, Michel Foucault, he most appropriately dwelt on the topic of power during the opening stages of his talk. In a now-familiar post-structuralist move, he spoke eloquently of the *ubiquity* of power, of its inescapability. But he also made a case for the word 'power' to be used in the plural – *powers*. In a passage reminiscent of Bakhtin on the monologic discourse to which Bakhtinian dialogism is opposed, he asks: 'What if power were plural, like demons?' He answers himself thus:

> 'My name is legion', it could say; everywhere, on all sides, leaders, massive or minute organisations, pressure groups or oppression groups, everywhere 'authorised' voices which authorise themselves to utter the discourse of all power: the discourse of arrogance.[1]

This is the more obvious face of power; it is the voice of *soi-disant* or real authority, but later Barthes will find power or powers to be present in any form of discourse, even the least obviously authoritarian; power is discernible in places where you might not expect it:

> Power is present in the most delicate mechanisms of social exchange: not only the state, in classes, in groups, but even in fashion, public opinion, entertainment, sports, news, family and private relations, and even in the liberating impulses which try to counteract it.[2]

This sounds extremely like a Bakhtinian notion of register; the list Barthes offers could be used as a basis for any linguist giving examples of the different sociolects and subvarieties of language: there is, after all, a 'language of fashion', one of sport, and one (or several) of family relations, and so on. But this coincidence is not at all coincidental, for Barthes goes on to equate, precisely, power with language: 'The object in which power is inscribed, for all of human eternity, is language.'[3]

Thus we have a useful short circuit: at a certain level of analysis language and power are virtually interchangeable; the place where we would find the power inherent in a given cultural structure is in the language that surrounds or forms it. Thus it would be in the grammar, syntax and lexis of 'news' that we would first look for signs of the power relations being deployed, in the textualising that puts a news item together and in the assumptions, values and nuances built into the discourse. Any change in the language implies a change in power relations. Barthes quotes both Mallarmé ('To change language') and Marx ('To change the world'); he goes on:

> From this there follows a certain ethic of literary language… We often reproach the writer, the intellectual, for not writing 'everyone's' language. But it is good that men, within the same language – for us, French – should have several kinds of speech. If I were a legislator (an aberrant proposition for someone who, etymologically speaking, is an 'an-archist'), far from imposing a unification of French, whether bourgeois or popular, I would instead encourage the simultaneous apprenticeship to several forms of French speech.[4]

Note how easily Barthes shifts from 'literary' language to political considerations. He sounds very like Bakhtin on the carnivalesque here (the carnivalesque being that disruptive force from the 'lower echelons' of society that subverts official discourses), and has the same broad view of the working of language. In his legislative fantasy he is not seduced into the left-wing myth that class freedom will flower if the various sublanguages of the classes, regions and professions of the French nation are allowed liberty of expression; rather, he sees a multiplicity of registers and dialects as being valuable precisely in their manifold nature. And all of them, not merely the speech of the 'masters', are constructs, and power-ridden:

> Once uttered, even in the subject's deepest privacy, speech enters the service of power... the signs composing speech exist only in so far as they are recognised, i.e., in so far as they are repeated. The sign is a follower, gregarious; in each sign sleeps that monster: a stereotype.[5]

Packed into this brief quotation is a range of ideas that exactly situate the power-text relationship (for Barthes is speaking of *text*, and not just of speech, as witness his remark that 'text is the very outcropping of speech'). Power is always already in speech, even the least public, for power is always already present in language; as soon as we recognise a sign, and repeat it or see it repeated, we are caught up in the noisy throng of its legion of meanings, and with it comes the cliché that we may or may not want, the stereotype of meaning with which power has invested this sign. We are in the world of inverted commas again here: am I in love, or am I 'in love'? Is the meaning (here = my feeling) *mine*, or is it subject to the stereotypical business of being-in-love? The powers that have created how-to-be-in-love-in-this-culture are here creating *me* through language. There are cultures in which the notion of being in love is incomprehensible.

So writing in general, and text in particular, are series of power-determined voices. These are, inevitably, not 'my own' voice, which would be nothing but White Noise or Zen silence, but the voices of stereotype and cliché, the registers of the society in which I live.[6] This need not be a depressing determinism; all linguistic activity is a mixture of constraint and freedom. Yes, I must speak in the language of others, but yes, also, I have the freedom to play among the multitudinous discourses of my culture, and it is this freedom that the 'an-archist' Barthes would want to maximise if he had power: let a thousand flowers bloom.

And power 'itself'? That is the inescapable legion that expresses itself in language and weaves its way through all my discourses; in summary: all power comes preregistered, all registers speak the voice of some source of power.

Bakhtin and Halliday

These Foucauldian equations (power = language; power determines the registers of language; the social is a series of power relations, and thus of register differences) bring together a range of well-known ideas in modern thought ('postmodern' thought, at any rate). There is little benefit in insisting that such ideas be kept separate, and there is a clear advantage in uniting them as our equations do. It is above all the hard-pressed reader or student of literature, who has enough to do to get to grips with the plot structure of a Toni Morrison novel or understand Renaissance English, who can gain by not being overloaded with distinctions which are, for his or her purposes, effectively meaningless. The synthetic (this belongs with this) has its place alongside the analytic (this is different from this).

Some of the most promising voices in the polyphonic chorus that has considered these matters in recent years are precisely those of scholars wishing to stress connections between ideas of differing provenance. Roger Fowler, for instance, writing on *Hard Times* in 1983, suggested that Halliday's linguistics meets Bakhtin's demand that styles of speech should be taken as embodying world-views, especially in so far as the concept of register is concerned. This is not explicitly a power analysis, but its closeness to Barthes should be obvious. Having observed that speech styles in Dickens are not merely 'caricatures', Fowler talks of 'dialogic' relationships in *Hard Times* – between the characters of course, and between the author/narrator and his characters. He goes on to observe that speech differences are 'semiotically significant stylistic oppositions' which permeate the novel. Then:

> Bakhtin provides no tools for analysing linguistic structure, but there is one linguistic theory which explicitly covers Bakhtin's condition that speech styles should be treated as embodying world-views: M. A. K. Halliday's 'functional' theory of language.... Halliday's main premiss is

that linguistic varieties within a community, or 'registers' encode different kinds of meaning, different orientations on experience.[7]

If language is a *social* semiotic (to borrow a Hallidayan phrase),
then registers ('significant stylistic oppositions') are social speech
types which embody world-views, generate meaning, and root that
meaning in the sociocultural ground. Here, to give another example,
is Ronald Carter discussing the teaching of literature in 1994:

> There are significant dangers for language and literary studies in too
> great a degree of formalism. Especially in respect of linguistics we
> need to go beyond formalism, to view language as social discourse and
> to embrace the orientation of language studies rather than linguistics.
> In this respect the work of descriptive linguists such as Halliday and of
> social and cultural theorists such as Bakhtin offer more relevant para-
> digms than either Chomsky or Saussure. By stressing language as closely
> related to historical and social change as well as to ideology such an
> orientation lays a valuable basis for a more fully integrated language
> and literary studies [*sic*].... To this end research in language studies
> needs to focus more sharply on areas such as repetition, vocabulary
> mixing and layering and on distinctions between speech and writing...[8]

Carter is not antagonistic to linguistics; what would be the good
of that, since linguisticians have their own massive and infinitely
interesting job to do? It is simply that the 'relevant paradigms' for
the study of language and literature may not always be those of
the formalist linguists. But this should not mean that those embracing the orientation of 'language studies' should either be
debarred from employing linguistic terms (repetition, layering,
speech, writing, *register*...) or be criticised if they choose to do so.

'Historical and social change as well as ... ideology' – these are
precisely the areas prioritised by Halliday and Bakhtin, and precisely the areas where a register analysis can be at its most fruitful.
Halliday and Bakhtin are entirely clear about the thrust of their
thinking. Writing of scientific English and its tendency to allow
nouns to take over the whole semantic content of a text at the
expense of verbal forms, which are relegated to the mere expression
of relationships, Halliday says that 'the whole configuration is an
immensely powerful resource for the semiotic construction of
reality'.[9] He thus sounds impeccably post-structuralist in his notion that language in some sense creates or constructs 'the world'.

Bakhtin, conversely, sees the world lurking behind every semiotic bush; for him, the voices to be heard in novels are not individual (though an individual may well express them) but the voices of identifiable social groups.[10] This double-headed coin is held together by the concept of register: science (for instance) develops a register to make the world one way (think of the apparent inexorability of the nominal 'law of gravity' as against the provisionality of the verbal 'things tend to attract each other'), and the world recognises itself and speaks to itself through the registers of 'identifiable social groups'.

Power, after all, as Barthes observes, isn't only a matter of vast institutions, nor even of the overt manipulation of language. Not all power relations are at the level of the national government, nor need they be as crude as the Soviet Communist attempt to reorientate language as satirised in Orwell's *Nineteen Eighty-Four*, where Newspeak is deliberately created to oppress the masses. Power is also deeply present in something as 'neutral' as scientific English, with its tendency to make things fixed, unassailable and causelessly static (the nominal structure 'the *achievement* of *equilibrium*' would be preferred in scientific writing to a verbal construction such as '*making* things *come* into balance'). Science has prestige in the modern world, and its power can be felt in the prestige attached to its mode of discourse. Theology and religious thinking in general, for instance, are attached to notions of becoming, development, emotion and change, but this can seem marginal or frivolous beside the scientific monoliths ('laws of motion', 'matter', even 'relativity') which just stand there, leaving religious thinking either to borrow them a little uncomfortably, so that God and Newton somehow become one, or to bypass them in some other way as best it can.

In the nineteenth century Lyell, Darwin, Huxley, and the others were in no obvious sense trying to exert power over others (their biographies, at least, lend no credibility to such a proposition); indeed, their thinking precisely promoted the idea of change and an unstable dynamic, but the fact remains that the overall thrust of their language, the ground rules of their registers, lead to an increased prestige for a certain sort of evidence generalisable into knock-down 'laws' which leave no room for other sorts of explanation. 'Evolution' got – and, spiritually at least, retains – a capital letter. The immediate result of this was a tremendous boost to a certain sort of education and the development of 'modern' sciences at universities at the expense of quite different priorities. The change – for instance, in Britain between, say, 1870 and 1970 – can be measured by the most casual enquiry about school and university curricula. To put it bluntly, how many of your friends and contemporaries are reading Classics or Theology/Divinity at university, or even have any secondary qualifications in these subjects? Now repeat the question for Physics, Chemistry, Maths, Engineering, Computing Science, Economics, Biology. The prestige of the 'new' registers of science in the nineteenth century has exercised enormous power over the world in the century-and-a-half since Darwin, precisely because it has become almost impossible, at the deepest level, to think in categories other than those provided by the scientists. Power resides in those things that can make us think in a particular way – the forces that establish the categories of thought – but this process cannot operate in some sort of non-linguistic, abstract realm; the difference between 'thinking in a category' and 'speaking/writing in a register' is one that eludes me.

Any register can become 'ritualised', according to Halliday, in a way that leads to its special features ceasing to make sense 'except as ritual' (Halliday has capitals for the whole word 'except' in the original, which reads 'EXCEPT', but I feel they would be too alarming to reproduce here – I've shifted register a little from his original).[11] Halliday gives the example of bureaucratic discourse, which often sounds 'received' and 'educated', but in a way that serves no purpose except that of power. The bureaucrat (especially before about 1970, in Britain at least) felt obliged to *sound official*, and he (usually *he*) achieved this by adopting the most official-sounding voice. This was a matter of accent, of course, in speech situations, but it was also a matter of non-phonetic elements of register: 'better-formed' sentences, constructions of a more 'written' or formal sort, 'correct' vocabulary choice and grammar. This might be quite without regard to the necessity for such a way of speaking or writing in the situation.

An example would be the discourse of 'the taxman' – officially known in Britain as the Inland Revenue, a change of name between popular and official versions that produces a register shift of fascinating origin: the impersonal body with the incomprehensible name ('Inland Revenue') is humanised and personalised ('taxman') in an attempt to specify more accurately the target of the usual (mildish) resentment of being obliged to part with a chunk of your earnings. 'He' gets it all; 'he' is greedy, and so on. This 'he', the taxman, technically the Inland Revenue, changed register quite consciously in the 1970s, and actually picked up the implications of his popular name (his not-so-popular popular name). Thus letters from the Inland Revenue started to adopt a more colloquial register in an effort to eliminate a language that might be called Bureaucratese. Third-person constructions ('Taxpayers are required...') were replaced with first- and second-person constructions ('I' will do this, 'You' must do the following); passives ('Forms will be sent...') were replaced by actives ('I will send you...'). The register shift was impressive, even amazing. To be addressed directly in the first person by a previously utterly impersonal institution was quite a change. The astonishment was not lessened by the fact that a moment's thought revealed that the 'I' in question was *nobody at all*, and that although the age-old process of bureaucratic depersonalisation was being reversed, the metaphorical *re*personalisation it was being replaced by was equally far from 'reality'. Of course, hidden not very far behind the surface of the new chummy register was another language of threats, imperatives and obligations – the language in which the fundamental legal position was spelt out in the small print. Power needs, uses, *is* language, but it can also hide its face behind language.

Our reading should become, perhaps automatically, that of 'critical discourse analysis': that is to say, we should be permanently aware of several unspoken questions threading their way through all texts, questions such as 'Who?' and 'Why?': 'Who is speaking here?', 'Why this formulation rather than another?', 'Where is the power here?', 'Where is the ideology that informs, that *has formed* this text?', 'Where does it come from?' The choices of lexis, grammar, and all other discourse features, *whether so intended by the author or not*, must be governed by some definite considerations, and these considerations must have their roots in some power structure. That is the target of critical reading: to identify registers, their provenance, the powers that make them, their users, their meanings. Foucault, in this context, quotes Nietzsche, repeating the latter's question 'Who is speaking?' and adding Mallarmé's answer: 'What is speaking… is the word itself.'[12] For the answer to these questions ('Who?') is not going to be an individual; we have not provided much of an answer if we simply name the speaker. 'Who?' is a question that asks for the status, place, significance and power of the voice; the voice's 'owner' is of no importance; what matters is where he or she or it is speaking from. 'Off with his head' is a joke if it is spoken by a small child playing a game in post-capital-punishment Europe, but it was very far from a joke if it was spoken by Queen Elizabeth I or Gengis Khan. The names (Elizabeth, Gengis) are without power, as are their orders, unless and until we inscribe them in a social-cultural matrix of, for instance, Absolute monarchy in a culture where beheading is not an act of insanity. So 'the word itself' turns out to be not an empty signifier drifting about in theoretical-linguistic space, but a word *registered,* socialised, acculturated, given a place in which to mean and to act. *That* is the word that speaks, and speaks power.

And literature? Where does the power-that-is-language-registered manifest itself in literature? Literature, that textualising that has 'a certain ethic', has to be (I mean, it has no choice but to be) the site of multiple and contending voices. What Bakhtin calls the 'novelising' quality of literature, and elsewhere its 'carnivalising' effect, is precisely its ability to celebrate the multiplicity of voices in a culture (though 'celebrate' may be a bit overenthusiastic here; the discourse of literature is at permanent war with itself, and ultimately the voices will sound more often cacophonous than harmonious). Literary discourse is, perhaps more than any other, intertextual, multivoiced, and, as Bakhtin would say, polyphonic. Literature is the site of register clash and thus constitutes, *ipso facto*, a culture's self-analysis.

Staying power: *Staying On*

After the heady theorising we have been discussing in this chapter so far, we need some concrete examples. Here is a section of Chapter 6 of the novel *Staying On* by Paul Scott, written in 1977. Lucy and 'Tusker' Smalley, a British couple, have decided to 'stay on' in India after Independence in 1947, and now, in 1972, they are getting old, although they are still enjoying their life with each other, and with their Indian servants and friends. Among these ambiguous elements Tusker has a genially bad-tempered manner that makes us like him and accounts in part for the improbable fact that his wife is still in love with him (one of the many 'themes' of the book). He has been out for a walk:

> When Tusker came back from his walk he seemed in a good mood. He asked cheerfully, 'Anything nice in the *dak*?'
>
> 'Only a letter from Phoebe.'
>
> 'Usual guff I suppose. What's the drill for lunch, old thing?'
>
> It was ages since he had called her that.
>
> 'Has your walk made you hungry, Tusker dear?'
>
> He said that it had but that he didn't want broth, nor a tray from the restaurant. He didn't want to go to the restaurant either. The very sight of Mrs Bhoolabhoy waddling from bedroom to kitchen and back again with one of her bloody headaches turned him off. He hadn't seen Mrs Bhoolabhoy since his attack. He didn't care if he never saw her again, the old bitch.[13]

What are the social–cultural–power implications of this short passage? What 'self-analysis' by 'our' culture ('Paul Scott's culture'?) is going on here? The names in themselves give us neither more nor less than any of the other words used, but the registers employed do a lot of work. In the longest paragraph quoted, starting from 'The very sight', it would now be critically conventional, and perfectly accurate, to identify free indirect speech. The words between 'He said' and 'the old bitch' are obviously Tusker's, not the narrator's; at first they are given in indirect speech ('He said that it had', for instance, replacing the direct speech that lies behind it: 'He said "It has…"'), but then there is a switch to free indirect speech with the image of the waddling Mrs Bhoolabhoy. We can demonstrate that this is not the narrator by pointing out the contracted forms used ('didn't', 'hadn't'), which are at variance with the narrator's 'own' practice, for instance, a few pages earlier, where 'he' writes: 'They did not see the end of the film…' instead of 'They didn't…'. Furthermore, it is Tusker, not the narrator, who employs such rude (and clichéd) colloquialisms as 'the very sight of', 'bloody', 'turned him off', and 'old bitch'. In other words, Tusker is being quoted here in a different register from that of the narrator; he is abrupt, bad-tempered (or pretending to be), and is presented through a kind of bluff-colonial-colloquial speech that exactly matches his register when he is in direct speech, as we see from such expressions as 'old thing'.

So far I have simply done a small amount of Bakhtinian analysis, looking for 'double-voicing' (Bakhtin has some fascinating examples from Dickens[14]), the process whereby we simultaneously read the voice of the narrator – for this paragraph is clearly 'written by' the narrator, and is not direct quotation of a character's speech – and the voice (that is, the register) of the character, here Tusker. But there is more: our question must now be: 'Whose *is* this voice?', or 'Whose are these voices?' To ask it another way: 'What *is* Tusker's register?', which is as much as to ask, since Tusker exists only on paper, 'Who is Tusker?' or – the same thing in another way – 'What does he mean?' What is the significance of his abrupt bad-tempered cheerfulness? Why is Lucy so touched by being called an 'old thing'? What is the reason for his attitude to Mrs Bhoolabhoy?

Well, Tusker is what is left of the Raj, the two centuries of British rule in India, a leftover colonial servant; he has mastered enough of the appropriate language to function in the country ('*dak*'), and he's a bit of an old elephant tusking about; he is thus both Indian (elephants are native to India) and very British in having that sort of public-school nickname. Lucy is the Britain that he loves, treats slightly cavalierly, neglects to some extent but relies on; Mrs Bhoolabhoy is the great fecund body of India itself; his 'attack', a heart attack, is the crisis of Independence, and his imminent death (the novel opens: 'When Tusker Smalley died of a massive coronary...') an allegory of the very end of British imperial involvement with India.

It has been a good life, but now he doesn't seem to want much more of it (he can't decide what to have for lunch), and has got fed up with the new India, which waddles and complains and is so different from what has been. Tusker is only just about 'staying on', hanging on in India and in life, and 'life' here means his position, his status and situation as an old Raj hand. What he is made of, since he is made of words, is the discourse of post-imperialist puzzlement, of being too old and out of place, of being expected to make room for the new India and/or the next generation. His voice is the voice of a class that has been passed over by the tides of history and a person passed over by the tide of time.

The register is made up of these and similar considerations. Tusker has affection for his wife (as he does elsewhere for the Bhoolabhoys, in spite of everything) but treats her in the genial hectoring manner of a good master with an old servant of whom he is fond (the Smalleys have a real servant called Ibrahim, a brilliantly conceived figure who is fascinated by his employers and whose registers reflect their language as well as his 'own' culture in a wonderful patchwork of voices). Thus Tusker operates in the modes of question, opinion and the statement of his desires; he asks about the post and about lunch in a way that shows the interrogatives to be politely concealed orders ('Give me my post' and 'Give me my lunch'); he passes opinions freely on other people; and he states his feelings about what to have for lunch without restraint. But in spite of this he is loveable, certainly loved by Lucy, respected by Ibrahim, liked by his Indian friends. There is some sense in having stayed on ('cheerfully' in spite of imminent death), and he obviously *does* care if he never sees the 'old bitch' again.

A good deal of what I have said here – and there could be quite a bit more of it – might be regarded as an old-fashioned reading for symbolism with a little added Bakhtin, but the crucial step towards seeing the meanings in this passage, and in the novel as a whole, is the identification of the registers involved. 'What's the drill', 'Old thing' and a certain use of 'bloody' belong to a specific cultural moment within which the Raj made good sense and its benevolence was demonstrable: the creation of a whole class of civil servants whose task, under trying conditions and for little reward, was to administer a vast country at the expense of their health and their families. The military basis for some of this activity is apparent in the 'drill' metaphor. Conversely, there is a faint hint in the passage of the more modern world in which, in spite of having 'stayed on', the Smalleys now live – this is 1972, after all. Tusker (rather than the narrator) is responsible for the phrase 'turned him off', surely a post-1960s Americanism at odds with the Raj-speak that dominates his usual way of talking; it suggests a mind not entirely closed to the new – a mind belonging to a man who can, for instance, be a good friend, in a non-patronising way, of the Indian Mr Bhoolabhoy, a fellow-male and one rather under the thumb of his enormous wife, with whom Tusker has drinks and gossips on a regular basis. Sensitivity to these small register shifts creates the possibility of the most useful understanding of the text. Even in remote Pankot, where the Smalleys live, the power of the media-based Americanisation of the postwar world can be felt; here its 'good' or soft side ('liberation' – turn on, drop out...) is to the fore, and softens what might be the harsh opinion of the reader of 1977 who has him- or herself been subject to the intense cultural pressure of anti-imperialist discourse. We are forced to *like* Tusker in this novel – to understand, as they say, where he is coming from. All the simplicities and naiveties and ignorances of our 'political opinions' and dogmatic views are dissolved in the infinite complexities of textual meanings such as these; the different registers we hear enable us to listen to the voices of other points of view; when we know where they are coming from, we can better understand them as well as the fictions in which they appear. Tusker Smalley is a fractured self, speaking in a mixture of registers, and the appeal and 'truth' of fiction, in contrast to the 'truth' of science, is that it can live with fracture and contradiction; indeed, it is obliged to do so, as its multiple registers make clear.

Taking power: *Pendennis*

Here is another example, again deliberately chosen from a novel not generally regarded as being among the greatest works of fiction in the history of literature: Thackeray's *Pendennis* (1848–50). In the early pages of this novel there is a sketch of the ancestry and relations of the hero, Arthur Pendennis, whose education we follow (after public school and a governor he goes to 'Oxbridge' – a term Thackeray coins perhaps without realising how useful it would become in the more general register of British university/education-speak). Then there is a passage that describes his feelings after the death of his father; the boy is only sixteen but is now, despite the continued existence of his mother and a guardian uncle, the squire of 'Fairoaks', the estate his father has bought and cherished because it is the outward sign of his belonging to that magic circle of Victorian society – the gentry:

I am not sure that in the very moment of grief, and as he embraced his mother, and tenderly consoled her, and promised to love her forever, there was not springing up in his breast a sort of secret triumph and exultation. He was the chief now and lord. He was Pendennis; and all round about him were his servants and handmaids. 'You'll never send me away,' little Laura [his sister] said, tripping by him, and holding his hand. 'You won't send me to school, will you, Arthur?'

Arthur kissed her and patted her head. No, she shouldn't go to school. As for going himself, that was quite out of the question. He had determined that that part of his life should not be renewed. In the midst of the general grief, and the corpse still lying above, he had leisure to conclude that he would have it *all* holidays for the future. How one's thoughts will travel! And how quickly our wishes beget them! When he and Laura in his hand [*sic*] went into the kitchen on his way to the dog-kennel, the fowl-houses, and his other favourite haunts, all the servants there assembled in great silence with their friends, and the labouring men and their wives, and Sally Potter who went with the post-bag to Clavering, and the baker's man from Clavering – all there assembled and drinking beer on the melancholy occasion – rose up at his entrance and bowed or curtseyed to him. They never used to do so last holidays, he felt at once and with indescribable pleasure. The cook cried out, 'O Lord,' and whispered, 'How Master Arthur do grow!' Thomas, the groom, in the act of drinking, put down the jug alarmed before his master.[15]

The register features of this generate its meanings at all levels: those of the character, the narrator and the reader. The cultural-social foundations of these register features are crucial to our understanding of the passage and, fascinatingly, elements of later, post-Thackeray discourses inevitably infect the reader's perception of what is going on here.

As young Pendennis realises that he is now 'head of the household', as the oldest male in the family that owns Fairoaks, the narrator moves into free indirect speech, doubling his own voice with the voice of his hero; and the register he adopts (*they* adopt) is of a biblical-dramatic kind: 'He was the chief now and lord. He was Pendennis.' These are the thoughts going through Arthur's head, and that may be enough to explain the slightly odd word-order ('chief now and lord' – he thinks one thing and then another, correcting or developing his first idea, improving 'chief', which is a bit primitive, to 'lord'), but there is more to be said. The rhythm of the sentences has a rhetorical effect, so that 'Pendennis' comes as the climax of a series of satisfactions – he is saying, in effect, 'I'm the boss, and I'm really the real boss – in fact I'm my father!' This technique is not original to Thackeray; it is part of a recognisable register connected to such expressions as 'God and lord of all' and 'The disciple is not above his master, nor the servant above his lord' from Matthew's Gospel, and to such rhetorically emphatic structures as this from a speech by President Roosevelt (making a promise, incidentally, that he did not keep):

> And while I am talking to you mothers and fathers, I give you one more assurance. I have said this before, but I shall say it again and again and again. Your boys are not going to be sent into any foreign wars.

This paratactic structure, where the syntax allows a division of the text into three sentences (where one could easily have sufficed), is clearly a device of the speech-maker, certain of not being interrupted and building up to climaxes that can be applauded. Pendennis/Narrator use this for the similar purpose of demonstrating and creating a certain excitement. But the biblical associations are the strongest, as will be emphasised by later biblical phrasings such as 'rose up at his entrance and bowed', because Thackeray goes on: 'and all round about him were his servants and handmaids'. This is fairly neutral until the word 'handmaids' which, instead of being nineteenth-century Standard English (which would be 'maids' *tout court*), is seventeenth-century Authorised Version; there *are* no 'handmaids' at Fairoaks, only 'maids', but Pendennis (or the narrator), caught up in the excitement of the power thrill he is receiving from his new position, slips revealingly into this patriarchal register. The result is that the words preceding 'handmaids' are infected by the biblical sonority of that expression, so that a member of the class 'servants' now becomes not just that usual Victorian thing, a servant, but something like a 'servant of the lord', which just faintly makes Pendennis God for a moment. And that seems right – his 'secret triumph and exaltation', already faintly hubristic and apotheosistic (if that word exists) – 'I feel I am becoming a god' – will become his 'indescribable pleasure' in the next paragraph; 'indescribable' ultimately means 'divine'. 'O Lord!' says the cook, upon seeing him.

Similarly, it is not enough simply to say that the description of the servants and others in the kitchen is 'from Pendennis's point of view'. It *is*, of course, very much so; we look with his eyes and mind as he sees the people and recognises them: 'There's Sally, the woman who takes the post, and that's the baker's man...'; the clumsy repetition of the place name 'Clavering' shows the un-digested nature of this process, and we might remember the point Ronald Carter makes about repetition, as quoted above. But there is a register consideration here to help us further with the scene. The expression 'The labouring men and their wives' belongs to the discourse, as well as to the point of view, of the new squire who isn't quite clear about the names of all his 'workfolk' (as Hardy would call them); it is now part of young Pen's voice, the free indirect speech of this hero-as-master, and it equates as a phrase, in register terms, to such expressions as 'the factory hands' and 'the servants'. For Pendennis is now master – not as in 'Master Arthur', but *master*, as the last word of our extract indicates.

Everything in a passage like this has a register that creates the ever-shifting 'tone' (surely a misleading singular, that) of the text. There are simple examples at the start of our second paragraph. Arthur pats his sister's head in an unmistakable gesture of patronis-ation, but Thackeray backs up this symbolic act with a register to match: 'No, she shouldn't go to school' is free indirect speech for 'you shan't go to school', which is a far stronger version of 'I don't want you to go to school' and, in fact, the emphatic version of 'you won't go to school'. The new young squire is asserting him-self here, as he also is in the expressions 'out of the question' (think how rarely we use that phrase – it's too strong for general consumption, almost implies bad temper) and 'he had determined', where both the lexical word ('determined') and the past perfect tense ('had') conspire to imply a *fait accompli* which nobody else's opinions will be able to shake.

Besides all this there is the interesting level of Freudian register which this passage must stimulate in a modern reader. How can we not enter the register world of psychoanalysis, specifically of the Oedipus complex (as ever, exactly locatable in time and place: in Vienna around 1900) when we read of a sixteen-year-old 'embracing' his mother, consoling her 'tenderly' and 'loving her forever' at the very moment when he is enjoying the 'secret triumph and exultation' after his successful 'killing' of his father – 'and the corpse still lying above'? The collocation of this tender scene with Pendennis's realisation and assertion of his new power is irresistibly Freudian; even his substitute mother, the cook (female provider of nourishment), spots the point, invokes God ('O Lord' – where Arthur is now calling himself 'lord') and imagines that the boy is larger than before (the young male grows at the expense of the old). Thomas, a mildly paternal figure, puts down the object from which he has been sucking liquid, being now in the presence of the new cock of the midden; the symbolic liquid that has hitherto been dedicated to other males is not to be impertinently imbibed in the presence of the new lord whose right it now is to drink first.

Is this a register? Am I not pushing the category too far? Surely this is just 'a psychoanalytic reading'? Well, it is certainly such a reading, but it can be better anchored in the text if we take a register approach. Look, for instance, at the opening sentence of the passage; there is an insistence, a particular style of repetitious focus, in the paratactic clauses 'and as he embraced..., and tenderly consoled ... and promised to love her...'; it is in the youth's 'breast' that new feelings 'spring up' (just as he seems to have grown and the male servants have to rise to meet him while the female abase themselves); he takes his female sibling in hand and commands her, and so on. If there is to be a Freudian reading undertaken here, it must be anchored in textual details which themselves 'belong', in one of their incarnations at least, to Freudian discourse.

Other terminology is always possible, and reading is unfinishable, but I would suggest that register is such a useful category for literary reading (and perhaps for all other kinds) that it cannot be left to a technicist linguistics.[16] The power-relations in particular, and the cultural meanings of a text, stand out much more clearly using this sort of approach.

Workpoints

> 'WHO SPEAKS?'
> Roland Barthes, *S/Z*

> This is a box
> Not actually a *box* but a 'text box'
> Who or what am I quoting when I say that?
> What are the power implications in late-twentieth-century wordprocessing?
> Who is Bill Gates?
> (What register is this box in?)

Notes

1 Roland Barthes, 'Inaugural lecture', reprinted in Susan Sontag (ed.), *Barthes: Selected Writings* (Fontana/Collins, 1982), p. 459.

2 *Ibid.*

3 *Ibid.*, p. 460. The Bakhtinian parallel can be seen in many places, among them this:

> At any given moment of its historical existence, language is heteroglot from top to bottom: it represents the coexistence of socio-ideological contradictions between the present and the past, between differing epochs of the past, between different socio-ideological groups in the present, between tendencies, schools, circles and so forth, all given a bodily form.

Mikhail Bakhtin, *The Dialogic Imagination* (University of Texas Press, 1981), p. 291.

4 *Ibid.*, p. 466.

5 *Ibid.*, p. 461.

6 Actually, it is easy to see that even White Noise or Zen silence are themselves voices too. One can give a very precise historical and cultural position to each of these formulations. White Noise (as I have capitalised it to help demonstrate) postdates the electronic revolution of the twentieth century, and Zen has a well-known history and locality.

7 Roger Fowler, 'Polyphony in *Hard Times*', in Ronald Carter and Paul Simpson (eds), *Language, Discourse and Literature* (Unwin Hyman, 1989) (reprints essay of 1983 with changes).

8 Ronald Carter, 'Language, discourse and literature: perspectives for teaching', *European English Messenger*, 3:2, Autumn 1994.

9 M. A. K. Halliday, 'On the language of physical science', in Mohsen Ghadessy (ed.), *Registers of Written English* (Pinter, 1988).

10 Bakhtin, *The Dialogic Imagination*, pp. 411–12.

11 Halliday, 'On the language of physical science', p. 177.

12 Michel Foucault, *The Order of Things* (Tavistock, 1970), p. 305.

13 Paul Scott, *Staying On* (1977) (Panther, 1978), pp. 74–5.

14 Mikhail Bakhtin, *The Dialogic Imagination.*

15 William Makepeace Thackeray, *Pendennis* (1848–50) (Penguin, 1972), pp. 55–6.

16 In an essay on Barthes, Julia Kristeva credits him with having undertaken a 'search for the laws of the practice known as literature', but warns that it is a 'technicist illusion' that 'literary science' is a real science that would conform to the requirements of linguistics or generative grammar. Julia Kristeva, 'How does one speak to literature?', in *Desire in Language: A Semiotic Approach to Literature and Art*, edited by Leon Rodiez (Columbia University Press, 1980).

5

Literary register

'Literary language'?

A commonplace discussion in academic literary circles in recent decades has concerned the existence or nonexistence of a thing called 'literary language' and, in general, the majority of votes have been in favour of its nonexistence. Nothing, it is pointed out, is so definitively unliterary that you might not find it in a book of poems – there is no longer anything that could be excluded *a priori* from a literary text on grounds, for instance, of 'decorum'.[1]

This attitude seems entirely reasonable – are we, after all, going to *police* our texts to make sure there is nothing 'unliterary' in them? What would be the criteria on which we could ever establish such a scheme of censorship? The prescriptive approach would be entirely out of the question. But even a descriptive approach runs into the sand, for who could say today what 'isn't literature' as far as linguistic choices and patterns are concerned? These questions suggest the difficulty of having 'literary language' as a working concept.

On the other hand, there is no doubt that most people who have read any literary texts at all can signal that they feel that there is something worth defining about the language they are reading or hearing when they are in the presence of the literary; they know it when they meet it. 'Literature', from *Beowulf* to Virginia Woolf, has a certain feel to it, wouldn't you say? Few people are likely to confuse Shakespeare's language, or that of Ben Jonson, with that of 'non-literary' writing, even when it is contemporary 'non-literature' such as, say, the political letters and speeches of Queen Elizabeth I's minister Robert Cecil. There will be similarities of historical dialect, of course, but where these similarities are very marked – say in the work of a linguistically inventive contemporary of Shakespeare such as Robert Burton of *The Anatomy of Melancholy* – we find that our culture is inclined to take, precisely, a literary approach to Burton (rather than, say, a medical-historical approach).

Most poetry is written in a noticeably special language. The work of Keats is unlikely to be mistaken for prose of any kind, not even 'poetic' fictional prose. But then, literary prose itself has an unmistakability about it. Dickens sounds like Dickens and rarely even like George Eliot or his more exact contemporary Thackeray, let alone like Mayhew or Newman or Carlyle. Most novels start with a recognisably literary formula of some sort:

It was a brilliant afternoon towards the end of May.
Mrs Humphry Ward, *Robert Elsmere*, 1888

Selden paused in surprise. In the afternoon rush of Grand Central Station his eyes had been refreshed by the sight of Miss Lily Bart.
Edith Wharton, *The House of Mirth*, 1905

These are unmistakably the opening sentences of narratives of a fictitious sort. We feel easily able to say with conviction that plays, novels, poems, 'sound like' something which we can perhaps not immediately identify but which we know ourselves to be in the presence of. It seems to be *literature* that they sound like.

The solution to this apparent contradiction (there is no such thing as literary language, yet we are able to recognise language as literary when we meet it) is that although there may not be a definitive category that can be named 'literary language', there are certainly literary registers (plural) available. The point is that a list of them does not exhaust the category 'literature', that is all. New registers, new literary formulae, are being produced all the time, and there is no limit to this, but those which have come to be associated with literature in the past continue almost unavoidably to signal a 'literary' text in the present. Register-associations may be formed in a partly arbitrary fashion, but once they are fixed they are difficult to shift entirely from their original place on the cultural map; 'Once upon a time…' is a phrase that we would be hard put to insert into any English discourse without conjuring up associations of the fairytale or childhood story. Literary registers sound like literature, they make texts sound literary, and this is true even though we are unable to come up with any convincing definition of what literature is (literary theorists frequently initiate their arguments with a chapter whose title is – or is a variant of – the question 'What is literature?' Various unsatisfactory answers are then canvassed[2]).

We should not be too exercised about the question of the nature or true essence of the literary. The best way to look at the matter might be that of John Ellis in *Theory of Literary Criticism* (1974). Ellis abandons the search for any objective or 'reference theory' of meaning which would answer for us the question of what the literary is, and settles instead for the formulation that that to which we take a literary approach is literary.[3] If we start looking at a text *out of immediate communicative context*, for something other than its communicative value, we are beginning to take a literary approach to it; commenting on a pun or some alliteration present in a public notice is to react to the notice in a literary way; instead of Minding the Step or Refraining from Smoking we are thinking about an aspect of the literary quality of the 'text' and, precisely, ignoring its communicative value. This is important for us, because the literary approach considers just those features that constitute the register of literature – or rather, *registers*, since there is clearly no single literary register.

The objection to there being a single 'register of literature' was made early in the history of our concept: Michael Gregory, writing about language varieties in 1967, observed that 'the language of literature is so unrestricted that to term it a register is apt to be misleading'.[4] He also refers – and thereby makes the same point twice – to the 'exotericism' of literature. The 'exoteric' is the opposite of the esoteric, and is given in the *Oxford English Dictionary* as a word of Greek origin, being a simple transliteration of the comparative form of the Greek 'exo', 'outside', and thus meaning 'outsid-er' or, better, 'more outside'. In another gloss the dictionary gives 'suitable to the uninitiate'. Literature, being exoteric, is suitable for outsiders, available to the uninitiate; it needs no special insider knowledge for its understanding; it has no restrictions.

One can see the point here: only someone versed in the technicalities of geology can readily deploy terms such as continental drift, tectonic plates and magma; only a player of real tennis knows what the tambour and the grille are – these are pieces of esoteric knowledge – but no special knowledge, no special *language*, is required to read Jane Austen; therefore Jane Austen does not write in 'a register'; such is the argument. But to this logic there are two objections, a weak one and a strong one.

First, weakly: in previous chapters I have tried to demonstrate how literature is made up of the voices of the culture from which it emerges, and one way of defining these voices is to call them registers; literature, in other words, being made of language, must be made of registers. One might say, therefore, that it is misleading to insist on avoiding the term altogether in literary studies. ·At the very least we should be allowed to identify registers *in* literature; texts must inevitably show signs of this or that externally identifiable register.

Second, and more strongly: literature is full of stylistic phenomena, at all levels, which cry out 'this is literature' just as loudly as talk of chemotherapy, appendectomies and junior housemen cries out 'medicine'. The examples given above of the openings of the two novels by Mrs Humphry Ward and Edith Wharton would be identified by ninety-nine out of a hundred reasonably experienced readers as belonging to narrative fiction; the same percentage, at least, would know that this was poetry:

> O Thou, who Man of basest earth did'st make
> And who, with Paradise, devisd'st the snake...

Even incomplete, as I have deliberately left it, this snippet of Edward Fitzgerald's translation of *Omar Khayyam* (1859) has the 'poetic', as one might say, written all over it; one need go no further than rhythm and rhyme to make the point. But most readers would also be able to go further than merely identifying it as poetry; certain archaisms, notably the second-person-singular pasts, with their interestingly awkward ''st' endings, would signal something of the Romantic tendency to an older, archaic style – a tendency, in fact, to, precisely, a form of 'poetic diction'. This is not '*the* register of literature', nor even '*the* register of poetry'; one can write poetry perfectly well without any recourse to these features, but they do none the less signal, correctly, that these lines belong to an identifiable register category which can be historically dated and placed in an intellectual context. A whole history of Victorian medievalism, not to say Victorian orientalism, stands behind this point; there is a sociocultural ground in which Fitzgerald's verses have their roots, a series of possible voicings in which he was participating.

Once again, the crucial question here is 'How do we think of register?' *If* we think of it narrowly, just as 'different ways of saying different things', if it merely tells us that we have a language for doing law and another language for doing farming or vulcanology, then we are faced with two possibilities:

> *either* there is a separate language of literature which exists alongside all the other registers of English and does not overlap with them (which is patently absurd, although there *are* languages in which poetry has sometimes tended to be written in a specialised register, including, I believe, Romanian);

> *or* there is no separate 'literary language', in which case literature is made *only* out of the 'normal' or non-literary registers of English (which is also absurd, since there is almost always something about the language of a literary text which is identifiably different and of which any half-competent reader can feel the presence, and which that reader is likely to want to call 'literary').

Neither of these alternatives corresponds to the realities of reading a literary text. We need to use the concept of register more broadly and flexibly so that, on the one hand, we are alive to all the voices of our culture(s) as they sound through the text and, on the other, we are also aware of how literature itself has a history, conventions, speech styles, languages, which themselves, through intertextuality and generic expectation, generate their own meanings and teach us how to read.

Thus: we poor exoteric uninitiates need to retain the breadth of the radically amateur, and listen to all the voices we hear in a text (we are amateurs because we are not professionally involved; we don't react to a piece of legalese in a literary text by attempting to solve the legal matter as a solicitor might, nor do we react to medical register by telephoning for an ambulance). But we also need to be aware (this has traditionally been seen as the one 'professional' skill possessed by students of literature) of the special registers of those texts to which we are taking a literary approach. Actually, of course, the real 'professionalism' – if that word has any useful meaning here (or have I dragged it in uselessly from another register?) – would be the ability of the reader to see the largest possible number of connections and interrelationships between *all* the different registers in the text, including both the literary and the non-literary ones; the meanings of a text are made by readers out of a weaving of the two. Reading for register should make us sensitive to all the recognisable accents, speech, languages and styles of the text, including the literary voice.

Perhaps the resolution to this dispute between the linguistician's way of using register (basically Halliday's rather monologic approach: different registers do different things) and the 'useful-for-reading-literature' dialogic way I am suggesting is once again to remind ourselves of the special nature of literature. This 'special' does not mean 'closer to God'. There is no claim being made that literary discourse is somehow better or more valuable or more refined or 'truer' than the non-literary; nor, as we have seen, is literature necessarily written in a special language. It is just that, for better or for worse, although one does not *have* to take a literary approach to a text, if one does do so, certain consequences follow. Notably:

- all the elements of that text become opened for an endless rereading;
- no fixed or final or stable meaning is to be expected *overall*;
- the parts of the text, however it is divided, are to be seen in constant play not only with each other but also with all other texts that touch them at any point and in any way (intertextuality)
- and with all elements in the culture from which the text arises and that other culture to which it returns (the locus of reading).[5]

Reading, in other words, should be semiotic, at least when it is literary, and one of the basic rules of semiotic reading is to inspect the medium closely and interrogate it. What better interrogation can we undertake than the one beginning with our questions 'Whose voice is this?' and 'What register is this?', remembering that there will be literary-conventional answers to these questions

('This sounds like romantic love poetry') as well as answers from the general world of registers ('This sounds pedagogic to me'; 'This is engineering-speak').

Literary magpie: *The French Lieutenant's Woman*

Well, putting this to the test, whose voice is this?

> An easterly is the most disagreeable wind in Lyme Bay – Lyme Bay being that largest bite from the underside of England's outstretched south-western leg – and a person of curiosity could at once have deduced several strong probabilities about the pair who began to walk down the quay at Lyme Regis, the small but ancient eponym of the inbite, one incisively sharp and blustery morning in the late March of 1867.
>
> The Cobb has invited what familiarity breeds for at least seven hundred years, and the real Lymers will never see much more to it than a long claw of old grey wall that flexes itself against the sea. In fact, since it lies well apart from the main town, a tiny Piraeus to a microscopic Athens, they seem almost to turn their backs on it. Certainly it has cost them enough in repairs through the centuries to justify a certain resentment. But to a less tax-paying, or more discriminating eye it is quite simply the most beautiful sea-rampart on the south coast of England. And not only because it is, as the guide-books say, redolent of seven hundred years of English history, because ships sailed to meet the Armada from it, because Monmouth landed beside it … but finally because it is a superb fragment of folk-art.[6]

This, the opening of John Fowles's *The French Lieutenant's Woman* (1969), sounds 'literary' because it presents us with the conventional features of the opening of a nineteenth-century novel: time, place, characters, the weather… The relationship between narrator and (implied) reader is established: both N and R know about cold winds, about the map of England, and we are both there together as the 'person of curiosity'. The length of that first sentence-paragraph alone, together with its embeddings and leisurely inclusiveness, signals a familiar register unmistakably that of classic realist fiction. And of course Fowles is having his joke here – this is pastiche, a 'pretend' classic opening, as children might say. At first you can easily hear the voice of Jane Austen – hinted at in the very locality, of course, for Lyme is famously the setting for part of *Persuasion* – with simple lexical echoes such as 'disagreeable' and 'a person of curiosity'; but even in the first sentence there is also the seemingly inevitable register polyphony at work, for Jane Austen would not talk about bites out of legs, after all. And is Henry James not present here too? The reluctance simply to *tell* us about 'the pair' (whose names and identities the narrator knows perfectly well) and the speculative deducing of probabilities are hallmarks of Jamesian style.

Then, in the next paragraph, a dozen subtle (and less subtle) register threads are picked up. There is still a little Austen ('The Cobb has invited…', 'well apart from the main town…'), but there is also slightly arch clichéd circumlocution ('what familiarity breeds…') and extended metaphor ('a long claw of old grey wall that flexes itself…', 'a tiny Piraeus to a microscopic Athens…') which are entirely unlike Austen, and signal a twentieth-century novelistic register. There is the colloquialism of the local resident ('real Lymers', 'it has cost enough in repairs') set against some definitely written formulations ('to a less tax-paying, or more discriminating, eye…', 'sea-rampart'). The pseudo-colloquial 'as the guide-books say' is followed by a parody of the register of those books: 'redolent of seven hundred years of English history…'. 'Sailing to meet the Armada' is a hybrid that reflects both the language of the guidebooks and the language of a certain late-imperial style of British historiography; 'Monmouth landed beside it' is a little bit less metaphorical-portentous, and lowers the register tone a touch. The last sentence I quote involves a register that is different again. 'A superb fragment of folk-art' comes from art criticism, I suppose – perhaps in its more journalistic manifestation.

Fowles, then, weaves his text from a number of register-strands and generates a secondary level of meaning from their interaction. Some of the registers at his command can most usefully be labelled 'literary' and their provenance (Austen, James) demonstrates this. It can be shown that Jane Austen's style has its own intertextual connections with Fanny Burney and with the theologians and moralists of the eighteenth century whom Jane read; nothing is static in these matters, there is no absolute register that 'goes back to Jane Austen' and stops there. But there is equally no doubt that the echoes that can be established between some elements of Fowles's first paragraph and certain elements in Austen's fiction are not mere chimeras. Fowles himself is aware of the registration of his prose and certain that not all of it is 'literary' ('as the guide-books say'); his intense post-modern consciousness of who is seeing what, who is saying what, what this clause sounds like, where he is coming from in all this, includes, involves, *is* a consciousness of register. The totality might add up to a quasi-mythological mix that we could call 'Fowles's own style', but the individual elements all come from somewhere else, including other literature.

Pretending to write unliterarily: *The Collector*

Here is another example from Fowles which is perhaps a more testing one for a literary-register approach. Indeed, this text might seem to be making a bid to sound altogether unwritten:

> When she was home from her boarding-school I used to see her almost every day sometimes, because their house was right opposite the Town Hall annexe. She and her younger sister use to go in and out a lot, often with young men, which of course I didn't like. When I had a free moment from the files and ledgers I stood by the window and used to look down over the road over the frosting and sometimes I'd see her. In the evening I marked it in my observations diary, at first with X, and then when I knew her name with M. I saw her several times outside too. I stood right behind her once in a queue at the public library down Crossfield Street. She didn't look once at me, but I watched the back of her hair in a long pigtail. It was very pale, silky, like burnet cocoons. All in one pigtail coming down almost to her waist, sometimes in front, sometimes at the back. Sometimes she wore it up. Only once, before she came to be my guest here, did I have the privilege to see her with it loose, and it took my breath away it was so beautiful, like a mermaid.[7]

This is the opening – in my view stunningly brilliant in its handling of register – of *The Collector* (1963). The narrator, Clegg, is emotionally deprived and disturbed, a monster and madman who will capture 'M', imprison her and keep her in his cellar until she dies of pneumonia, because he loves her, in his fashion, and knows no other way of relating to her satisfactorily. But he is not altogether hopeless as a person; he is capable of holding down a job, and is clearly something of an expert entomologist (he collects butterflies, which teaches him how to *collect* women). Fowles works, through register, to present the disturbing and dangerous mind of this Calibanesque lover in all its limitations; from the first words we are made to feel that there is something wrong, that the writing *shouldn't be like this.*

At times Clegg can operate in the literary-narrative mode that we expect in first-person fiction from a competent writer (and there is no doubt about Fowles's competence). Thus he employs the simple past, handles the time-setting very efficiently (we learn a lot here about what has happened and when), moves from subjective to objective narration with great ease ('she' – 'I' – 'her' – 'she' – 'I' – 'I' – 'her', and so on), and sees the need for literary figures (the similes 'like burnet cocoons' and 'like a mermaid'). This is some sort of literary register. We might be tempted to take it instead for a confession to the police, in many places possibly even a spoken or dictated confession (the first two or three sentences? the whole paragraph up to the last sentence? the whole paragraph?), but on rereading it is evident that it is in literary mode. There is just slightly too much subordination for a confession or for mere private musings: the first sentence has three clauses, two being subordinate; the second ends with a subordinate clause; the last sentence embeds a subordinate clause and manages an inversion ('Only once ... did I').

On the other hand, this paragraph also catches the banal, obsessive, monotonous voice of the psychopath in a register that is quite unliterary. In spite of the hypotaxis (the subordination), there are strings of paratactic elements that show Clegg's mind circling round his prey. Either sentences repeat a simple grammatical structure ('I saw...', 'I stood...' 'I watched...') or Clegg returns helplessly to an obsessing topic without regard for grammatical completeness; here I've added, subtracted and highlighted to make the patterns stand out more clearly:

> I watched the back of <u>her hair</u>...
> > <u>It</u> was very pale...
> > > [<u>It</u> was] All in one pigtail...
> > > > [<u>It</u> was] *Sometimes* in front...
> > > > > [<u>It</u> was] *Sometimes* at the back...
> > > > > > *Sometimes* she wore <u>it</u> up...
> > > > > > > Once [I saw her] with <u>it</u> loose
> > > > > > > > <u>it</u> took my breath away
> > > > > > > > > <u>it</u> was so beautiful...

This haunted, fixated voice that suggests a hypnotised state is only a shade away from the flat, colloquial ordinariness of much of the passage. The ordinariness is set against a series of 'literary' elements in a bizarre stylistic cocktail. Clegg's mixed mind becomes apparent through the register choices which show us a man who, though capable of the figurative 'silky, like burnet cocoons', which has probably sent us to our dictionaries, seems otherwise content to talk (or write) the dullest, most Spoken English – a kind of Estuary English before its time.

Its features include *colloquial phrasing*:

every day sometimes [instead of, say, 'there were occasions when I saw her every day']

used to … used to … used to

right opposite … right behind her

sentences with strings of adjuncts after the verb, unpunctuated:

I stood   right behind her
           once
           in a queue
           at the public library
           down Crossfield Street.

'lazy' omission of clause-constructing elements, creating ambiguity:

'I watched the back of her hair [*which was*] in a long pigtail'

The unease generated by this opening paragraph could be summarised by listing these two opposing register tendencies.

- On one side are the 'higher' registers, Educated, Literary (first-person narrative) and Entomological, which come together in a sentence such as 'In the evening I marked it in my observations diary' and in the specialist simile 'like burnet cocoons'.
- On the other side are 'lower' registers, the Uneducated, Colloquial Police-Confession style, the obsessive Private Musing, the clichés and the grammatical incompletenesses.

The two tendencies overlap beautifully in clauses such as 'Only once … did I have the privilege to see her with it loose', where the inversion ('did I') is 'literary' and 'having the privilege' the most appallingly clichéd piece of grovelling Uriah-Heep-speak (i.e. *both* colloquial and 'Dickensian'), while 'I saw her with it loose' is the normal colloquial version used to express the vision of a woman's crowning glory unbound. Equally, the banal 'it took my breath away' is utterly can't-think-of-anything-more-interesting-than-that colloquial, and is supported by the ungrammaticality of 'like a mermaid', which should be 'like a mermaid's', but he can't manage that possessive; on the other hand, the very idea of the comparison with mermaids has a literary flavour, as if Clegg is striving for something 'poetic' to encapsulate his feelings about the magic of M's tresses.

A test that can be employed here is to read the passage aloud to someone else. The 'voicing' required is very specific. To some extent it is a matter of geographical dialect (but, as we shall see in Chapter 9 below, dialect *in literature* has the same function as register, and only that function), and Clegg must belong to an area of central or southern Britain, with its casual suburban tones; for my money he's Home Counties sub-Cockney (now 'Estuary'). It is also a matter of class, that is, 'social dialect' or, as we would say, the register of a particular social grouping. Clegg is lower middle class at 'highest', a clerk in the Town Hall. Consequently, an accent and an intonation are demanded by the passage, a 'voice' to match phonetically what Fowles has written graphically. But the person reading this aloud will then have a moment's doubt and hesitation when they come to 'higher' register points; how does one do 'burnet cocoons' in Estuary English? In my experience it is almost impossible to read the last sentence without putting an extra emphasis on 'did I have the privilege' to indicate that Clegg is here 'putting on' a style more elevated than 'his own'. This is a wrong instinct, I think, because what is sinister about Clegg is that he can flatly and monotonously proceed in the same intonation whether the register is high or low. The putting on to one plane of at least two registers, in other words, constructs his frame of mind for us; he cannot distinguish between private thoughts of a rambling and vague kind ('I fancied this girl once…') and the scientific pursuit of butterflies. In the next paragraph he delivers himself of mixed-register voicing of a kind that entirely confirms this analysis:

Another time one Saturday off when I went up to the Natural History Museum I came back on the same train. She sat three seats down and sideways to me, and read a book, so I could watch her for thirty-five minutes. Seeing her always made me feel I was catching a rarity, going up to it very careful, heart-in-mouth as they say. A Pale Clouded Yellow, for instance. I always thought of her like that, I mean words like elusive and sporadic, and very refined – not like the other ones, even the pretty ones. More for the real connoisseur.[8]

The point here is that writers – at least, writers like John Fowles – *play* with registers including literary registers. Here entomology ('Pale Clouded Yellow') mixes with a vulgar spoken voice ('going up to it very careful, heart-in-mouth as they say'), but we are also, in however concealed a manner, in the presence of literary narrative complete with scene-setting, self-analysis ('Seeing her always made me feel...') and reflection ('More for the real connoisseur'). In other words, Clegg sometimes sounds like a writer writing literature, sometimes he sounds like a collector, and sometimes like a particular sort of young Englishman talking to you about his girlfriend. It may sound paradoxical, but literary register is only one of many that a writer of literature can use. It doesn't even have any special status in the gamut of registers at the writer's disposal.

Words such as 'parody' and 'pastiche' may come to mind here, and that is probably a good reaction. For what is Fowles doing except parodying the voices of the clerk, the psychopath, the butterfly collector, *the novelist*? What else can he do?[9]

Borrowing styles

In *The Dialogic Imagination* Bakhtin summarises the situation of the novelist thus:

The writer of prose does not meld completely with any of [his or her] words, but rather accents each of them in a particular way – humorously, ironically, parodically and so forth...

The stratification of language – generic, professional, social in the narrow sense, that of particular world views, particular tendencies, particular individuals, the social-speech diversity and language-diversity (dialects) of language – upon entering the novel establishes its own special order within it, and becomes a unique artistic system, which orchestrates the intentional theme of the author.

I have quoted this from Pam Morris's *Bakhtin Reader* rather than from the original in order to include Morris's footnote to this passage:

> The words are not to be understood as the author's direct speech, but as words the author 'exhibits' as it were from the distances appropriate to humour, irony, parody, etc.[10]

Some things need to be thought about in these quotations; we might nowadays be less concerned to establish the author's 'intentional theme', for instance, and Bakhtin seems to want to talk only about the novel when he might as well talk about all artistic prose; furthermore, he has not here established the notion of literary register as merely another register available to the writer alongside all others. But the overall thrust of this sort of thinking is crucial to an understanding of register in general. In particular, the three expressions 'not meld with', 'upon entering the novel' and 'exhibits' are worth very serious consideration.

'*Melding*' with any voice in the text is not merely undesirable for an author, it is impossible. The voice in the text is never *mine* in some uncomplicated old-fashioned notion of expressivity. At most the voice we hear is that of the implied author, but even he (or she, and the implied author may not be of the same gender as the 'real' author, or of any gender at all) has to speak in some register – in some 'social-speech diversity'.

'*Entering the novel*' means that language changes in nature on becoming part of a literary work. It becomes voiced, self-conscious, parodic, exhibitionist. It is part of a game that the author is playing, with this difference: the author can never come forward through the curtain and take a bow *in propria persona*; it is only in *another persona* that we can meet him or her. Anything, any piece of language, any protestation of sincerity, comes from a distance, belongs elsewhere too.

'*Exhibits*' is a good word for what literary writing does. It 'puts on a show' of a particular voice, a particular register. All writing is *play* in this circus or theatrical sense. All words involve a 'play on words'. All language is figurative. The beggar who holds out his hand to us in the street might be seen as seriously involved, without play, in trying to keep body and soul together (though he *might* be playing, too), but the beggar on page or stage, say Edgar as 'Tom' in *King Lear*, or the Old Cumbrian Beggar in Wordsworth, or Jo the Crossing Sweeper in Dickens, or the 'face on the Waterloo Steps' in John Cowper Powys's W*olf Solent* – these are 'exhibits', verbal constructs whose meaning may be something quite different and who may represent anything at all; this collection of examples, as it happens, representing, playing the part of, respectively:

'Tom' – Honest Filial Loyalty Forced to Disguise Itself
Old Cumbrian Beggar – Sturdy Perseverance, Nature
Jo – Uneducated Poverty, Neglect, Instinctive Christianity
'The face' – Desperation, the end of the tether.

There is almost nothing in common between these characters. Interestingly, considering Bakhtin's comment, none of these four can be taken altogether seriously – not in the way we take a 'real' beggar. If we do. If we can.

The point is that parody and pastiche wouldn't work if we did not already recognise the literary sources to which they refer. Katie Wales, writing in 1989, appeals for a more Bakhtinian sort of reading:

What is needed is a kind of analysis for any type of text or discourse that arises from the focus on inherent or internal dialogism, the inter-action of word with word, and which probes deeper than traditional concerns of 'tenor' of discourse at the interpersonal level.[11]

This can help us to see the necessity for a more connected reading than the word 'text' might indicate. The concept of intertextuality is a good reminder of where we should be looking (outside the text and inside simultaneously), but it is easy to see intertextuality as a sort of second or supplementary notion, an 'extra' to be considered after the 'text itself' has been inspected. This must be a mistaken perspective, however, as texts do not stand proud and independent in some glorious Romantic isolation and then, addi-tionally, perhaps even optionally, happen to have a few points of contact with other texts. Connectedness is *inherent*, to use Wales's word; dialogue is always already going on even as we approach the text, it is not merely orientated in a particular direction under the general notion of 'tenor'; and the registers of which it is made are the key element in this web-like fact about meaning. This is because connectedness, 'answerability' and interaction are inherently in the nature of *all* language use.

Here is Bakhtin, using the word 'genres' where I think we would now use 'registers' (we shall have to come back to genre, but for the moment it is worth noting that 'genre' and 'register' can be interchangeable):

> Like Molière's Monsieur Jourdain who, when speaking in prose, had no idea that was what he was doing, we speak in diverse genres without suspecting that they exist. Even in the most free, the most unconstrained conversation, we cast our speech in definite generic forms, sometimes rigid and trite ones, sometimes more flexible, plastic and creative ones.... We are given these speech genres in almost the same way that we are given our native language, which we master fluently long before we begin to study grammar.... Speech genres organise our speech in almost the same way as grammatical (syntactical) forms do. We learn to cast our speech in generic forms and, when hearing others' speech, we guess its genre from the very first words.[12]

We have learned to speak in 'speech genres', that is, in registers, and they are interactive, they form part of a dialogue of such power that our meanings are rendered meaningless unless they are situated in a dialogic context:

> Each utterance is filled with echoes and reverberations of other utterances to which it is related by the communality of the sphere of speech communication. Every utterance must be regarded primarily as a *response* to preceding utterances of the given sphere... It is impossible to determine its position without correlating it with other positions.[13]

Now Bakhtin is talking about speech here, but what he says is just as true for other forms of text and, *a fortiori*, for the literary text. Language comes to us registered, preformed to some degree, and so do the genres of literature and the kinds of writing that go with them. Literature exists, like all other kinds of text, in a *communality* that is the absolutely essential ground for the emergence of any meaning whatsoever.

Jay Lemke, in his work on intertextuality, is particularly good at arguing the case for this sort of extensive connectedness; he has developed the notion of a 'contextualising practice' whereby we process texts according to our knowledge of where they fit in the practices of a community (or 'culture'). Lemke observes that our knowledge is equally a knowledge of where to fit things in and where *not* to fit them in; contextualising practice is 'a making sense of the texts, or portions of them, by placing them in the context of only some and not other texts or recurring discourse patterns'. He continues:

> All meaning making may be described as such **selective context-ualisation** … because it is only insofar as all possible combinations of signs and their contexts of use are *not* equally likely that meaning itself is possible.[14]

Now if this process is true for texts in general (Lemke is concerned in this article with a science lesson), it is true to an even greater degree of literary texts (or, to be consistent, those texts to which we are taking a literary approach). The 'selective contextualisation' involved in reading a novel is remarkably clear: first one is powerfully aware of the genre *novel* involved (Here's a new novel by William Boyd! Or: I'm rereading Proust… – 'Proust' here meaning 'writer of a long fictional work'), and that genre is quickly subdivided. (It's about time I read some of those big Victorian novelists again. Or: I love a good thriller – have you seen the latest Wilbur Smith?) The phenomenon of the fashionable genre proves the point rather well. After the stunning success of J. R. R. Tolkien's *Lord of the Rings* in the 1960s, for instance, a whole host of imitators was spawned, many of them almost plagiaristically related to Tolkien. But of course Tolkien himself was deeply indebted to the Old Norse, Old English and later medieval texts which he was professionally engaged in studying and teaching; doctoral theses – indeed, whole monographs – have been written tracing the 'influences' on his *magnum opus*. It is impossible not to contextualise his work by making an explicit, or at least a subconscious, appeal to vast tracts of cultural stereotypes, ideas, images, details (all coded as language, in other words as a register or series of registers) which can be extensively documented and displayed. Equally, one automatically brackets out, when reading Tolkien's sort of romanticising fantasy, all notions of, say, contemporary political commentary, all 'gritty realism', and so on. The context for reading is given to us, as Bakhtin says, 'from the very first words.' Since Tolkien (or since William Morris, Bullfinch and the Victorian resurrection of the medieval? or since Malory? or since Chrétien de Troyes?) the 'fantasy' register has been available. And then, subsequently, the genre takes on a life of its own – a new fantasy can satisfy if it sounds sufficiently like Tolkien, who himself gained 'authenticity' by *sounding like* the sagas and romances in whose register he wrote. Here is a 'literary register' at work clearly enough, but of course it is not simply that in isolation. When, for instance, Sam Gamgee relates to Frodo Baggins in a loyal-servant-to-good-master manner, we can equally clearly read the register of the culture in which Tolkien wrote – a register with its roots well buried in the cultural soil of the British class system of the nineteenth and early twentieth centuries.

Literature between literary and non-literary registers

All texts are inclined to start *in medias res* (*not*, dear spell-checker, *in medusa roes*, which would get us into some rather fishy territory) and not merely in deference to Sir Philip Sidney and his classical antecedents, who prescribed this way of beginning. Texts come as Bakhtinian responses to preceding texts or, in Randolph Quirk's terms, as 'continuations' of an existing dialogue. As he says, 'beginnings do not exist: we have only continuations'.[15] With the dubious exception of 'existential openings' such as 'There was once a princess...', all beginnings involve some form of tacit agreement that the topic introduced 'exists as *a priori* common ground' between speaker and listener (poet and reader) and, usually, directly imply some preceding dialogic element. Quirk cites the opening of *The Tempest* ('Boatswain!' – 'Here master. What cheer?' – 'Good. Speak to the mariners. Fall to it yarely, or we run ourselves aground.') as an example of a text that presupposes a large amount of previous action assumed by the audience (the actors tend to shout these words as they are, after all, responding to an imagined storm). He also has a good reading of Shakespeare's Sonnet 116, 'Let me not to the marriage of true minds', of which the opening, by being polemical and in the negative, 'obliges us... to supply the essentials of unwritten argument that precedes it'.[16] Quirk also says, of our capacity to understand what is being talked about, even when (perhaps especially when) we are being addressed by strangers, that 'the seeds of this beginning lie darkly hidden in our common knowledge of the language'.[17] This 'common knowledge' is both literary and non-literary.

Helga Geyer-Ryan, writing in Willie Van Peer's *The Taming of the Text* (1989), and wanting to be as Bakhtinian as possible – that is to say, to keep her texts as firmly grounded in the social as possible – is wary of the notion of intertextuality precisely because it sounds too much as though it belongs to the realm of the 'poetic' and is thus insufficiently social. She quotes Brecht and Tony Harrison to show real sociolects at work (good grimy working-class stuff seems to guarantee a superior authenticity of social analysis). Quoting Brecht's 'Questions from a worker who reads', she finds voices that question official historiography ('The young Alexander conquered India./ Was he alone?'), but in Tony Harrison's 'Them & [uz]' she finds voices raised against the official poetics. This dialogue between the official and the unofficial queries the notion of a literary register but does so, paradoxically, by writing, in the entirely literary form and genre of poetry in a (partly) 'non-poetic' register. The Harrison poem includes such expressions as 'So right, yer buggers, then!' and, with reference to 'T. W. Harrison' as a name, 'I'm *Tony* Harrison, no longer you!' This is not literary register, but it is a perfectly legitimate – indeed, very effective – part of a well-known poem that is widely read in a literary context.

These 'answers' and 'continuations' of a class struggle, of a dialogue between monoglossia and heteroglossia, demonstrate clearly enough the open and non-'literary' nature of literature. The literary registers available to writers are not compulsory, any more than it is obligatory to see Alexander as the sole conqueror of India or obligatory to write poetry in 'RP' or any other official accent, dialect or register.

Geyer-Ryan makes her point, but it clearly implies that we cannot do without the concept of the literary. Sufficient attention to the notion of register should achieve the necessary compromise. Literature has indeed developed registers of its own, surely for good sociocultural reasons, and there would be no Brechtian dialogue with official registers if it had not, but it is also substantially made up of the registers of everyday life. 'Register' covers both the sociolectal (which is surely nothing other than the social-intertextual) and the poetic-intertextual. The necessary simple first step is to ask what the register of the text is; later we can ask whether the register we have identified is entirely social in origin or entirely 'poetic' ('literary'), or a mixture of the two.[18]

Ruqaiya Hasan, perhaps the strongest Hallidayan of them all, has devoted some time to the topic of the specifically literary. In her paper 'The place of stylistics in the study of verbal art' (1975),[19] and her book *Linguistics, Language and Verbal Art* (1985),[20] she makes an intriguing compromise between the linguistic gospel of Halliday and the special concessions needed to deal with the phenomenon of literature. It is fascinating to watch her use the powerful functional-systemic machinery to approach the literary text, and then to see the adaptations and exceptions she needs to introduce. She is aware that there is something not quite tameable in the literary, making a difference between 'style' – for instance, in a sermon or a lecture – and 'artistic style'; the question 'what is this lecture about?' just isn't the same sort of question as 'what is this novel about?' – so much so that even the specification of field becomes problematic in literature. Literature, for Hasan, is just a good deal more complicated than other forms of text. And a good deal more free; she suggests, for instance, that the 'symbolic articulation' of a theme in literature is *arbitrary* in much the same way as, for Saussure, the symbolic meanings in language are themselves arbitrary.

This is all most reassuring, and we can see here a first-class linguist exercising the necessary caution, even humility, in the face of the literary. Hasan has not quite been liberated by the postmodernist enterprise, though, as is revealed by her resort to the myth of depth in an otherwise excellent comment on, as it happens, *As You Like It*. She starts to consider what would be 'the deepest level of meaning' in that play, canvassing 'order' as a possible answer; this would be the 'theme' of the text. Well, perhaps.

In spite of such thinking, Hasan's work is a good first step towards the sort of liberation we need. She is aware that a linguistic analysis of a text (= stylistics in action) is a vast undertaking. Even as simple a sentence as Robert Frost's 'I wonder about the trees' needs 'exhaustive analysis at the levels of semantics, syntax, lexicon and phonology', and she imagines the 'innumerable tables listing frequencies of tokens of different types from the various levels of language'. But she rejects this method, and she objects that without any 'hypotheses' one can *do* very little with such tables.

How could one form an interpretation from them? Straight linguistic analysis can say nothing about the text as art. Her 'Stage One' is inadequate.

In these circumstances Hasan reaches, for a solution, to... register. 'Style', she says, has been used to cover much the same territory as 'register' in Hallidayan thinking. This is 'Stage Two'. But even this is not enough. As Hasan asks, is the 'contextual construct' around a literary text 'non-language' (as it is for a non-literary text) or 'literary genre'? Events and states of affairs, in literary texts, have no 'inherent qualities which logically determine the range of meanings that can possibly be assigned to them'. Here is a promising loosening of the linguistic straitjacket in which literature is in danger of being caught by too technical a linguistic approach.

Julia Kristeva, often credited with being the 'inventor' of intertextuality, was one of the earliest – following Barthes's groundbreaking ideas and the rediscovery of Bakhtin, both phenomena principally of the 1960s – to offer a reasoned summary of the implications of their thought for literature and literary study. In several essays – but notably in 'Word, dialogue, and novel' (1969) and 'How does one speak to literature?' (1971) – Kristeva stresses the multiplicity of the literary text and its place in the great web of all texts. For her, Bakhtin was the first to see that :

> Any text is constructed as a mosaic of quotations; any text is the absorption and transformation of another. The notion of *intertextuality* replaces that of intersubjectivity, and poetic language is read as at least *double*.[21]

The idea of text as a series of quotations (Barthes will make the same point, and use the alternative metaphor 'a *tissue* of quotations') begins to indicate the seriousness with which Bakhtinian thinking takes the idea that texts are *shot through* or woven by elements 'outside' themselves. Just as the vocabulary of English stands in some sense separately and independently from any given text in which it appears (though at one level the text is made of nothing other than words), so the registers, voices, genres and *other* texts in English (and more than just English – there are intertexts for English literature in French, Spanish, Latin...) stand independently, at least as theoretical structures, from the actual text in which they are instantiated. If English lexico–grammar is an armoury from which writers draw, then the semiotic structures of intertextuality constitute another, equally indispensable armoury.

Examples of literary intertextuality are not hard to find. The most obvious ones may be the least interesting, but as a test, let us look at this straightforward example from *Pendennis* (1848–50); Thackeray is writing about the tendency for young boys at Victorian public schools to learn about sex very early, and in a way that would make their parents blush:

> Before he was twelve years old little Pen had heard talk enough to make him quite awfully wise upon certain points – and so, Madam, has your pretty little rosy-cheeked son, who is coming home from school for the ensuing holidays. I don't say that the boy is lost, or that the innocence has left him which he had from 'Heaven, which is our home', but that the shades of the prison-house are closing very fast over him, and that we are helping as much as possible to corrupt him.[22]

This is hardly a 'difficult' or deeply hidden intertext, in fact it's more or less just the old-fashioned quotation of one text inside another, complete with inverted commas. Thackeray is deploying his 'armoury', and getting a further dose of meaning by putting in some Wordsworth. The implication seems to be roughly: 'You and I know Wordsworth – well, here is a hint that when I am talking about childhood innocence I am doing so in the quasi-Christian way that he did in the "Intimations of Immortality" Ode which, I have no doubt, you, as a good Christian Victorian of 1848–50, have read and admired, although this poem will be displaced as the nation's favourite very soon (1850) by Tennyson's *In Memoriam*; of course, like that poem, this one is shot through with Doubt, but we'll ignore that for now...'. But, as this implies, perhaps intertextuality is always more complex and interesting than just this – perhaps it is always doubled in some way. After all, Thackeray himself was not by any means an orthodox Christian, writing *Vanity Fair*, for instance, in a conscious attempt to write 'without God in the world'. This makes his notion of 'innocence' the more striking, as it is one element only, taken from the full range of Christian beliefs, that he has chosen to single out (here we are obeying Bakhtin's injunction to listen to 'the ordering of

all the other ideological voices of the era'). The ‹
'purity' is so great that it remains intact even wh‹
Christianity is a little shaky (in this context one m
Angel Clare, Tess of the D'Urbervilles's husband,
no longer a Christian – he becomes an agnostic – is unable to
tolerate Tess's lapse from 'purity').

And then, of course, Wordsworth himself was by no means an
orthodox Christian, either, so that Thackeray's direct address to
'Madam', characterised just a few lines earlier as one of the 'tender
mothers and sober fathers of Christian families', takes on an extra
ironical edge. What is more, it is by no means clear that the
Immortality Ode is thinking of sex at all, certainly not when it
talks about the shades of the prison-house which Thackeray
chooses specifically to refer to; it seems much more likely that the
prison-house is connected with sin only very generally, if at all,
and has far more to do with 'getting and spending' (as in Wordsworth's poem beginning 'The world is too much with us, late and
soon / Getting and spending we lay waste our powers'). The prison
is that of the later life of the boy who rowed on Windermere or
listened to the cataract or saw the daffodils; now he is obliged to
do 'mortal' things, deadly things – to take a job, to live in a city.
It is an image from natural religion or pantheism rather than from
Christianity in the poet; why, then, has it become an emblem of
chastity for the (actually not very Christian) novelist?

Then again, Thackeray *misquotes* Wordsworth, who wrote: 'From
God, who is our home', which seems to me to be some sort of
Freudian slip – Thackeray was happier with the vaguer 'heaven'
than with the more definitely committed 'God'. And again, why
precisely is a boy 'lost' (not a word used by Wordsworth) just
because he has found out about what the nature poet might possibly have regarded as a 'natural' development among young male
humans? And who are the 'we' who corrupt him? It seems very
odd, this 'we', since the reader cannot be supposed to be at school
him or herself and, if he or she were at school, would presumably
be an innocent bearing no responsibility for the situation to be
found there. This 'we' sounds to me a lot like Carlyle, at the
height of his fame at the time Thackeray is writing, hectoring his
generation and wringing his hands, in *Signs of the Times* and other
texts, over the sorry state of Victorian culture.

What this amounts to is that the 'literary intertext', while it is just that (Thackeray is profiting from belonging to the same profession, at some level, as the great Wordsworth – about to become more famous still by dying in 1850), cannot be only a *literary* intertext. There is no such thing as the purely literary. On further inspection, it turns out that the elements on the basis of which the literary comparison between Thackeray and Wordsworth is made reveal differences and similarities which inevitably send the reader back to the cultural and historical conditions in which the intertextuality is taking place. So 'shades of the prison-house' is undoubtedly 'in' a literary register – it isn't journalese or sociology, and is undeniably a borrowing from a literary text; but the analysis cannot be left there: there really were prisons of a certain sort in the nineteenth century, and there is a discourse surrounding them separable from that of literature.

Workpoints

[The poet's] medium is language, with the possible admixture of unfamiliar terms and metaphors and the various other modifications of language that we allow to poets.

Aristotle, *Poetics*

If the same register appears in two texts,
they are intertextually related.
Discuss

Notes

1 A recent theorist to argue the case against 'literary language' is Paul Simpson, in *Language through Literature: An Introduction* (Routledge, 1997, Introduction). For a good introduction to the topic, see Jeremy Tambling, *What is Literary Language?* (Open University Press, 1988).

2 For instance, besides Sartre's entire book entitled *Qu'est-ce que la littérature?* (Gallimard, 1948), there are: R. Wellek and A. Warren, *Theory*

of Literature (Jonathan Cape, 1949), Part I, chaps 1 and 2; John M. Ellis, *The Theory of Literary Criticism: A Logical Analysis* (University of California Press, 1974), chap. 2; David Lodge, *The Modes of Modern Writing* (Edward Arnold, 1977), Part I, chap. 1; Terry Eagleton, *Literary Theory: An Introduction* (Blackwell, 1983), Introduction; Jeremy Hawthorn, *Unlocking the Text* (Edward Arnold, 1987), Introductory; and Sylvan Barnet, Morton Berman and William Burto (eds), *An Introduction to Literature*, 1993, p. 1, 'What is literature?'

3 Ellis, *The Theory of Literary Criticism*.

4 Michael Gregory, 'Aspects of varieties differentiation', *Journal of Linguistics*, Vol. 3, 1967.

5 This list could be applied to non-literary texts, too. I don't care about that. The claim I am making here is simply that it *should* be applied to texts when we are taking a literary approach to them.

6 John Fowles, *The French Lieutenant's Woman* (Panther, 1969).

7 John Fowles, *The Collector* (Jonathan Cape, 1963).

8 *Ibid.*

9 On this topic, see Dennis Freeborn, *Style* (Macmillan, 1996), chap. 20, 'Parody and pastiche'.

10 Pam Morris (ed.), *The Bakhtin Reader* (Edward Arnold, 1994), p. 115.

11 Katie Wales, 'Back to the future', in Willie Van Peer (ed.), *The Taming of the Text: Explorations in Language, Literature and Culture* (Routledge, 1989). For an excellent example of register analysis, see William Downes's chapter in this same volume, 'King Lear's question', which includes criteria for distinguishing 'high style' and a demonstration that it is the register of Lear's questions that enables Regan and Goneril to reply to him satisfactorily but prevents Cordelia from doing so.

12 Mikhail Bakhtin, 'Speech genres', in C. Emerson and M. Holquist (eds), *Speech Genres and Other Late Essays* (University of Texas Press, 1986).

13 *Ibid.* There is a good Bakhtinian essay on polyphony in Dickens's *Hard Times* by Roger Fowler, in Ronald Carter and Paul Simpson (eds), *Language, Discourse and Literature: An Introductory Reader in Discourse Stylistics* (Unwin Hyman, 1989).

14 Jay L. Lemke, 'Intertextuality and text semantics', in M. Gregory and P. Fries (eds), *Discourse in Society: Functional Perspectives* (Ablex, 1995) (bold print in the original).

15 Randolph Quirk, 'Focus, scope, and lyrical beginnings', in *Style and Communication in the English Language* (Edward Arnold, 1982).

16 *Ibid.*

17 *Ibid.*

18 Helga Geyer-Ryan in Van Peer, *The Taming of the Text*, pp. 193–221.

19 Ruqaiya Hasan, *The Place of Stylistics in the Study of Verbal Art* (Skriptor, 1975).

20 Ruqaiya Hasan, *Linguistics, Language, and Verbal Art* (Deakin University Press, 1985).

21 Julia Kristeva, *Desire in Language: A Semiotic Approach to Literature and Art* (Columbia University Press, 1980).

22 William Makepeace Thackeray, *Pendennis* (1848–50) (Penguin, 1972), p. 51.

6

Register and genre

Unnecessary difficulty

Here is the sort of text figure I do *not* find immediately useful for the reading of literature:

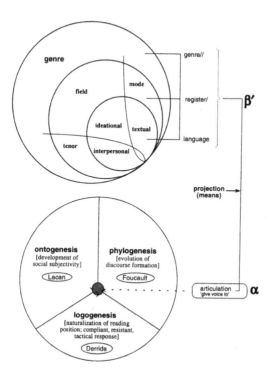

This figure is an attempt to show in visual mode the relationship between genre and register, and it comes early in a chapter that discusses the 'functional parameters' of genre in a text in the Cassell 'Open Linguistics' series.[1] The author, J. R. Martin, teaches linguistics in Australia, home of much recent work in systemic functional linguistics since Michael Halliday's arrival in that country in 1976. There is nothing wrong with the work that has led to this figure, which I find quite fascinating, and I have no complaint or objection whatsoever to J. R. Martin's purposes, techniques, interests or accomplishments. It is just that I do not think we should be faced with the choice of *either* swallowing such work whole 'before' undertaking literary reading *or* feeling obliged to eschew linguistics in its entirety.

Looking at the figure leads to the following logic:

- Here we have a sophisticated analysis in a complex area. In order to understand the relationship between genre and register in any written or spoken text across the full spectrum of texts in English, an analysis such as this may well be useful.

- But it is too general, and surely too complex, to be used readily in the reading of a literary text. There seems, in particular, no point in trying to hold the detail of this sort of work in mind while grappling with meaning in a complex structure such as a poem, novel or play.

- 'Register' and 'genre', however, have their place, and a very useful one, in literary analysis.

- We therefore seem to have a dilemma: either to stop using these terms in literary work altogether, which denies us useful tools, or to import into that work large edifices, such as the figure we are looking at, on the grounds that 'that's what register and genre *are*'.

- The solution is to refuse both horns of the dilemma. What is suitable for linguistics in general may not be suitable for literary texts in particular. Indeed, something may be lost in applying broad-brush techniques to the specifically literary question of meaning, although elements in those techniques may still be of use.

- We should not be frightened by the complexity of linguistic analyses into flying the field. We need not take an all-or-nothing approach in considering 'the application of linguistics to literary texts'.

- In general terms, this logic might provide a solution to the problem of 'linguistics and literature'. Perhaps there will never be a linguistics that is completely useful for literary study – there will never be a model that enables literary analysis to be subsumed into linguistic analysis. But there certainly is overlap.

Text and literary context

When we read the (linguistic) literature on genre, it is immediately clear that the problem posed concerns the relationship between text and context. Genre and register are defined as 'mediating phenomena' between various forms of context on the one hand ('context of situation', 'wider context of culture') and the linguistic forms of the text on the other. Roughly speaking, culture or society produces generic forms and registers which are then 'realised' in texts, and the task of functional linguisticians is to find the best way of describing this process. The debate concerns when and how to use the terms 'register' and 'genre'.

A substantial part of Helen Leckie-Tarry's posthumous study *Language and Context: A Functional Linguistic Theory of Register* (1995) is devoted to this debate.[2] Reviewing the subject from its appearance on the scene in the 1970s, she stresses the socially bound nature of both genre and register, quoting Hallidayans such as Kress and Hodge, for whom the relationship between text and context is seen in the form of 'a nexus between language and society'. Then the only question to be addressed becomes the one of when it is most useful to see the formations of this nexus as generic, and when they are best considered as registers. Her conclusion is that there is a major overlap between the two terms, and that both are none the less useful. She takes on two points in particular:

1. Registers have commonly been associated more with the linguistic properties of the texts in question, and with the immediate context of situation, while genres have seemed to be more on the social side of the nexus and thus less immediately linguistic.

2. There is also a suggestion that genres are *complete* and relatively *fixed*, while registers can be found in partial sections of a text, and can be somewhat variable.

But both these distinctions are relatively weak. Genres and registers are both perceived as being 'in the middle' – mediating – between text and context, between language and society; they are both looking both ways: into the language of the text one way and into the social order the other. Leckie-Tarry concludes:

> What seems to emerge, therefore, is that while registers are free to mediate in any communicative event, socially identified or informal, complete or incomplete, genres are taken to represent those events which have been culturally recognised.[3]

That is all the difference she finds it necessary to retain. Her point could be expressed in a formulation such as: register can appear anywhere (in this book I have been at pains to point out that all language always comes to us already registered), but genres are a bit more official and larger-scale, so the term 'genre' may not be quite as flexible as 'register'.

But, in truth, although there is sometimes some point in distinguishing between these two terms, for the most part they are almost interchangeable. For the power of genre exercises itself throughout a literary text and, as we have often said, register is likewise ubiquitous; and the two interact ineluctably. Consider this, which I shall not for the moment identify except in the endnote:

> 'Quite like old times,' the room says. 'Yes? No?'
>
> There are two beds, a big one for madame and a smaller one on the opposite side for monsieur. The wash-basin is shut off by a curtain. It is a large room, the smell of cheap hotels faint, almost imperceptible. The street outside is narrow, cobble-stoned, going sharply uphill and ending in a flight of steps. What they call an impasse.
>
> I have been here five days. I have decided on a place to eat at midday, a place to eat at night, a place to have my drink in after dinner. I have arranged my little life.[4]

Here, inextricably intertwined, are strands of register information and generic information, meanings at several levels, none of which could be placed definitively 'above' the other. For instance, take the short opening sentence. There is perhaps nothing in its lexis to indicate immediately much about either register or genre, but what can we say of the tense of the verb in 'the room says'? Surely it limits the *genre* possibilities to something confessional, in fact to something first-person and narrative? It is also entirely metaphorical.[5] What genre could this be other than novelistic? And, as we soon discover, first-person, 'autobiographical' novelistic at that. But the 'says' could just as well be described as characteristic of certain fictional *registers*. If the 'generic' fact it suggests ('this is a confessional narrative') is supported by the word 'I', which appears in the third paragraph, then the 'register' fact ('this *sounds like* a confessional narrative') is supported by the tense of the next verb after 'says' ('are' rather than 'were'), which is also in the present, and is part of a fairly extensive description.

Whether we see them in terms of genre or in terms of register, a number of definable characteristics of this prose extract become apparent. The style of the second paragraph is for the most part an exercise in artful simplicity, with short declarative sentences, mostly using no verb more elaborate than 'to be'. Very few genres or registers work like this – only elementary diaries, confessions, the writings of the supposedly mad trying to keep a grip on sanity; or, of course, fictional texts trying to sound like or trying to echo or represent these voices.

On the other hand, these first two paragraphs indicate the artifices of literature, too, thus narrowing the possibilities still further. For there is personification ('prosopopoeia') in the idea of the room *saying* anything, especially in its capacity to insist on an answer ('Yes? No?'), and there is an unmistakable hint of the symbolic in the last word ('impasse') which immediately, in the most usual of literary gestures, acts as part of a semantic field by relating to lexical sets concerned with *difficulty of locomotion* ('cobble-stoned', 'sharply uphill'), with *restriction* ('shut off by a curtain', 'narrow', 'ending in a flight of steps') and overall, both literally and metaphorically, with something like *the end of the road*: there is no 'monsieur' to occupy the other bed here (hence 'I', not 'we' in the third paragraph) and the hotel, despite the size of the room, is 'cheap'. So the genre here is that of confessional fiction, the sort of novel that has the hero-narrator at the end of the road, looking back, crawling forward, *voyage au bout de la nuit*, good morning midnight. One might think of Beckett's *Molloy*, which opens: 'I am in my mother's room. It's I who live there now. I don't know how I got there.'[6]

The passage quoted is the opening of Jean Rhys's novel *Good Morning Midnight* (1939). If one wants to begin to understand this text, one needs to be aware of its position at a specific place and time as a piece of late-modernist or even early postmodernist fiction, connected with the situation in Europe in the 1930s, with the feeling of *Angst* and rootlessness of that period and rather strange position of women between Victorianism and 'early' feminism on the one hand, and Women's Liberation on the other. It is the world of Katherine Mansfield, but it is also the world that had recently been overwhelmed by Proust and Joyce; it is the world of Kafka, too, as well as that of Colette, Woolf, W. H. Auden... Intertextualities indicate the ever-changing nature of the genre. Rhys enters the genre she has chosen at her own angle – re-creating it while being created by it.

Register *as* genre: Pope and Scott

The question thus occurs: is there really any very useful distinction to be preserved between register and genre for the purposes of literary analysis? Of course, if one wishes to distinguish between a sonnet and an epic, between a one-act play and *King Lear*, or between Mills & Boon and *Middlemarch*, one can use the word 'genre' to make the point, but when we are reading for meaning, analysing the text, there will in practice be few differences in what can be said using either term.

The crucial idea in all this – one that is not widely canvassed by stylisticians – is that of literary register, as discussed in Chapter 5. There, instead of trying to define literature, I suggested (a) that a 'literary approach' was possible towards any text whatever – something very similar to Jakobson's 'set towards the message'; and (b) that certain texts, not all of them necessarily those categorised conventionally as literature, showed signs of a literary register. Now, every register hints at, sounds like, belongs to a genre; it is impossible to imagine the one without the other. Gibbon sounds as he does (register) because he is writing classical history (genre) in the eighteenth century; if we are asked to iden-

tify some or all of T. S. Eliot's *Four Quartets,* or the choruses from
The Rock, we could equally well say that they belong in part to
the genre of 'Christian religious poetry', or that they employ the
registers of Christian religious poetry. The evidence in either case
would be the same.

The only difference would come in terms of certain structural
features such as scale and organisation. The length of the *Four
Quartets,* for instance (neither a thousand pages nor one), keeps
them within the generic bounds of 'Christian religious poetry',
and for this rather banal point the word 'genre' is obviously better
than 'register'. Equally, although the pastiche epic language sometimes employed in *Ulysses* is indeed an invocation of epic register,
one could not quite say that *Ulysses* is generically an epic: it does
not employ the epic style *in extenso* over several hundred pages,
nor is its organisation confined to the epic mould. But the logic
of the analysis remains the same whether we think of register or
of genre. What Joyce is playing with in his novel is simultaneously
(and indistinguishably) the epic genre and epic register; both are
invoked for the parodic purposes of art (art made out of art – *ars
est revelare artem,* perhaps?) and his game works in both ways at
once.

Literary registers are the languages in which literary genres have
their being. Were one to write an epic in Brooklyn slang, one
could hardly characterise what one had done in two sentences
('It's an epic. It's in Brooklynese' – as if one were saying: 'It's an
epic. It's in Latin'). One would be obliged to define one's mon-
strous/hilarious creation in one single sentence ('It's an epic in
Brooklynese!'), complete with exclamation mark to signal that the
work is not in the 'right' register for its genre. The meaning of the
text in this case would lie substantially in the fact of its status as
'mock-heroic' pastiche. Examples such as *The Rape of the Lock* spring
to mind; in Pope's poem there is a fair degree of fidelity to the
epic genre, including invocations, a quasi-divine machinery, epic
similes, a focus on military action, and so on, but the register is
at odds with this at the level of lexis (though grammar, syntax and
metaphor are often quite Homeric) because Pope has miniaturised
and feminised the elements of his plot, and this clashes with the
large-scale masculine norm for epic-writing. The result is a list of
nouns that do not belong to the epic genre:

> And now, unveil'd, the toilet stands display'd,
> Each silver vase in mystic order laid...
> This casket India's glowing gems unlocks,
> And all Arabia breathes from yonder box.
> The tortoise here, and elephant unite,
> Transformed to combs, the speckled and the white.
> Here files of pins extend their shining rows,
> Puffs, Powders, Patches, Bibles, Billet-doux...[7]

'Toilet', 'vase', 'box', 'combs' and 'pins' have no place in the world of the epic and, in the famous line quoted at the end of this extract, Pope lists the ephemera to be found on a young lady's dressing-table in 1712. It is often commented on that the word 'Bible' is out of place here, among the make-up and the love-letters, and so it is, but it is *doubly* out of place if we take a register approach to a text such as this, for the Bible has as little place alongside the pagan epic themes as it does among the powder-puffs. In general, though, the point of mock-heroic (Pope called his poem 'heroi-comical') is that the epic genre is imitated very largely in an epic register, but lexical sets are introduced that are ridiculous in this framework. The *Dunciad* has the Funeral Games of Homer all right, and very athletic they are, but they consist of competitors diving into a sewer which, as one might say with perfect accuracy, rather *lowers the tone*.

As a schoolboy Pope had started translating the *Thebaid* of the Roman poet Statius. Here is a flavour of his serious 'heroic' mode from early in that rendering. The poet promises to write a really heavyweight epic about the current Caesar (Domitian), but contents himself for the present with the old story about the House of Thebes:

> The time will come when a diviner flame
> Shall warm my breast to sing of Caesar's fame:
> Meanwhile permit that my preluding Muse
> In Theban wars an humbler theme may choose:
> Of furious hate surviving death she sings,
> A fatal throne to two contending kings,
> And fun'ral flames that, parting wide the air,
> Express the discord of the souls they bear:
> Of towns dispeopled, and the wand'ring ghosts
> Of kings unburied in the wasted coasts:

When Dirce's fountain blush'd with Grecian blood,
And Thetis, near Ismenos' swelling flood,
With dread beheld the rolling surges sweep
In heaps his slaughter'd sons into the deep.[8]

Here the vocabulary (largely but not exclusively nouns or nominal constructions) belongs to the lexis that forms an essential part of the epic register. Although in *The Rape of the Lock* there are parodic versions of divine flames and muses, only in real epic are you likely to get 'furious hate', 'death', 'fun'ral flames', 'towns dis-peopled', 'wand'ring ghosts', 'blood' or 'slaughter'd sons'. Here, in short, the lexis supports the rest of the register, and the register is precisely that of the genre – epic. In summary: if a text is not a parody or pastiche, its register will always support genre, and be so closely bound to it that the distinction between the two will only rarely need to be invoked.

In Walter Scott's *Ivanhoe*, the registers and genres employed are very clearly marked. He borrows the lexis, even the polyglossia of foreign or alien words, of the twelfth century in which his story is set; the novel is stiff with the quasi-French vocabulary of her-aldry, the Latin of Friar Tuck and medieval-sounding English in general. But the narrative voice works in some kind of eighteenth-century Johnsonian or Gibbonian (does that word exist?) prose that gives rein to Scott's rather orotund tendencies. As a result, we get a kind of trifocal vision: an English written in 1830, based in the heavyweight prose of the previous century, but also sprinkled with twelfth-century English and other things from earlier periods.

Thus we get this kind of thing in a letter from a Cistercian monk to a Templar knight, asking to be rescued from captivity:

Aymer, by divine grace Prior of the Cistercian house of Jorvaulx, to Sir Brian de Bois-Guilbert, a Knight of the Holy Order of the Temple, wisheth health, with the bounties of King Bacchus and of my lady Venus. Touching our present condition, dear Brother, we are a captive in the hands of certain lawless and godless men, who have not feared to detain our person, and put us to ransom; whereby we have also learnt of Front-de-Boeuf's misfortune, and that thou hast escaped with that fair Jewish sorceress, whose black eyes have bewitched thee.[9]

This can be contrasted with utterly unmedieval – indeed, clearly eighteenth-century – narratorial interventions such as:

> The spoils were indeed very large; for, notwithstanding that much was
> consumed, a great deal of plate, rich armour and splendid clothing had
> been secured by the exertions of the dauntless outlaws, who could be
> appalled by no danger when such rewards were in view.

It might be thought that this is a simple case of the single-voiced
narrator writing in a different register from the single-voiced Prior
(diegesis in one style, mimesis in another). But that would be to
overlook the cross-infection that can occur between the two
categories, as in the following:

> There was brave feasting in the castle of York, to which Prince John
> had invited those nobles, prelates, and leaders, by whose assistance he
> hoped to carry through his ambitious projects upon his brother's throne.
> Waldemar Fitzurse, his able and politic agent, was at secret work among
> them, tempering all to that pitch of courage which was necessary in
> making an open declaration of their purpose.

Here, in what is generally highly measured eighteenth-century
prose, three small words indicate interference from the 'medieval'
register. 'Brave' feasting hints at the Frenchness of those Plan-
tagenet years (the word then, as now in French, does not refer to
courage); the castle *of* York, rather than York Castle, is archaic
even for the eighteenth century; and 'tempering *all*' has a positively Shakespearian ring to it, in place of 'everything' or some
alternative locution.

The genre point here is this. By playing about among these
registers, Scott invokes genres that in themselves carry meaning.
The Prior's letter is a pastiche of prose that can be found in
Jocelyn of Brakelond, the *Carmina Burana*, Gower, Chaucer and
elsewhere; it has a specific generic origin in known texts which are
not, among other things, novels; Scott actually refers in the Introduction and his footnotes to 'the Wardour Manuscript'. Similarly,
the Gibbonian prose is making a bid for 'historical' status – this
is how, since Smollett, Gibbon, Burke, we treat historical topics.
The genre is known and it is, again, not a fictional genre. The
combination of these elements in 1830 is intended to invoke the
new, fictional genre, the historical novel, invented by Scott himself
with *Waverley* in 1814. It must be firmly set in the past, with
constant hints at the existence of (non-fictional) texts from the
period in question, and it must be treated in the archly serious way

devised by Gibbon. These genres are needed to underpin the new one, and Scott's main method of doing this is to use appropriate registers.

Workpoints

A little linguistics can go a long way in the illumination of a literary text.

Graham Trengove in Willie Van Peer,
The Taming of the Text (1989)

Notes

1 J. R. Martin, 'Analysing genre: functional parameters', in Frances Christie and J. R. Martin (eds), *Genre and Institutions: Social Processes in the Workplace and School* (Cassell, 1997).

2 Helen Leckie-Tarry, *Language and Context: A Functional Linguistic Theory of Register* (Pinter, 1995).

3 *Ibid.*, p. 15.

4 Jean Rhys, *Good Morning Midnight* (1939) (Penguin, 1969), p. 9.

5 Rooms could be said to have a register of their own, or a series of registers. Don't they 'speak to us' at times? Are we here approaching the same point that Roland Barthes reached forty years ago when he discussed the grammar of fast food? Where there is grammar, there is register also.

6 Samuel Beckett, *Molloy* in *Molloy, Malone Dies, The Unnamable* (Calder & Boyars, 1959), p. 7.

7 Alexander Pope, *The Rape of the Lock*, Canto I, lines 121–38

8 Alexander Pope, *The First book of Statius His Thebais*, lines 47–60

9 Sir Walter Scott, *Ivanhoe* (1830), chapter 35.

Translating register

The impossibility of translation

Translation is impossible, and literary translation even more so. There are several reasons for this, most of them based on the Saussurean insight – which has been seen as the foundation of structuralist thought, and of all that has followed it – that different languages make different distinctions; that they divide up the world in different ways. In French a *mouton* on the hillside is *mouton* on the plate while in English the *sheep* on the hill becomes *lamb* or *mutton* at the butcher's. Famously, Eskimo-Aleut languages have lots of words for snow, Arabic lots of words for camels. Distinctions, of an obvious sociocultural nature, are made in these languages that are not made in those other languages which have emerged in parts of the world where camels and snow are of lesser importance. There is no one world, no single language, no universal '*découpage*' of reality.

If I wish to write or speak of a camel, therefore, I have fewer terms at my disposal, fewer nuances, than an Arabic speaker; this has the consequence that if I am translating a text about camels *from* Arabic I must be restricting my possible range of meanings, and if I am translating *into* Arabic I find it hard to decide whether to use a generic term or to avail myself of the greater specificity that that language offers. In translating, six into three hundred doesn't go; if there are six words for the same area of 'reality' in one language and three hundred in another, how can translation be accurate?

One can similarly imagine difficulties that would present themselves in translating a love poem written in Estonian, or some similar language, in which the gender of the described beloved is not made clear. Here one into two doesn't go: the pronouns 'he' and 'she' are both '*ta*' in Estonian. In these circumstances, how do I translate '*ta*' as it appears in that poem? For if '*ta*' in Estonian means 'he or she', then, unless there are other grounds for doing so, I am unable to decide whether the 'wonderful smile', say, of the poet's beloved is that of a man or a woman; is it *her* smile or *his* smile?

The solution to this puzzle might perhaps present itself to an English speaker as follows. In English there are gendered third-person pronouns, but there is no gender in the second person. Third persons are 'he' or 'she', but 'you' can be male or female. One might therefore transpose the Estonian poem so that, instead of describing 'she' or 'he', it is now recast to address 'you' directly. Other changes would almost certainly have to follow, but something of the original ambiguity would be preserved. On the other hand, an *address* (to 'you') is a rather different thing from a *description* (of 'him' or 'her'). This is as much as to say that a choice between two imperfections would be forced on the translator. Either the gender ambiguity is preferred – in which case the descriptive nature of the poem is lost – or the descriptivity is preferred – in which case the gender ambiguity is lost. Translation is impossible.

Samuel Beckett, in his late text *Company*, self-translates his expression 'Cloudless May day' into French as '*journée d'avril sans nuages*'.[1] Here there is no need to reach, for an explanation, to the notion of Beckett as a specially privileged self-translator. Even the humblest journeyman translator would be well advised to consider such apparently radical departures from 'the original'. After all, Beckett was Irish, and I would challenge anyone to find an account of cloudless days in Ireland (or Britain, for that matter) in April; May is another matter. Conversely, in many parts of France cloudless days are quite common in May, so to gain the same effect English 'May' has to become French '*avril*'. This merely reflects the problem experienced by more mundane translators of French who, faced with the phrase '*les giboulées de mars*', feel obliged to talk about 'April showers', which have a lot more clichéd clout about them than 'March showers' would.

It is easy to see, under these circumstances, that translation has to be a translation of the register or tone qualities of the original into the nearest approximation to those same register or tone qualities in the target language. Too great a fidelity to the mere lexico-grammar of the original is the greatest besetting sin of translators, and even of commentators on translation. Brian Fitch, for instance, an expert on Beckett, uses the May/*avril* crux as evidence that the two texts of *Company* – one French, one English – are simply different; that they represent a 'heterocosm'.[2] This seems to me to be quite right, but not for the reason that Fitch suggests. His idea is that Beckett tampers with his 'original' text and wilfully changes it when translating, thus creating a new or different text. But this is not the reason for the radical difference in meaning between the French and the English; it is not a matter of Beckett's *intentions*. The reason for the difference is that Beckett is trying to match a register in one language with something like an equivalent register in the other. From a *register* point of view, in this context, '*avril*' is a *better* translation of 'May' than '*mai*' would have been, even if no dictionary (or other part of the lexico-grammatical apparatus) would ever tell you so.

Here is another example. For Fitch, the 'classic shift' from the simple past of the English of *Company* to the *passé composé* of the French constitutes a rewriting of the text by Beckett, the creation of a new text; but that seems wrong. The French is indeed a different object, but this is not because Beckett has used author's privilege to change it; it is because, despite the changes that can be made to accommodate differences by using such considerations as register, no two languages are commensurate. None the less, Beckett does his best. Thus his 'For some reason which you could never fathom' becomes in French '*Pour une raison que tu n'as jamais pu expliquer*', and Fitch sees this as a shift in the perspective, as the creation of a second, different fictive universe, one in which 'you' *had been* unable to explain rather than one in which you *could* not do so. But it is not, and sensitivity to register can demonstrate that it is not. For the *passé composé* is the normal translation of the English simple past *in colloquial speech*. Evidently Beckett is simply trying to keep the voicing of his text colloquial; the English is acceptable as colloquial, and the use of the second person almost guarantees that it should be read as such ('For some reason *you* could never fathom'). Only insensitivity to the register implications of the spoken/written distinction could lead one to suppose that Beckett is trying to create a different fictive universe here.

Again, in another example, Fitch tries to establish different universes implicit in the translation of *Company* by quoting both versions of the first sentence of the text:

> A voice comes to one in the dark. Imagine.
> *Une voix parvient à quelqu'un dans le noir. Imaginer.*

He points out that 'Whereas the English "one" could refer to the speaker, the French "quelqu'un" suggests a third (or second) person other than the speaker.'[3] But a careful reading, bearing register in mind, shows that 'one' cannot really refer to the speaker here, because if it meant 'me' it would smack of a kind of Jeevesian pedantry that is quite out of keeping with the tone of the rest of the text in English. *This* narrator is not the person to refer to himself as 'one' in the way that Wodehouse's manservant is able to when he says things like: 'So one should be supposed to imagine, sir' as super-polite code for 'I agree.' So the 'one' is 'someone' – '*quelqu'un*'.

The translator has an impossible task, but part of that 'pensum' must be to read for register as much as for anything else.

Sociocultural constraints mean that languages develop terms that do not equate to similar terms in other languages. What is the '*Ecole Normale Supérieure*' in English? Normally (ha!) we simply leave that name in French, untranslated, which is as good a demonstration as one could find of the thesis that translation is impossible. Similarly, we talk of 'the burning of the Reichstag', rather than of 'the German Parliament' (or some similar term), for a complex of reasons, mostly political, thus leaving subeditors with the problem of whether to put 'Reichstag' in italics as a foreign word or leave it unmarked, thus implying that it is a loanword now established in English.

And, of course, it is not only at the level of lexis that languages differ. It simply is a fact that Arabic has a dual as well as a singular and a plural; that Spanish and Portuguese prefer to omit nominative pronouns, at least in the spoken form of those languages; that the definite article is almost nowhere as complex in its behaviour as in English. Grammatical differences are so great as to be more common than grammatical similarities. Partly in consequence of this, syntactical differences are also the norm. Few sentences can be translated from any one language into any other while keeping the same word order and using the same grammatical categories in each slot. Here is the sort of very simple sentence that can manage this:

The ink is on the table.
L'encre est sur la table.
La tinta esta sobre la mesa.

Even here there are nuances. Tables in French and Spanish are feminine, which they aren't in English; and in Spanish I have used one of two possible versions of 'to be', '*estar*' (less permanent existence), rather than '*ser*' (more permanent existence), a distinction unavailable in French or English. '*Sobre*' doesn't cover exactly the same semantic territory as '*sur*' or 'on'; '*tinta*' is etymologically connected to wine and colouring, which 'ink' and '*encre*' aren't; and so on. More importantly, this sort of direct translation is possible only

(a) in such artificially simple sentences as these; and
(b) where the languages have strong historical links with one another.

Among these difficulties, compounding them but also offering some hope of a solution, is register.

'Levels of language'

The French Canadians J. P. Vinay and J. Darbelnet, working in the 1950s and 1960s, set up some basic *points de repère* (but could one translate that as 'landmarks' in this highly metaphorical usage?) for the stylistic comparison of French and English.[4] Their book opens with the story of its own genesis: driving along a motorway from New York to Montreal, the linguists were struck by the oddity, to French speakers, of American road signs: KEEP TO THE RIGHT. NO PASSING. SLOW MEN AT WORK. STOP WHEN SCHOOL BUS STOPS. THICKLY SETTLED. – and others. These sorts of injunctions they considered to be 'almost paternal' and only '*doucement autoritaire*'. Considering the nature of French-language road signs, they were moved to observe:

'Pour des Français, tout cela n'a guère de résonance officielle. C'est plutôt comme si nous venions d'avoir, avec l'administration des ponts et chaussées de l'Etat de New-York, une courtoise conversation muette…'[5]

[For someone French, this didn't really sound very official. It seemed more as if we had been having a polite (though silent) conversation with the New York State Roads Department.]

In other words, Vinay and Darbelnet's starting point is that there is a difference in *register* between English road signs and French ones. Note their word '*résonance*', which I have translated, typically transposing a French nominal structure into an English verbal one, by the verb 'sound' (as in 'to sound like') and their notion of a '*conversation*'. This is the very language of register analysis, as we have seen. The *tone* of the English signs, according to these two Francophones, is simply different from that of their French equivalents: French signs are in a sort of French-bureaucratic-officialese which, backed with the authority of a very self-conscious and rationalist state, sounds formal and written in contrast to the English. Actually – for this Englishman, at least – the American signs, although not as directive as their French equivalents, sound pretty bald and direct too, almost rude; they can get away with this only because they *are* written. I can think of many softer ways of proclaiming these injunctions, including the use of a few 'pleases' and 'thank-yous', which would greatly improve the matter from a '*courtoisie*' perspective. Certainly these instructions, if *spoken*, could easily cause offence.

So it is a matter of *comparative* stylistics. Only by looking at what they do in other languages can we see what the stylistic emphases of our own may be. Not surprisingly, the authors of the book, who have not come across the term 'register', have to develop an equivalent term of their own. They choose '*niveaux de langue*', levels of language. Their overall purpose is to provide some sort of guidance to the hard-pressed translator, and they have come across this problem of the road signs. Translating, they see, is evidently not just a matter of fitting one word over another, nor even of fitting one phrase or clause over another, there are broader considerations.

Vinay and Darbelnet, who are Saussureans, distinguish their

'levels of language' from one another in a structuralist pattern of binary oppositions. There are, in particular, the pairs:

bon usage versus *langue vulgaire* (say: 'correct' English versus 'everyday' English – already, in these very imperfect translations, we can feel the pressure of the different sociocultural circumstances of the two languages; English doesn't quite have '*bon usage*' – 'good usage' against which some other 'common-or-garden English' can be set).

préoccupations esthétiques versus *préoccupations fonctionelles* (say: registers defined according to their quality or class – 'high'/'low', and so on – against registers associated with occupations, such as medicalese).

Their schematic presentation of these differences looks like this[6]:

Les nivaux de langue

		tonalité esthétique	spécialisations fonctionnelles.			
Bon usage	Langue commune	langue poétique				
		langue littéraire				
		langue écrite	adminis-trative	juridique	scienti-fique	etc.
		langue familière				
Langue vulgaire		langue populaire	les jargons			
		argot				

Rather against the run of what I am trying to establish here, I have to admit that the terms used as labels for these 'levels' are themselves in very little need of translation for the Anglophone reader. But that, I suppose, is because they are terms in a 'scientific' specialist area (linguistics) which uses Greek-based or Latin-based words in both languages (*esthétique* = aesthetic; *littéraire* = literary, and so on). The only potentially difficult word is '*argot*' which, mercifully, we have borrowed into English without changing either the spelling or the meaning (we haven't really changed its pronunciation, either, saying 'ah-goh' rather than 'ah-gott', although we don't pronounce the 'r' in the French manner).[7] In fact, even terms such as '*littéraire*' are false to their English friends; the French word includes some definitely non-'literary' texts in a way that needs no apology, whereas in English 'literature' has to be explained, delimited or widened. But, if we are to say anything at all, we can accept the obvious English translations of the words in this figure as being accurate enough for our purposes.

'Levels of language', as presented by Vinay and Darbelnet, make a very good start on the topic of register. The notion is introduced by the two French-Canadian authors because '*le traducteur doit garder la* tonalité *du texte qu'il traduit*' (the translator should preserve the *tone* of the text he or she is translating). The meaning of the text resides not merely in its lexico-grammar but in its discursive structure, which includes such delicate and nuanced notions as intertextuality, voicing, tone. A translation is often a pretty good piece of literary analysis in that the translator has had to 'read' or to 'hear' the voices of the text accurately, and this will mean being sensitive to the 'levels' of the languages in question. Of course, the translator then has to be able to transfer the '*tonalité*' to the target language, and one can seriously wonder whether that is ever fully possible.

'Tone' is not merely a direct function of 'level' in the Vinay and Darbelnet scheme, but the two terms are very close, and it is difficult not to think that 'register' would do in place of both of them:

> Le niveau peut être apprécié indépendamment du message, bien qu'il s'exprime en fait par des signes concrets: mots spéciaux, syntaxe particulière, ordre des mots, etc. Il pourra, lors des opérations de découpage, être porté en marge du texte, un peu comme on inscrit la tessiture d'un morceau de musique à la clef.[8]

> [Levels can be perceived separately from the message even though, *de facto*, they appear in such concrete signs as specialised words, syntax created for the occasion, word order, and so on. When the text is being divided up for purposes of analysis, levels could be noted in the margin rather as the nature of a piece of music is written after the key-signature.]

Here we see Vinay and Darbelnet defining the features of a concept that they do not possess; like musical *registration*, the 'level' or tone can be added to the margins of the 'score' that is the text in the hope, presumably, that the translator will remain faithful to the original in this respect. The missing term, of course, is simply 'register'. It is the register that can be defined independently of the message and it indeed becomes apparent in the special vocabulary, unusual syntax and other features of the text. Even the musical analogy is the same.

Vinay and Darbelnet make good use of structuralist oppositions in their analysis, following Bally[9] (the very scholar, surely, satirised by name by Beckett in *Molloy* and eleswhere). But they go too far when they oppose language with *'tonalité'* to a language, the *langue commune*, whose words are *'dépourvus de tonalité'*. Clearly they intend to assert that there is a normal French which is 'without style'. I do not see much need to enter very far into this debate, but for our purposes no such colourless, toneless language need be supposed to exist, however important such a distinction may be in general linguistics. For literature, at least, *all* language comes registered, and is available for reregistration. The reader of the literary text is aware that some words are more ordinary than others *in certain contexts*, but the same reader is simultaneously aware that those words therefore carry a particular tone and colouring. There is no 'literature degree zero', no transparent language. What this means is that every word can be weighed and reassessed according to the context it finds itself in ('water' means different things depending on whether we find it in the Old Testament, the New Testament, the *Rime of the Ancient Mariner* or Graham Swift), and that the most ordinary piece of vocabulary can take on quite spectacular meanings if it is unusually collocated with the 'wrong' lexical set. An elementary example is the word 'Bibles' in *The Rape of the Lock* as quoted in Chapter 6 above, and there are the well-known thrusts of Dorothy Parker:

> Four be the things I'd been better without:
> Love, curiosity, freckles and doubt.

And, at the end of her poem on being sent perfect roses:

> Why is it no one ever sent me yet
>   One perfect limousine, do you suppose?
> Ah no, it's always just my luck to get
>   One perfect rose.

Freckles and limousines belong to the wrong... You've got it.[10]
Of course, in the second extract here, 'do you suppose?' and 'just
my luck' are already bending the register a little.

Thus when our French analysts imply that in the opposition
'*décès/mort*' the word '*mort*' is without tone, being the '*mot usuel*',
I would reply that '*mort*' could be a strongly marked or toned term
if it is employed in any unusual context and, anyway, comes to us
in French with a large baggage of intertexts and overtones that are
different from those of 'death' in English. Which shows that it
cannot simply be ignored as the 'normal' word.

The most difficult problem for a translator, according to Vinay
and Darbelnet, is that of '*la situation*'. By this term they mean the
metalinguistic situation, the facts of the cultural moment in which
the text appears or is received or consumed. Metalinguistic knowledge, beyond the formal details of language, together with the
'context of culture' and the situation, all play a large part in understanding a text and, therefore, in translating it. For Vinay and
Darbelnet, this knowledge is '*la connaissance de l'homme, de sa philosophie
et de son milieu ... la traduction est donc vraiment un humanisme*' ['knowledge of mankind, of his philosophy and his environment ... translation is thus a true humanism']. One could not go this far in the
post-structuralist world that has replaced the existentialist–
structuralist world that our French linguists inhabited in 1958; at
the very least one would have to add the female gender (*l'homme?
Il faudra chercher la femme...*) and the notion of *culture* (metalinguistic
knowledge is knowledge of the cultures of humanity, that is, precisely, of their languages). But the idea is instructive: all reading
(and translation is simply reading to the power of two) must operate
not merely with 'background knowledge' as a sort of optional extra
but with maximum knowledge of the full range of the significances
of culture as they form and in-form language. 'Full' knowledge
cannot ever be, but must be the aspiration. No translation is perfect;
no reading of any text is perfect. Hence the 'infinity' of the text.

Circumnavigating another culture:
David Mourão-Ferreira

Here is the first stanza of a poem by the Portuguese poet David
Mourão-Ferreira, published in 1950. The poem has the same name

as the collection, his first, in which it appeared: '*A Secreta Viagem*'
– the secret voyage.

> No barco sem ninguem, anonimo e vazio,
> ficamos nos os dois, parados, de mão dada…
> Como podem so dois governar um navio?
> Melhor é desistir e não fazermos nada![11]

Literally translated, word-for-word, this becomes:

> In the boat without anyone, anonymous and empty,
> stay we the two, stopped, of hand given…
> How can only two govern a ship?
> Better is to desist and not we do nothing!

Or, in a more usual style of English, something like:

> Alone in the boat, anonymous and empty,
> the two of us stand, unmoving, hand in hand…
> How can just two people sail a ship?
> It's better to give up and just do nothing.

Because Portugal and England, homes of the two languages in
question, are – or were – maritime nations, there seems to be an
easy correspondence to help the translator with the title of the
poem and with some of this stanza; a *voyage* is a recognisable entity
in either language, and '*barco*', for instance, is 'boat' in distinction
from '*navio*', which is 'ship'. We make the same distinctions in the
two languages and, although there are subtle differences here, we
probably think that these translations will serve. There is the same
promotion of size whereby two-people-sailing-a-boat, which seems
possible enough, becomes the impossible two-people-controlling-
a-ship. But already there are problems.

'*Viagem*' means 'journey' as well as 'voyage'; in other words, it
can be used of land or air travel as well as of sea travel. '*Navio*',
on the other hand – cognate, of course, with the verb '*navegar*', to
sail or go on a voyage – carries with it in Portuguese a hint of
Vasco da Gama, of Magellan: of, precisely, '*Os Navegadores*', the
(Renaissance) Navigators to whom there is a monument of that
name overlooking the Tagus at Lisbon. At the time Portugal had
a king known to history as Henry the Navigator. Now this is

something that we can sympathise with, given English history of the period (Drake, Raleigh, & Co.), but it is not quite as firmly present in the culture of the English language as it is in Portuguese. Here is Mourão-Ferreira writing of himself as Portuguese in another poem:

> Eu venho de Portugal:
> mesmo é dizer que venho
> de longe, do litoral, e um sabor, no corpo, a sal
> definiu meu fado estranho...
>
> Trago nos labios o mar,
> cheio de vento e de espuma...

[I come from Portugal, which is as much as to say that I come from afar, from the coast, and a taste of salt in the body defined my strange fate... I carry the sea on my lips, full of wind and spray...]

I do not think that many English poets could have defined themselves this way; in the different cultures in question there are different registers available concerning national self-definition and the sea. For a Portuguese to set out on a *viagem* is stronger, more adventurous, more *journeysome*, than for an Englishman to set out on a voyage; it is more a matter of defining himself according to one of the central cultural myths of his 'people'. There is something 'deeper' about the sea and its ships for this Atlantic lover than there would be for an English poet working in the tradition of Matthew Arnold, for instance.[12]

Mourão-Ferreira's 'secret voyage' is, then, a secret journey, as in 'life's journey' in English, but also a heroic and romantic undertaking, something almost imposed on him by his nationality. He becomes, along with his beloved, a king, or at least a captain (in a later stanza the lovers are the '*aparentes senhores*', the apparent bosses of the ship) adventuring on uncharted seas, born with the taste of salt on his lips, gazing forward like the figurehead of a ship, fixed forever in a position of hope, endurance, determination. The poem '*A Secreta Viagem*' goes on, indeed, to describe the lovers as wooden sculptures passing the sea through their hands, fixed in eternity.

In the registers of Portuguese, among the lexical sets around maritime activity in that language, there are meanings not quite available in English. What, then, is the translator, restricted by definition to the registers and lexical sets of English, to do? Let us return to the first stanza, quoted and translated above, and consider just two words of it: '*governar*' and '*fazermos*'.

I have translated the first of these words, '*governar*', as 'govern' in the word-for-word version and as 'sail' in the slightly more English version. Neither is right. The Portuguese word means both 'govern' and 'steer', as in the Latin '*gubernare*', to steer, from a Greek root to the same effect. This makes considerable sense in the context of a poem where the lovers are and are not the masters of their fate – on the one hand the '*aparentes senhores*' of the boat; on the other inadequate as a crew, and thus better doing nothing and just drifting; the play between the masterful 'governing' and the much less certain 'steering' echoes this situation.

Similarly, '*fazermos*' is a verb in a tense unknown, almost unimaginable, in English, the future subjunctive. One tends to giggle or add exclamation marks the first time one encounters this rare object when learning Portuguese. The future subjunctive?! Well! It is actually a doubly uncertain tense, and thus of great use for the uncertainties of poetry. The phrase '*Se Deus quiser*', for instance, equates to 'If God wills' but is literally 'If God might in the future will' or, rather horribly, 'If God might will will'. The subjunctive doubt ('might') is compounded by the mention of that most uncertain of times, the future. What can be done to convey this sort of meaning into English? '*Não fazermos nada*' literally means 'not we might in the future do nothing'. Leaving aside the special untranslatability of the double negative, how can we convey the delicacy of this suggestion that we cannot control ourselves as time goes, and will go, by? The very employment of the future subjunctive is a register feature of Portuguese, not merely a grammatical problem to be solved. Only by the most extensive circumlocution could we capture something of its evanescent spirit in another language.

Workpoints

> There has been a growing awareness that translation is not just a matter of item-to-item equivalence, or indeed of group of items to group of items, or structure to structure; rather it is a matter of text-to-text equivalence which involves variety and register considerations.
>
> Michael Gregory and Susanne Carrol,
> *Language Varieties and their Social Contexts*
> (Routledge & Kegan Paul, 1978)

> The system of register will not correspond one-to-one between languages. In the translation of literature, especially poetry, there is likely to be a *range* of potential register equivalents.
>
> Ure, Rodger and Ellis, 'Somn: sleep.
> An exercise in the use of descriptive
> linguistic techniques in literary translation'
> (paper originally delivered in 1964)

Notes

1 For further discussion of Beckett as self-translator see Lance St John Butler, 'Two darks: a solution to the problem of Beckett's bilingualism', in *Samuel Beckett Today/Aujourd'hui*, 3, Rodopi, 1994.
2 Brian Fitch, 'The relationship between *Compagnie* and *Company*: one work, two texts, two fictive universes', in Alan Friedman et al. (eds), *Beckett Translating/Translating Beckett* (Pennsylvania University Press, 1987). See also Fitch's *Beckett and Babel: An Investigation into the Status of the Bilingual Work* (University of Toronto Press, 1988).
3 Fitch, 'The relationship between *Compagnie* and *Company*', p. 29.
4 J. P. Vinay and J. Darbelnet, *Stylistique comparée du français et de l'anglais* (Didier, 1958; new edition 1969).
5 *Ibid.*, p. 18.
6 *Ibid.*, p. 34.
7 If we had gone the other way, pronouncing the 'r' in the French manner and the 'got' in the English, we would almost have ended up with the German exclamation 'Ach Gott!'
8 Vinay and Darbelnet, *Stylistique comparée*, p. 33.

9 Charles Bally, *Précis de stylistique* (Geneva, 1905).

10 I apologise for the gameshowese.

11 David Mourão-Ferreira, *A Arte de Amar* (Verbo, 2nd edn 1973), p. 50.

12 Where English has become the language of other cultures (Australia, India, the USA, etc.) it can operate in quite different ways, naturally. Just as Brazilian Portuguese has inherited some but not all of the cultural meanings of '*Portugues do Portugal*', so North American Englishes are both the same as and different from English English. It is not difficult to find Canadian writers for whom the sea and fishing in it have something of the mythological characteristics of the Portuguese affair with the ocean.

Part III

Case studies

8

'Pestling the unalterable whey of words': Samuel Beckett's attempt at unstyle

Indigestion: *A Dream of Fair to Middling Women*

Reading early Beckett is liable to give one a sort of register indigestion. For instance, the poem *Whoroscope* (1929), the essay on Proust (1931), the novel *A Dream of Fair to Middling Women*, written in 1932, and the short stories, partly quarried from *Dream*, published as *More Pricks than Kicks* in 1934, all break new ground in the field of register collocation. This is the sort of thing one can be faced with; it is from *Dream*, unpublishable in its day:

> The Empress Wu of China took the chair at Cabinet council wearing a false beard. The lily was nearly as fair as the rose as lovely as God Almighty the Empress Wu.
> 'Bloom!' she cried to the peonies 'bloom, blast you!'
> No. Not a stir out of them. So they were all extirpated, they were rooted up throughout her dominions, burned and their culture prohibited.
> Now, having got so far, our opinion is that we might do worse than slip, in the elegant phrase, our sad spaniels and let them quest. We durst not, our taste, the literary cui bono, precludes it, make a sudden leap, princum-prancum!, from the pleasant land of Hesse, the German garden, to marshy Dublin, its paludal heavens, its big winds and rains and sorrows and puddles of sky-flowers; from the merely snout-fair Smeraldina, that petulant, exuberant, clitoridian puella, who has not the first glimmering of an idea of how to set her cold bath on fire, whom now it is high time to turn round and dislike intensely, like collops of pork gone greasy, to Alba, Alba, royal diminutive, Du, dust of a dove's heart, the eyes the eyes black till the plagal east shall resolve the long night-phrase. Can't hop about like that, really can't, must make

> lull somehow or other, let a little breath of the fresh into the thing
> somehow, little breather all round. Nik?[1]

The first words of this (highly characteristic) extract disorientate
us not only because of the bizarre image they conjure up (an
empress in a beard) but because of their instability at the level of
register. Empresses don't 'take the chair' – chairmen of companies
or those presiding over meetings do that; empresses are 'seated on
thrones' or 'throned in state'. The second sentence appears to be
an unacknowledged quotation taken from the conventional praise
the empress receives; it involves a formulaic comparison, supposedly common on the lips of courtiers, between the empress
and lilies or roses (hyperboles of floral beauty). But either the
courtier or the narrator, overwhelmed by rebellious anger, boredom or lust, drops in a random 'God Almighty', a sort of blas-
phemous aside taken from a quite different register.

Similarly, in the next sentence we shift from possible empress-
speak (the imperative 'Bloom!') to an upper-class English register
of, say, bluff army officer getting annoyed over some misdemeanour
among his troops: 'Blast you!' The 'No. Not a stir out of them'
is free indirect speech (possibly free direct speech) representing
the thoughts either of the empress or of the narrator, but then the
archaic register of the official historian is brought in: 'throughout
her dominions'.

The 'Now' could belong to several possible registers but is
located as the voice of the self-conscious narrator by the first-
person-plural 'our' (though that is marked as archaic too, of course,
since nowadays the academic or narratorial 'we' has become 'I'),
while there is an 'elegant phrase', as we are told, available in
'slip[ping] our sad spaniels'. Then 'we', instead of 'not daring' or
'not having the courage to', indulge in 'durst not', which seems to
come from a definite range of registers including the Authorised
Version and Bunyan but not, for instance, the late nineteenth
century when homosexuality, we remember, was the love that *dares
not* speak its name.

The indigestion gets worse as one goes on, so dense is Beckett's
style in these early texts. Whence gets he 'princum-prancum', for
instance? Obviously cognate with some such verb as 'to prance'
and thus connected with horses, it has no discernible place in any

dictionary I have consulted. We *can* say about it, however, that it belongs to a register (that of Elizabethan slang?) different from anything else in the passage quoted, and we have thus accounted for its oddity and out-of-placeness in some degree. One possibility is that it is a coinage, and here we are faced with an interesting fact about register: even invented words can signify by imitating a particular tone – that is, by evoking a particular register.

The register shifts become most striking at the end of the main paragraph; the self-conscious narrator admonishes himself to stop 'hopping about', a slang term reinforced by the contraction ('can't' for 'cannot'), by the typically colloquial repetition ('really can't') and by the lack of expressed subjects ('*I* can't'; '*I* must'). This colloquialism, situated several stylistic light years away from 'paludal' or 'puella', reaches a climax in the Cockney contractions of 'a little breather of the fresh [air]' and 'little breather all round'. That 'little', which means something rather different from 'small', is the voice of an absolutely identifiable London (or possibly Dublin) working-class persona, adopted by Beckett's narrator for the nonce.[2] (The 'Nik?', incidentally, I take to be a form of the German interrogative tag 'Nicht?' as in 'Nicht Wahr?' – 'Isn't it?' – 'Don't you agree?')

The result of this sort of indigestion is not entirely unpleasant – although *Dream of Fair to Middling Women* has usually been seen as virtually unreadable – but the reaction is similar to that provoked by the early performances of *Waiting for Godot*. In that play, it was often felt, Beckett had succeeded only too well in staging boredom and purposelessness; the first audiences, made to experience this boredom and futility, often felt that the best bet was to leave at half-time. Similarly, in *Dream*, Beckett presents an utterly unstable and unanchored consciousness struggling in an incomprehensible world, and he does so by making the reading an unstable, virtually impossible experience (as Paul de Man said, the impossibility of reading should not be taken too lightly). To involve the reader in the instability he deploys various devices, and one of these is register. If reading early Beckett feels like the opposite of reading Jane Austen, it is partly at least because he never allows us to settle into a register at any point and thus, in a profound sense, prevents us from knowing where we are. Jane Austen is, as it were, always the same; Beckett is always different.

Escaping into French

After the Second World War Beckett turned to writing in French, an unusual choice for someone with neither French blood nor French schooling. Asked why he had done so, he replied: '*Parcequ'en français c'est plus facile d'écrire sans style*' – because in French it is easier to write without style. Such a motive is consistent with Beckett's general 'art of impoverishment' and with the aesthetic summed up in his breathtaking minimalist manifesto: 'Less is more.' But – as the lengthy quotation from *Dream* above demonstrates – in his earlier, Joycean phase, it almost seemed as if he was writing to achieve the *maximum* style, so something clearly happened between his last 'overloaded' work (*Watt*, written during the war and completed in 1945) and the beginning of the trilogy (*Molloy*, probably begun about 1948; *Waiting for Godot*, incidentally, was already being worked on in 1947). There are good accounts of this 'turn' in Beckett's stylistic programme,[3] but for our purposes it makes him a fascinating example of someone battling to change the register in which he could work, to limit and reduce his register potential; indeed, an example of a writer trying to write *without* register.

What basis might there be for Beckett's feeling that he could somehow manage to write 'less' in French? Is it possible that French, for all its beauties and range of expression, has fewer registers than English? In Vinay and Darbelnet's now classic *Stylistique comparée du français et de l'anglais* (1958) the impression given is that in some areas English has more resources, more nuances, a greater range of possibilities (English distinguishes between the intellectual and affective senses of a term, for instance – as in French *maigre* which has to serve both for 'thin' and for 'meagre' in English); but that, *en revanche*, there are plenty of areas where French has a greater range of expression, such as the many possible translations into French, depending on context, of the simple word 'brown', which can be *marron*, *roux*, *bistre*, *brun* or even *jaune* or *gris*. Yet Beckett seems, intuitively, to have a point in his attempt to destyle his writing by his change of language.

English, after all, has a larger vocabulary and a more complex etymological structure. Such estimates are hard to substantiate, but it is generally assumed that English vocabulary extends to at least half a million items, while the vocabulary of French, calculated on a comparable basis, is usually taken not to exceed 300,000 words. The greater etymological variety of English is an accident of history: the Old English basis of the language was supplemented in the years after 1066 by Norman French, and during the Renaissance large numbers of words were added that had been taken directly from Latin and, to a lesser extent, Greek. Imperial expansion between the Renaissance and the nineteenth century brought a range of new words from all sorts of other languages, too, with the result that modern English is a wildly heterogeneous lexical morass. Contrastingly French, derived from Latin in the early Middle Ages (the first French literary text is generally thought to be the *Cantilène de Sainte Eulalie*, composed at the end of the ninth century) and also provided with new Latin vocabulary in the Renaissance, has a more coherent and consistent etymological nature.[4]

Besides these possibilities it is conceivable that English, being more widely-spoken than French, has a larger range of regional and even dialectal expression which, for literary purposes, is the equivalent of an extended register structure. Thus if small details recognisable as 'Wessex' or Australian or Californian generate particular literary meanings, and if there are more such places in the Anglophone world than in the Francophone, it would follow as likely that the Anglophone world has more register possibilities.

It is also the case that Beckett, who became bilingual but was not truly a 'native speaker' of French, may have felt less confident of handling all the registers of his adopted language than he was of handling the infinite subtleties and complexities of his 'own' (highly educated) Irish English. He was a disciple of the great wordsmith Joyce, after all, and if one compares Joyce's language with Proust's (the obvious comparison in terms of date, genre and literary aspiration) it is at once apparent that French prefers a certain chastity of expression in contrast to the overblown linguistic monster that is, for instance, *Ulysses,* let alone *Finnegans Wake.* Early texts, such as *Dream,* show Beckett experimenting with Joycean excess:

> The tense passional intelligence, when arithmetic abates, tunnels, sky-mole, surely and blindly (if we only thought so!) through the interstellar coalsacks of its firmament in genesis...

Which of the two, Joyce or Beckett, wrote that? There seems to be such a thing as Joycean register and sometimes Beckett employed it.[5]

But most Beckett critics assume that he was referring, when he spoke of the relative 'stylelessness' of French, to the fact that English has a stronger tendency to retain the *associations* of words – in fact *to see them as registered.* Thus many English speakers are amused to discover that the perfectly ordinary French term for 'riding' (as in riding horses) is '*l'équitation*'; the amusement stems from the fact that to Anglophone ears this word sounds rather too grand, too precise, too *learned* for the activity of just going for a hack or a canter or a trot (or any of the other expressions used to convey the idea of sitting on a horse and moving along). The point is that English has the translation 'riding', but has 'equitation', too, and although this latter term means, indeed, riding or horsemanship, it carries an extra baggage of meaning that comes from its belonging to a different register, in this case a learned or even pedantic one. 'Indulging in equitation' is a joke version of 'going for a ride', and is credible as a serious alternative only in certain contexts such as the letters of the headmistress of an Academy for Young Ladies writing about her school in, say, the 1780s or 1840s. I suggest that *l'équitation* does not carry the same baggage as its English equivalent perhaps because, there being fewer terms available in French, an expression like this has to do general duty, and cannot be reserved for a particular *registration.*

Even if this view of the relative register richness of French and English is inaccurate, however (and these comparisons are difficult to establish with any certainty), it remains the case that Beckett certainly thought, for whatever reason, that he would escape from some of the metaphorical and associative overload of English by switching languages. The switch is at least fairly good evidence that he was, as he claimed, trying to minimise (minimalise?) his style according to his apophthegm 'Less is more.' *Dream, More Pricks* and the other early texts are wildly register-unstable. In looking for *less*, for an art of impotence and 'indigence', the very last thing he wanted to do was to give any impression of mastery, of knowing, of having an answer. So his early strategy was to write well beyond the limits of most readers' register tolerance, and his later was to go in exactly the opposite direction. He chose to pursue this negative path, the path of unenlightenment, both at the level of direct statement (his narrator can refer to his own narrative as 'All balls invented to prove I forget what...') and at

the level of register. In the early texts one is never allowed to
penetrate the narrator's mind-set as one is, for instance, with classic
pre-modernist texts, and this unsettled quality is partly attributable
to register variation of an unpredictable kind. This is from *More
Pricks than Kicks*:

> Now it began to rain again upon the earth beneath and greatly incom-
> moded Christmas traffic of every kind by continuing to do so without
> remission for a matter of thirty-six hours. A divine creature, native of
> Leipzig, to whom Belacqua, round about the following Epiphany, had
> occasion to quote the rainfall for December as cooked in the Dublin
> University Fellows' Garden ejaculated:
> 'himmisacrakruzidirkenjesusmariaundjosefundblutigeskreuz!'
> ⸺ Like that, all in one word. The things people come out with some-
> times![6]

Apart from the Bakhtinian polyvocality here (German in an English
text), the newscaster's tone of the second half of the opening
sentence, and the almost random moment of Old Testament register
('upon the earth beneath'), the instability of the narrative is apparent in the contrast between the formal, almost official tones of
'incommoded' and 'without remission', the arch and archaic eight-
eenth- and nineteenth-century precious poeticism 'a divine creature',
and the banal colloquialism of the last two sentences. One might
also consider the register status of 'native of' and 'cooked'.

Before monologue: *Murphy*

As we have seen, Beckett did not 'solve' his stylistic problem until
after the war when, alongside the switch to 'styleless' French, it
suddenly came to him that *monologue* was the technique he needed;[7]
the result was, among other things, those immense monologues
that constitute the trilogy *Molloy*, *Malone Dies* and *The Unnamable*.
Meanwhile, he continued to struggle with the infinite temptations
of overregistered English. Here is the opening of *Murphy* (1938),
showing Beckett more controlled than in earlier fiction but still
unwilling or unable to settle to a 'voice'. It is interesting, none the
less, that this is unmistakably *Beckett* that we are reading and, in
general, that there is, in spite of his efforts, a recognisable 'Beckettian register':

The sun shone, having no alternative, on the nothing new. Murphy sat out of it, as though he were free, in a mew in West Brompton. Here for what might have been six months he had eaten, drunk, slept, and put his clothes on and off, in a medium-sized cage of north-western aspect commanding an unbroken view of medium-sized cages of south-eastern aspect. Soon he would have to make other arrangements, for the mew had been condemned. Soon he would have to buckle to and start eating, drinking, sleeping, and putting his clothes on and off, in quite alien surroundings.

He sat naked in his rocking-chair of undressed teak, guaranteed not to crack, warp, shrink, corrode or creak at night. It was his own, it never left him. The corner in which he sat was curtained off from the sun, the poor old sun in the Virgin again for the billionth time. Seven scarves held him in position. Two fastened his shins to the rockers, one his thighs to the seat, two his breast and belly to the back, one his wrists to the strut behind. Only the most local movements were possible. Sweat poured off him, tightened the thongs. The breath was not perceptible. The eye, cold and unwavering as a gull's, stared up at an iridescence splashed over the cornice moulding, shrinking and fading. Somewhere a cuckoo-clock, having struck between twenty and thirty, became the echo of a street-cry, which now entering the mew gave *Quid pro quo! Quid pro quo!* directly.

Here is a brief attempt at a register-analysis of some aspects of these two paragraphs:

The sun shone   Simple past tense, with focus on the weather as in the opening of a thousand banal novels.

The nothing new   There is 'nothing new under the sun' according to Ecclesiastes, so this is an overt intertext, but the added definite article ('the') is 'wrong' because it 'should' refer to some preceding or following element in the text; as it doesn't it tends to become general and refer to the world or even to the whole universe, or 'Life'.

Medium-sized [property] of north-western aspect commanding an unbroken view of medium-sized [properties] of south-western aspect...   Estate agent's particulars with a rather grandiose flavour ('commanding') interrupted fatally by the out-of-register word 'cage'.

To make other arrangements   Landlord giving euphemistic notice.

The mew had been condemned   Local-government-speak; journalistic version of same. False singular of 'mew' emphasises the 'caged' theme – 'mewed up' comes to mind – possible register of imprisonment here, as also in 'no alternative', and 'as though he were free'.

Have to buckle to and start eating... and putting his clothes on and off Nanny- or mother-speak; easy to translate into direct speech ('Soon you'll have to'...) Possible Irishism in 'putting *off*' your clothes; flavour of Irish nanny speech?

Alien surroundings This has several possible readings, but it is certainly in a register that is different from that of 'buckle to' – there is a formality about the phrase that might be found in a social work report.

Naked... undressed teak Here register permits a joke. 'Undressed' when collocated with a wood becomes timber merchants'-speak or the language of furniture or antique dealers.

Guaranteed not to... Language of the manufacturer's guarantee, of course, but undermined by the fact that 'corrode' shouldn't collocate with anything wooden and the fact that night-time creaking would have to be voluntary on the part of the chair – an unlikely circumstance.

It was his own Is double-registered: as in 'a poor thing but mine own' from *As You Like It*; it is personal ('it never left him'), but it is also inventory-speak, and is to be seen as a contrast to the landlady's furniture as provided.

The billionth time Is also doubled: on the one hand it evokes the enormous numbers by which we are astounded in astronomy; on the other hand it echoes the casual speech of pub and playground, where 'billions' can mean 'three'.

Seven scarves held him in position As in 'Four flying buttresses supported the tower', Murphy is made an object rather than a person. There seems to be something *imminent* here, as if he is about to be blasted off somewhere, or tortured.

Only the most local movements... Either a mountaineer who has fallen and is stuck in a gully or a medical account of a patient's condition, for example: 'In osteoarthritis of the hip the range of motion is impaired.' The special usage of 'local' inclines me to the second of these possibilities.

> *The breath was not perceptible* Same medical register. Doctor reporting.

One could go on, but it is perhaps enough just to point out that in the remaining sentences of these two paragraphs there are further elements that would repay register analysis: 'cold and un-wavering' is reminiscent of a cliché from a certain type of romantic fiction; 'the cornice moulding' is a shade too technically archi-tectural; *Quid pro quo!* is a polyvocal element of dubious prov-enance, but its register significance is *at least* to signal ambiguity, as it belongs at once to a learned Latin register (we feel tempted, in the context, to translate it) and to a middlebrow tone in which we think of it as quintessentially mercantile: 'It's a deal!' There is something horribly cold and indifferent about it, as in 'You don't get anything for nothing in this world.'

It is noticeable that the register instability in *Murphy* has subtle or 'delicate' aspects as well as these more obvious features. The tense of the first verb of the text is a case in point: 'the sun shone', we read, but surely *narratives* should start in the past con-tinuous? There may be some static introductory material, but the story 'proper' usually needs a continuous form. Thus – to take two Brontë examples – *Villette*, after four paragraphs of explana-tory scene-setting, opens its narrative proceedings with 'In the autumn of the year - I *was staying* at Bretton...'; and *The Tenant of Wildfell Hall*, after a similar preamble, starts its storytelling: 'With such reflections as these I *was endeavouring* to console myself...'. This is the convention that gives us such classic openings as 'It was raining and...'. Yet Beckett chooses instead to employ the simple past ('The sun shone'), which gets us off immediately on the wrong foot. As Beckett would say, the right wrong foot.

Monologue achieved?

Beckett, of course, failed. He failed to 'write without style' – that is, to eliminate register – because the aspiration so to do is tan-tamount to declaring one's intention to 'write without language' or write without ink. As the trilogy goes on, and in subsequent texts, the failure is less marked, the style flatter and less dense with allusion, but the registers are still there to be found, for all the new chastity of the Beckettian text. He fails, but this failure is a big success, for if he had a motto it would surely have been his own injunction: 'Fail again. Fail better.'

The first volume of the trilogy, *Molloy*, is divided into two sections, one narrated by Molloy and the other by a private detective hired to seek him out, one Moran. Many critics have considered that there is an incoherence in the arrangement of these two parts in that the Moran section, which comes second, is more 'normal', more anchored in the conventions of realism, than Molloy's narrative, which precedes it; thus Moran should come first, because that would put him at the furthest distance from the *telos* of the trilogy (presumed to be the end of the third volume, *The Unnamable*.) The order of narration should, according to this argument, run: Moran–Molloy–Malone–the Unnamable, instead of the order actually chosen by Beckett: Molloy–Moran–Malone–the Unnamable.

But from a register perspective, things are not so clear. The *register* of the Molloy section of *Molloy* is further away from the register of *The Unnamable* than the register of the Moran section is. Here is Moran, sounding very like the Unnamable:

> *Moran [on the Sabbath]* I've always loved doing nothing. And I would gladly have rested on weekdays too, if I could have afforded it. Not that I was positively lazy. It was something else. Seeing something done which I could have done better myself, if I had wished, and which I did do better whenever I put my mind to it, I had the impression of discharging a function to which no form of activity could have exalted me.[8]

> *The Unnamable* And I await my turn. Yes indeed, I do not despair, all things considered, of drawing their attention to my case, some fine day. Not that it offers the least interest, hey, something wrong there, not that it is particularly interesting. I'll accept that, but it's my turn, I too have the right to be shown impossible.[9]

The short sentences, the staccato clauses and phrases, the insistent self-absorption, and the rather Johnsonian complexity of clause structure alongside a straightforward lexis, make these two passages similar in tone. Molloy 'himself', on the other hand, can sound very different:

> *Molloy [after his arrest at the start of the novel]* I took advantage of the silence which followed these kind words to turn towards the window, blindly or nearly, for I had closed my eyes, proffering to that blandness of blue and gold my face and neck alone, and my mind empty too, or

> nearly, for I must have been wondering if I did not feel like sitting down, after such a long time standing, and remembering what I had learnt in that connection, namely that the sitting posture was not for me any more, because of my short stiff leg, and that there were only two postures for me any more, the vertical, drooping between my crutches, sleeping on my feet, and the horizontal, down on the ground. And yet the desire to sit came upon me from time to time, back upon me from a vanished world.[10]

The styles here are recognisably Beckettian, but the third extract has a fluency, an inclination to metaphor and an optimism denied to the other two. Molloy 'himself' is thus 'further out' into the world, less enclosed in a claustrophobic nightmare, than the later 'avatars' who populate and narrate the trilogy, including Moran. This is demonstrable from the registers employed, even if it is not evident from the supposed situation in life of the narrator. The register becomes steadily flatter as the trilogy progresses, something which would not be true were it reordered.

After *Molloy*, with *Malone Dies*, the process is continued: the gaps between the registers become smaller, the text becomes increasingly smoothed into the hypnotic babble of a single voice – *monologue* wins in the very Bakhtinian sense that there is only one voice, one source of discourse available. At least, one can see that monologism may be something like Beckett's aspiration, but the result is, naturally, failure. The style becomes flatter, the register shifts become less noticeable, but a monotone seems simply unavailable in this kind of music (or in any kind). Here is Malone imagining himself as his own *alter ego* and trying to tell us something about this rather monstrous being:

> And as he rolled on he conceived and polished the plan of continuing to roll on all night if necessary, or at least until his strength should fail him, and thus approach the confines of this plain which to tell the truth he was in no hurry to leave, but nevertheless was leaving, he knew it. And without reducing his speed he began to dream of a flat land where he would never have to rise again and hold himself erect in equilibrium, first on the right foot for example, then on the left, and where he might come and go and so survive after the fashion of a great cylinder endowed with the faculties of cognition and volition. And without exactly building castles in Spain, for that [*sic*][11]

As my '*sic*' indicates, there's something odd here; the narrative breaks off exactly as I have printed it; after 'for that' there is a gap during which we are to presume that Malone – who is dying, after all – has some sort of cardiac or similar crisis which he thinks may herald his death. After the equivalent gap in the text he continues:

Quick quick my possessions. Quiet, quiet, twice, I have time, lots of time, as usual. My pencil, my two pencils...

The style changes; this new section is meant to be some sort of 'truth' after the fictionalising and fabulation of the earlier extract. The clauses shorten and there seems to be an effort at simplification:

My exercise book, I don't see it, but I feel it in my left hand, I don't know where it comes from, I didn't have it when I came here, but I feel it is mine.

These clauses are linked by the most elementary cohesive ties ('My exercise book' – 'it' – 'it' – 'it'...) and march along in a breathless paratactic chain, creating the impression of a string of thoughts written exactly as spoken. This is a different text-world from the rather contrived, pedantic and leisurely subordinations of the earlier extract ('which to tell the truth...', 'endowed with the faculties of...') That first extract is heavily *written* in contrast to the 'spoken' (or 'thought') quality of the more desperate sentences after the break. The narrator continues: 'I continue from memory. It is black dark. I can hardly see the window.' These, incidentally, actually *are* sentences, but there is almost no difference, at this level of parataxis, between a string of clauses separated by commas and a string of sentences separated by full stops. Either way the impression given is of the rather desperate thoughts of an individual mind coming to the end of its tether.

Yet Malone, as we can see from the number of pages that we still have to read at this point of the novel, does not die immediately after this crisis. He will continue his maunderings for a good while yet. And we cannot live in a state of permanent crisis; old habits of life reassert themselves as soon as the threat of death has passed. So it is for Malone, who quickly gets back into his manic narrative stride where he is talking and inventing like mad, to fill the time, to stave off the inevitable. Looking through his 'possessions', he finds the bowl of a pipe:

> The bowl of my pipe, though I never used a tobacco-pipe. I must have found it somewhere, on the ground when out walking. There it was, in the grass, thrown away because it could no longer serve, the stem having broken off (I suddenly remember) just short of the bowl. This pipe could have been repaired but he must have said, Bah, I'll buy myself another. But all I found was the bowl. But all that is mere supposition. Perhaps I thought it pretty, or felt for it that foul feeling of pity I have so often felt in the presence of things, especially little portable things in wood and stone, and which made me wish to have them about me and keep them always, so that I stooped and picked them up and put them in my pocket, often with tears, for I wept to a great age, never having really evolved in the fields of affection and passion, in spite of my experiences.[12]

This starts in the relatively simple post-break, more 'serious' mode but then starts to change. The register shift is more of a register evolution (to borrow Beckett's word). At first the text seems to continue in the usual desperate-narrator string of paratactic clauses and phrases:

> The bowl of my pipe
> I never used a tobacco-pipe
> I must have found it somewhere
> On the ground
> When out walking
> There it was
> In the grass
> Thrown away...

(which I have doctored only to the extent of omitting the 'though' before 'I never used' on the grounds that it functions here more or less as a mere conjunction) but it gradually modulates into the more fluent and complex structures of the fiction (the 'supposition') inspired by the narrator's discovery of the pipe-bowl. Thus things become a little more complex with the 'because' clause, the parenthesis ('I suddenly remember that') and the direct speech ('Bah'). Then, with the 'Perhaps' sentence, which is suddenly much longer than any of its predecessors right back to 'And without reducing his speed' in the first extract a whole page earlier, Malone takes stylistic wing. He gets into his other stride and now sounds like a man with plenty of time on his hands, a non-desperate man, a *writer* who can elevate his style with subordination ('which made me wish'), inversion ('keep them always') and a degree of formal, even biblical, language ('for' meaning 'because'; 'wept' for 'cried'; and so on).

The alteration here is perhaps not easy to spot. And Beckett is notoriously capable of shifting about in register even in these mature works. But there is no doubt that some account needs to be given of the sense of discomfort, detachment and 'failure' in the trilogy in terms of style; the tool to hand for this account is register.

Here is Malone going the other way. This time the text-break is between a section of desperate possession-counting and a section of narrative 'supposition'. So we are going from the simple-and-desperate to the more leisurely and complex. As usual, the pencil is well to the fore in the narrator's consciousness.

> The pencil on the contrary is an old acquaintance, I must have had it about me when I was brought here. It has five faces. It is very short. It is pointed at both ends. A Venus. I hope it will see me out. I was saying I did not depart from myself now with quite the same alacrity. That must be in the natural order of things, all that pertains to me must be written there, including my inability to grasp what order is meant. For I have never seen any sign of any, inside me or outside me. I have pinned my faith to appearances, believing them to be vain. I shall not go into the details. Choke, go down, come up, choke, suppose, deny, affirm, drown. I depart from myself less gladly. Amen. I waited for the dawn. Doing what? I don't know. What I had to do. I watched for the window. I gave rein to my pains, my impotence. And in the end it seemed to me, for a second, that I was going to have a visit!

[Beckett has a gap at this point.]

> The summer holidays were drawing to a close. The decisive moment was at hand when the hopes reposed in Sapo were to be fulfilled or dashed to the ground. He is trained to a hair, said Mr Saposcat. And Mrs Saposcat, whose piety grew warm in times of crisis, prayed for his success. Kneeling at her bedside, in her nightdress, she ejaculated, silently, for her husband would not have approved, Oh God grant he pass, grant he pass, grant he scrape through!

When this first ordeal was surmounted there would be others, every year, several times a year. But it seemed to the Saposcats that these would be less terrible than the first which was to give them, or deny them, the right to say, He is doing his medicine, or, he is reading for the bar. For they felt that a more or less normal if unintelligent youth, once admitted to the study of these professions, was almost sure to be certified, sooner or later, apt to exercise them.[13]

These two passages are of almost identical length. The first of them, where Malone 'himself' is talking about himself, before the gap in the text, has twenty-one orthographic sentences (that is to say, twenty-one full stops). The second has eight. Immediately we should suspect ourselves of being in different register worlds, and so it is; in the first part we are listening to the colloquially registered thoughts of a dying man thinking about his situation. In the second we are in narrative mode, with register to match: past continuous as the first verb describing the context (here of time) in which the ensuing action is set ('The summer holidays *were drawing*'); the representation of the speech of others ('said Mr Saposcat', 'she ejaculated'); including free indirect speech ('When this first ordeal was surmounted'); subordination (the final sentence beginning 'For they felt that'; and metaphor ('reposed', 'dashed to the ground', 'grew warm', including some terribly clichéd examples such as 'drawing to a close', 'this... ordeal was surmounted', 'exercise' a profession, and so on).

In the first part parataxis reigns; in the second there is some hypotaxis. In the first part Malone speaks to himself in grammatically incomplete sentences ('Amen', 'What I had to do'), while this is avoided in the second part. In terms of vocabulary the colloquial talking-to-himself of the first part is conducted in what might be called basic English with educated lapses. In the second part it is the reverse: educated, though utterly clichéd, written-storytelling mode ('But it seemed to the Saposcats', 'For they felt that') is interspersed with banalities such as 'in her nightdress', 'several times a year', 'He is doing his medicine'.

Frequently in passages such as these we notice that the discourse tends to get infected with the register of the other part. Thus even 'Malone', in the first part, can rise to the register heights of 'pertains to' and 'impotence' at the level of vocabulary; while in the second part there is a tendency, in spite of all, to revert to paratactic simplicity, as in 'The summer holidays were.... The decisive moment was...' or: 'He is trained to a hair, said Mr Saposcat. And Mrs Saposcat...'.

But in spite of this tendency to a degree of cross-infection, there is no doubt that these two styles of Beckett's are distinct, and can be shown to be so. He has, in other words, more than one register at his command, in spite of his ambition to write 'without style'. An interesting point, of course, is whether this shifting about in register as late as the trilogy is present in the original French versions of the three novels. My impression – and that is all it can be – is that his French, in keeping with the different register structure of that language, is rather more consistent (in register) than his English. If this is so, it may be that Beckett proved his point about the two languages: perhaps it *is* easier to write *sans style* in French.

Maximum monologue?

The Unnamable, in some sense the climax of the trilogy, is also a sort of climax in Beckett's *oeuvre*; it is, anyway, monologue at its most intense and unrelenting, and it breaks the greatest number of stylistic conventions in his work up to the point at which it was written. Here, if anywhere, register will be at a minimum, and thus of least use as an explanatory tool. Here, surely, the monologue wends its weary way without benefit of pause or alteration in – as Beckett himself might have said – a Calvary with no limit to its stations and no hope of crucifixion.

And yet. Has Beckett eliminated style – that is, has he managed to write in a sort of no-register, in a passage such as the following?

> For it is difficult to speak, even any old rubbish, and at the same time focus one's attention on another point, where one's true interest lies, as fitfully defined by a feeble murmur seeming to apologise for not being dead.[14]

Here, if we read the sentence omitting 'even any old rubbish', it appears a good deal more register-consistent (though not register-free); 'even nonsense' would seem a little more decorous and in-place, and 'even random thoughts' would be 'better'. The 'one' who stands in, in this sort of discourse, for the speaker first and for the reader second, seems to be, indeed, some sort of speaker, a lecturer or preacher perhaps, capable of lengthy and beautifully balanced complexities such as the end of the sentence (from 'as fitfully'), with its alliteration and metrical cadences. This speaker seems highly unlikely to slip 'any old rubbish' into his (I feel it *is* 'his') series of phrases and clauses in this unmotivated way. Then again, is the subordinate clause 'where one's true interest lies' not the most tremendous cliché? It is a quotation, from whatever source, of such unoriginality that it immediately manages to defeat itself in a way that leaves the reader feeling that whatever 'other point' one is focused upon, it *isn't* the locus of one's 'true' interests, whatever those may be.

It is hard to keep up one's courage when doing register analysis of Beckett. Around any corner an entirely unexpected animal may suddenly spring out, a beast quite different from the one one thought one was tracking. But one can try out some ideas. For instance, is there perhaps a pattern, a register pattern, whereby Beckett's narrator, even in a text like *The Unnamable*, has at his disposal a 'low' mode (say, approximately, spoken and informal) and a 'high' mode (say, written and formal), so organised that the former dwindles into useless silence while the latter reveals itself as a hollow sham?

Such a pattern will not be a simple one. Beckett can slip into banality and cliché when he is in either 'low' or 'high' mode, to unsettling effect. Each mode, to complicate matters, is conscious of itself and of the other, and each can comment on the other. What is more, each can employ the rhythms or the syntax of the other in a most disconcerting manner.

Here is some 'low' register from the novel: 'Years is one of Basil's ideas. A short time, a long time, it's all the same. I kept silence, that's all that counts, if that counts...'[15] A string of thoughts, short clauses and phrases strung together with quite a lot of the logical connections taken for granted; a man grumbling into his beer in a pub. Now some 'high' mode; the Unnamable, limbless, is stuck in a large pot outside a restaurant by way of advertisement:

> I realised darkly that if she took care of me thus, it was not solely out
> of goodness, or else I had not rightly understood the meaning of good-
> ness, when it was explained to me. It must not be forgotten that I

represented for this woman an undeniable asset. For quite apart from
the services I rendered to her lettuce, I constituted for her establishment a kind of landmark, not to say an advertisement, far more effective than for example a chef in cardboard, pot-bellied in profile and
full-face wafer thin. That she was well aware of this was shown by the
trouble she had taken to festoon my jar with Chinese lanterns, of a
very pretty effect in the twilight, and a fortiori in the night. And the
jar itself, so that the passer-by might consult with greater ease the
menu attached to it, had been raised on a pedestal at her own expense.[16]

The clauses and phrases are generally longer, the sentences much
longer than in Beckett's 'low' mode. The vocabulary is educated
('thus'), polysyllabic, and includes learned expressions ('a fortiori').
The order of elements within the sentences is sometimes unusual
or 'marked', notably in the last sentence quoted, which in its normal
or unmarked version would run: 'And the jar itself had been raised
on a pedestal at her own expense so that the passer-by might
consult the menu attached to it with greater ease.' There are
figurative elements here, too, such as both alliteration and chiasmus
in the phrases 'pot-bellied in profile and full-face wafer thin'.

So far so good, but then the complications appear. First, the
unnerving resort to cliché and set expression: 'solely out of good-
ness', 'rightly understood', 'services I rendered', 'a very pretty
effect', and so on. This subtly undermines the 'high' register, making it more banal and less serious. Then the self-conscious lapse
into the 'low' style occurs; the Unnamable goes on, after 'at her
own expense':

> It is thus I learnt that her turnips in gravy are not so good as they used
> to be, but that on the other hand her carrots, equally in gravy, are even
> better than formerly. The gravy has not varied. This is the kind of
> language I can almost understand.

Here the lexical items (carrots, turnips, gravy) seem not to belong
to any sort of elevated discourse world, although the sentence in
which they appear is an example of almost classical balance and
antithesis: A plus B is C, but D plus B is not C; therefore B is
a constant while A and B must vary. So here the rhetoric is 'high'
while the lexis is 'low'; this is, as we are told in 'low' mode, the
'sort of language' that the narrator can 'almost' understand. But
does he mean that he finds it more nearly comprehensible because

of the classical syntax ('high') or because of the carrot-and-turnip topic ('low')?

If there were no such thing as register, these confusions, so necessary for the creation of the sorts of meaning (including meanings about the unmeaning of 'meaning') that we get from a Beckett text, would be impossible. With register in mind, we can at least see where the trouble lies; it lies – as Beckett will say towards the end of the trilogy – in the words.

Workpoints

On translating French into English and vice versa:

Les registres d'expression des deux langues coincident exactement sur peu de points, en dépit d'apparences.
J. Bélanger, *Les Langues modernes* (1950)

Notes

1 Samuel Beckett, *Dream of Fair to Middling Women* (Black Cat Press, 1992), pp. 111–12.

2 'Nonce' in prison slang is 'a sexual offender; esp. one who assaults children'. He's in the *nick*, anyway.

3 See Deirdre Bair, *Samuel Beckett: A Biography* (Jonathan Cape, 1978), pp. 350–1; and James Knowlson, *Damned to Fame: The Life of Samuel Beckett* (Bloomsbury, 1996), p. 352 (coincidentally).

4 One must not exaggerate the etymological coherence of French, a language whose history substantially resembles that of English in that it, too, has a group of *mots de base*, derived from late Latin, equivalent to the Old English/Norman French core vocabulary of modern English, around or on top of which a huge superstructure of words from the most varied sources has been piled during the last millennium. The Larousse *Dictionnaire Etymologique* has several sections which contain few words of Latin origin; the ten words between *bakchich* (Turkish) and *balalaika* (Russian), for instance, are interrupted only by *bal* as a word of Latin provenance and include Germanic and Arabic elements. On the other hand, whole pages of the same dictionary can be found which contain nothing but words of Latin origin, as for instance in such sections as that stretching in uninterrupted Latinity from *ablative* to *absence*. *Larousse: Dictionnaire*

étymologique et historique du français (Paris, 1964).

5   The answer is Beckett in *Dream*. The giveaway is perhaps the parenthesis.

6   Samuel Beckett, *More Pricks Than Kicks* (1934) (Calder & Boyars, 1970),
pp. 86–7.

7   John Montague told Deirdre Bair that Beckett had told him, in response to a complaint that he was finding a particular poem hard to
write, 'Ah, Montague, what you need is monologue – *monologue!*'
Beckett apparently held up 'one thin finger to emphasise his point',
and added: 'That's the thing!' This anecdote relates to the point in
Beckett's life immediately after his experience on a pier one stormy
night while staying in Dublin when, like Krapp in *Krapp's Last Tape*,
he had some sort of visionary or mystical experience, and saw 'the
whole thing'. His vision of how to write seems to have coincided
with a vision of the nature of the universe, which he would certainly
not have called a vision of the nature of the universe. See Bair, *Samuel
Beckett*, p. 351.

8   *Molloy* in Beckett's Trilogy (John Calder, 1959), p. 93.

9   *The Unnamable* in Beckett's Trilogy (John Calder, 1959), p. 379.

10   *Molloy*, pp. 22–3.

11   *Malone Dies* in Beckett's Trilogy (John Calder, 1959), p. 74.

12   *Ibid.*, p. 75.

13   *Ibid.*, pp. 34–5.

14   *The Unnamable*, p. 310.

15   *Ibid.*, p. 311.

16   *Ibid.*, p. 331.

9

Register and dialect:
Thomas Hardy's voices

Dialect as register

In linguistics, and in language study generally, a clear separation is made between dialects and registers. A dialect is usually a subvariety of a language spoken in a particular area, while a register need have no geographical limitations. Halliday sees dialects as being, like languages, '*different ways of saying the same thing*', as in 'church' – 'kirk' – 'église' where the words, though different, 'say the same thing' respectively in Standard English, Scots and French. Registers are then '*different ways of saying different things*'. Sometimes 'social dialect' has been used to cover some of the territory which is, surely, better referred to as register, but the basic idea in dialectology is the establishment of geographical areas in which subvarieties of languages are spoken.[1] There would not be much sense in a register atlas but there is a huge amount of fascinating work summarised in a dialect atlas. Fieldwork – especially in a country such as Britain, where different dialects are crowded together in a relatively small area – yields maps of great complexity where 'isoglosses' trace the incidence of certain expressions as recorded.

There are arguments, of a largely political kind, between those who would call certain dialects 'languages' and those who would insist that they are dialects. The usual criterion is mutual intelligibility: if one speaker can understand the other, then they speak the same language even if there are dialect differences; if not, they speak different languages. On this basis there are quite a lot of grey areas. Spanish politicians interviewed on Portuguese television are not usually given a voiceover translation; Danes can understand Norwegians as well as Londoners can understand Glaswegians, or rather better. Yet Spanish, Portuguese, Danish and Norwegian are all considered separate languages, while London and Glasgow have only different dialects of 'English'. Some of the languages of southern France – now sadly disappearing – were considered dialects of French, although Provençal or Béarnais are definitely not mutually intelligible with French. One can see the political importance of these distinctions; they are also good examples of how arbitrary and culture-bound such things are.[2]

In theory, every dialect could have every register. For our purposes here, we may as well think of all languages as dialects and put them all on to one plane, for after all, one does not speak or write English or Arabic or German, one speaks or writes Standard English or classical Arabic or 'Kolsch' (Cologne German). Each of these dialects could have as many registers as the most register-prolific language in the world. In the eighteenth century a range of more and less formal registers was clearly developing in Scots, for instance, and there is absolutely no *a priori* reason why Scots should not today have all the registers of Standard English, and more. Modern medicalese could have been created in the remotest dialect, provided only that its speakers had access to the relevant modern medicine; religious language can be found as a special register in numerous cultures.

De facto, as we know, internationalisation has tended to limit the register development of many dialects; someone learning air traffic control instructions in Bolivia will get them neither in an Amerindian language such as Quechua nor in local Bolivian 'Creole' Spanish, but in a mixture of Standard Spanish and English. But that, obviously, is only a matter of cultural and political history. If Greek had had a history similar to that of English, most languages of the world, instead of talking down planes in a version of English, would do so in Greek and instead of referring as they now do to a game called football (or 'futebol' or another variant) might all have had to incorporate a thing with a name from Greek something like '*Sphairistike*'. Only the subtle flows of power determine these things, nothing in the languages/dialects themselves.

In practice, then, many dialects (even many languages), for historical and political reasons, do not have certain registers, or have registers that others do not. Middle English has no space-exploration register; modern English has not developed a new register for courtly love. And, in literature, it is the practical, not the theoretical that counts in such matters. The practical fact, for instance, that the register of space travel is very modern means that a writer could not employ it without connoting the second half of the twentieth century and all that that implies. Similarly, any touch of the register of courtly love must bring with it something of the medieval world. I do not know of much specialist legalese in Geordie (Newcastle 'dialect') nor, presumably, does vernacular Black American English have many very formal registers

If every dialect had every register to the same extent and to the same degree of development as every other dialect, then dialects might not be very interestingly employed in literature. There would still be the supposed regional characteristics attached to different dialects, but that would be all. Thus the famous Scottish carefulness with money could still be evoked more strongly through a character speaking in the Aberdonian fashion than through the laid-back tones of a flower child of the Californian 1960s. But many other limitations and associations would be lost. The notion of rustic innocence, for instance, crucial in Hardy's use of Wessex dialect in *Tess of the D'Urbervilles* and elsewhere, would not be available if 'Wessex' included a register of high finance, another of sensation journalism, another of the penal system (legalese, police-speak), and so on. The high financier doing his dubious and self-orientated deals in a rich Wessex patois is simply incredible – not in itself and *a priori*, but because we have come to associate 'Wessex' with cows and gentleness; and that is because there happens not to have been much high finance going on in Wessex since the development of modern English. So 'Wessex' dialect does not merely connote the supposed qualities of the locals who live there but also, in a structuralist series of oppositions, excludes and denies values and ideas more usually presented through other dialects.

Thus it comes about that the employment of dialects, like the employment of those dubiously different entities 'languages themselves', *in literary texts*, carries a charge of meaning entirely different from the meanings a dialectologist would be looking for. The dialectologist is concerned to record and systematise differences which exist as ends in themselves – the furthest such studies can go is to the point of a complete recording of differences and the explanation, where it is possible, of the etymologies of varying locutions. This is a rational and surely praiseworthy objective, but it leaves the meaning of dialect in literature quite untouched.

When Donald Farfrae appears in *The Mayor of Casterbridge*, his Scots dialect isn't very convincing and has little to teach the student of language variation; his exact provenance (Scotland) is of some importance, though his origins in a particular part of Scotland are never made clear; what is most significant is that he has a different view and status from the Wessex people he is among – a point already made in his surname and merely emphasised by his accent (much 'dialect' in literature turns out to be little more than accent difference). Perhaps some romanticised notion of Scottishness hangs about him which helps him in winning the hearts of the female characters in the novel, but for this purpose he could as well be a Spaniard and, certainly, would do better to be French. In his case, then, dialect merely signals *difference*, and has an effect of similar force to the effect that a gentleman would have entering the Casterbridge world and speaking in Standard English in Received Pronunciation – the obvious example here being Angel Clare in *Tess of the D'Urbervilles*, whose alien status also wins him the affections of most of the unmarried females on the farm where he is living, quite out of his class context, to learn the trade of farming. Angel is much remarked on by the narrator for his manner of speech; so is Farfrae. The point being made is the same – *different* voices/accents/dialects/registers mean different expectations, the pull of the exotic, freedom from local constraints. In the one case (Farfrae) the difference is dialectal; in the other (Clare) the difference is in register (class) as well as in dialect (in so far as the farm folk at Talbothays actually speak Wessex). My overall point, then, is that there isn't any difference between register and dialect in terms of the kinds of meaning they generate *in literature*.

In the case of Donald Farfrae Scottishness itself, though inevitably significant up to a point, need not be the most important part of what he means. He is a fairly extreme example of how dialect in literature is not very dependent for its meaning on anything that would interest a dialectologist; but there are many other cases where there is considerable meaning to be found in the mythology surrounding the dialect used. Different dialects have associations and connotations that give them an extra layer of significance – usually a pretty obvious one – in literary texts. One has only to think for a moment of the meanings engendered by words such as 'Australian' or 'Irish' to get the point. We are in the presence of the crudest form of stereotyping here, but that is how language works in literature: by invoking, playing on and, perhaps, contradicting stereotypes. It does it with dialects in exactly the same ways as with registers. Mr Squeers in *Nicholas Nickleby*, mouthing the platitudes of the brochures of the Victorian 'Yorkshire Schools', is clearly stereotypically representative of a particular rhetoric (concealing in this case a reality which is the exact opposite of what is being said), while Joseph in *Wuthering Heights* employs the broadest Yorkshire dialect to connote the narrow-minded puritanical intransigence associated stereotypically with a certain sort of Yorkshireman of the period. In the one case the job is done by register, in the other by dialect; it comes to the same thing.

Dialects within registers: Anthony Powell

A form of Welsh English is used systematically throughout Anthony Powell's *The Valley of Bones* (1964), the seventh volume in the *Dance to the Music of Time* series. The narrator, Nick Jenkins, signs up, to fight the Second World War, as an officer in a Welsh regiment. Being highly educated and belonging to the class that speaks Standard English, and perhaps above all being the self-conscious narrator of a novel, he represents his 'own' voice as that of a narrator who is at home with sentences such as the following (which describes the Welsh coastal town where he has been quartered and where there is a house which had belonged to his ancestors):

> The cliffs below the site of the house where all but foundations had been obliterated by the seasons, enclosed untidy banks of piled-up rock against which spent Atlantic waters ceaselessly dissolved, ceaselessly renewed steaming greenish spray: *la mer, la mer, toujours recommencée*, as Moreland was fond of quoting, an everyday landscape of heaving billows too consciously dramatic for my own taste.[3]

The register here is staking a claim to a sort of qualified aesthetic mode, bidding for a very specific tone of 'literary' semi-detachment. It is not merely written but positively literary to omit definite articles in such phrases as 'all but [the] foundations' and '[the] spent Atlantic waters'; also to omit the conjunction in 'cease-lessly dissolved, [and] ceaselessly renewed'. The lexis shows signs of this same poetic register, of a very specific period, roughly that of late Romanticism – the period of Matthew Arnold in England and the Symbolists in France; of the Aesthetic Movement and Debussy: 'spent', 'ceaselessly', 'billows' and, of course, the whole lexical set connected with water which echoes both Matthew Arnold's almost obsessive use of water imagery and Valéry's *Cimetière Marin*, from which 'Moreland's' quotation comes. Further-more, the whole business of quoting poetry, of having friends who can quote it at you, belongs to this same world. But this is a novelistic narrator, not a poet, so a different tone is also struck: the note of ironic quasi-detachment to be found in such comfort-ably 'low' lexis as 'untidy', 'was fond of' and 'an everyday land-scape'. The narrator is 'present' here, consciously watching himself watching the scene, aware of his own reactions as well as of the coast and the sea. He seems to me to be rather amusedly present, also, in the epithets 'steaming greenish' and in the '*heaving* bil-lows'. Then, of course, he makes a gesture characteristic both of this sort of narration and of the British 'come-off-it' school of thinking: he concludes that this is all 'too consciously dramatic for my own taste'; the qualification applies to the Symboliste language he has been using as well as to the 'landscape' itself. He has played with some registers here, adopted the voices of Valéry, Moreland, a certain poetic period; and, without rejecting them, has expressed a preference for something else. This is Derridean 'play' of the clearest kind – it both plays among the registers and asks the question 'how far can I shake this thing?' – 'how far will it bend?' – 'how convincing can I make it?' The answer to the last question seems to be: *Not very. But I shan't cross out what I have written for all that.*

Now against all this, Powell sets the Welsh voices his narrator is surrounded by. In the barracks, a couple of pages later, the soldiers are singing (this *is* a Welsh regiment) and the officers come to look round; when a soldier starts banging on the bed-steads with his broom, he has become too noisy: "'All right, all right, there," shouted the Sergeant-Major, who had at first not disallowed the mere singing. "Not so much noise am I telling you.""[4] Those last four words, especially in their unusual order, at once signal a multitude of meanings generally assignable to Welsh dialect. First they separate the Sergeant-Major from Nick Jenkins and the other Standard-English-speaking officers present; Nick, for all his Welsh ancestry, is a stranger in a strange land. Second, and as a consequence of this, they establish the basic Us-and-Them social structure of the British Army in the 1940s: the Sergeant-Major speaks in the same way as the men; he may shout, but he does so in a dialect that he has in common with them. His Welshness also permits him to soften the order in another way: by adding 'am I telling you', where syntax supports accent. He may appear to stress his own authority, but in fact he is subtly undermining it by saying, in effect, either 'It's only me saying this, a fellow Welshman, so be good chaps and keep quiet or I'll get into trouble' or, alternatively, 'I don't want just to shout "Not so much noise" so I'll add something to make it seem less harsh.'

Then again, the order isn't 'Silence!' (a very different register) but merely a limitation on the number of decibels (the soldier has been banging his broom 'with all his force against the wooden legs of one of the bunks') which specifically permitted *singing*, the stereotypical Welsh male activity. There is an impression here of gentleness beneath the order, a Celtic softness perhaps that would seem entirely different if the dialect were that of Yorkshire or New York.

But, above all, it is the relationship between this dialect and the other voices of the text that generates the extra meanings we are looking for. In these first pages of *The Valley of Bones* we encounter not only the qualified aesthetic and the Welsh but also Army officialese, a quotation from the Bible, a song (including Spanish: 'For it was *mañana*/ And we were so gay/ South of the border/ Down Mexico way…'), another French quotation, references to painters, and several other elements. What is crucial here is that the dialect (and the foreign language) works in this continuum in exactly the same way as a register: Aesthetic – Welsh – Biblical – French – Officialese… In each case we read the different voice both for its difference and for its connoted meanings. In literature, dialect *is* register. Or – better, perhaps – dialects are registers.

Education: narrator versus characters in *Jude the Obscure*

Jude the Obscure starts with the following sentences:

> The schoolmaster was leaving the village, and everybody seemed sorry.
> The miller at Cresscombe lent him the small white tilted cart and horse
> to carry his goods to the city of his destination, about twenty miles off,
> such a vehicle proving of quite sufficient size for the departing teach-
> er's effects.[5]

This is Standard English operating in at least two registers. The
first voice seems pretty average, of uncertain class or 'none at all'
(these scare-quotes pose the question: is that possible?). It is written in the sense that it smacks of the scene-setting opening of a
fictional work complete with the past continuous tense (though
there is ambiguity here – the 'was leaving' need not mean 'was in
the process of leaving' but, rather, 'was to leave'). It is also spoken
inasmuch as 'everybody' in this sort of sentence is likely to be a
gossipy collective meaning 'everyone around here – you know, all
the villagers, your neighbours and mine'.

The second sentence starts in the same way ('The miller at
Cresscombe' sounds as if he belongs to the beginning of a novel,
but '*the* white tilted cart' is the voice of the gossip again – we are
supposed to know about that cart), but then at 'the city of his
destination' it becomes more educated, more 'literary' and more
formal. Colloquial alternatives easily spring to mind as we go
through the rather calmly written phrases:

the city of his destination = the town he was going to (verbal form
– colloquial – replacing the more formal nominal form)

such a vehicle = a vehicle like that (or just 'that')

proving of quite sufficient size = turning out to be quite big enough
(phrasal verb from core vocabulary replacing Latinate 'proving',
etc.)

the departing teacher's effects = the things he was taking with him
(avoiding the complex genitive; verbalisation to avoid nominal
construction)

So far so good – a bread-and-butter register analysis. It could be
continued through the following paragraphs, which describe the

reactions of the various villagers to the schoolmaster's departure. One problem is that he cannot take his piano with him, and the blacksmith and the farm bailiff are trying to help him decide what to do with it. They are 'standing in perplexed attitudes in the parlour before the instrument' when a boy joins them and makes a suggestion: 'Aunt have got a great fuel-house, and it could be put there, perhaps, till you've found a place to settle in, sir.' Suddenly there is a touch of dialect among the registers (this is to put it wrongly, of course, since all the Englishes used are dialects, and it would be better to say 'another dialect'). At any rate, a new voice speaks, and it is marked as a Wessex voice, quite different from the voice of the narrator. In this dialect there is no need for a possessive to specify a kinswoman (it isn't '*My* aunt'), 'have' serves for the third-person singular present of 'to have' (instead of 'has'), 'great' (pronounced 'gert', though with a retroflexed 'r') replaces 'big'; that's about all, but it is enough to change the overall orientation of the text. The voice we are now obliged to hear is that of the uneducated village boy; a whole rural world is invoked of narrow horizons, natural beauty, peace, a harsh life in bad weather, man integrated into the landscape, agricultural depression, happiness, lack of opportunities, gentleness, unsophistication. The dialect, sketched in with a few touches of non-standard grammar and lexis, opens a large door, and this other world pours in, speaking to us, undeniably, in its 'own' voice.

But this is to claim for dialect exactly what one would claim for register, neither more nor less. The register features of the two opening sentences, discussed above – also inevitably in a dialect, of course, Standard English – *open a world* in every bit as significant a way as this irruption of a Wessex English voice into the text. It may not seem quite as obvious in the case of these first sentences, but it isn't difficult to find register examples just as clear as the arrival of dialect in the text. For instance, when the narrator wants to indicate that the other schoolboys and girls – unlike the offerer of the 'fuel-house', who is Jude himself and can come to school only in the evenings – have failed to appear to help the departing schoolmaster or see him off, he comments: 'The regular scholars, if truth must be told, stood at the present moment afar off, like certain historic disciples, indisposed to any enthusiastic volunteering of aid.' This is not a *dialect* variation from the surrounding text, it is a register shift, but it does exactly the same thing as young Jude's voice does, with its Wessex grammar and tones. It opens a whole world of Christian history or mythology for the reader, and it does so more or less compulsorily. Just as one is limited as to how one can read young Jude's dialect, so one is limited with this sentence; it cannot, at any rate, be dissociated from Christianity, which means that Hardy is hinting at some employment of or questioning of Christian values in his novel. Of course, there is more than just the Christian voice in this sentence; there is direct quotation from the New Testament ('afar off'), but there is also a slightly arch exaggeration of another kind of tone generated by such Latinate words as 'regular', 'enthusiastic' and 'volunteering' which, combined with the public speaker's 'if the truth must be told', preserves an ironic distance between the narrator and the Christianity to which he refers and, of course, also keeps him well away from the world connoted by Jude's dialect.

And, indeed, it is precisely these worlds opened up by Jude's dialect and by the narrator's registers here that will occupy large parts of the novel. Jude Fawley is *the wrong class* to get an education at Christminster (= Oxford), and he will also be defeated in various attempts to *lead the Christian life*. These points are initiated by the registers and the dialects of this opening. Rather than try to preserve a difference between the function of these terms, it is better in literary study to recognise them, acknowledge that they do the same job, and then continue the analysis without anxiety about the distinction between them. Both are subsumed under the concept of *the voices of the text*. There is a polyphony of voices in a Hardy novel, and the meanings of it lie not only in what those voices say but also in the way they say it and in the relationship *between* the voices. Thus the blacksmith responds to young Jude's suggestion of his aunt's fuel-house with: 'A proper good notion', showing that he speaks much as the boy does; a little later the narrator paraphrases the opinion of this blacksmith by saying that the fuel-house was 'eminently practicable'. This is virtually a synonym of 'proper good', but is in a very different register (and dialect). Hardy's meanings, like the meanings he tried to impose on his own life in his autobiography,[6] lie in part along this fault-line in his voicing, in this polyphony of tones.

The narrator in Hardy characteristically operates in a 'high' or formal-educated register, and thus appears at first to patronise his 'low' or uneducated characters; then he dignifies the world-view or aspirations or wisdom of the low characters to the point where this taking-of-sides is neutralised. In *Jude the Obscure*, for instance, the narrator sounds more like the schoolmaster than the black-smith – only he and the absent rector would be capable of using some of the lexis of this opening chapter, which includes 'depu-tation', 'whimsical' and even '*impedimenta*' (the italics are Hardy's, indicating that this is meant to be Latin, not just a loanword). The narrator is writing for the gentry – for nobody 'lower' than the educated middle class, anyway – and sounds as though he has been to school, perhaps even university. So he seems to be 'on the side of' the gentlemen, clergymen and schoolmasters – Phillotson in this novel, Angel Clare in *Tess of the D'Urbervilles*. But his 'lower'-class heroes and heroines have a natural ability to rise, and their education often occurs or continues in the course of the novel, so that their registers become closer to the narrator's own. Jude, Tess, Clym Yeobright, Grace Melbury and others are on an upward social – and therefore linguistic – curve. Their capacity to express themselves in educated tones is one of the main things that make them stand out from the 'rustic chorus' of happily uneducated villagers and countryfolk. Jude, with immense effort, gives himself the education of a clergyman or an Oxford undergraduate; Tess is clever, has had more education than usual for her class and gender at the time, and is a quick pupil of Angel Clare's, learning his agnosticism if nothing else. Clym Yeobright's tragedy is in part brought on by near-blindness preventing him from pursuing his studies; Grace Melbury has been sent away to a smart boarding-school to finish her education, thus being put at least one whole class above her parents and her lover, Giles Winterborne. In every case the character rises in register and echoes the narrator's educated tones.

Tragedy in any language: *Tess of the D'Urbervilles*

There is something terrible in Hardy's major fiction: tragedy, pes-simism, things tending to go badly, the wrong man meeting the wrong woman, 'too late, beloved', death, suffering and all the well-known elements that lead some readers to wonder if they can tolerate reading, say, *Tess* again. And yet Hardy is not melodramatic, an exaggerator of effects; he does not seek to indulge in the wringing of hearts for its own sake, nor to employ purple passages. All of which can be expressed in another way: he does not often deploy the resources of the romantic or Gothic genres and, inevitably therefore, does not use the various romantic registers to promote his emotional effects. On the contrary, he works with a rich lexico-grammatical palette, including all sorts of registers (and some dialects), to generate highly complex patterns. Lots of voices can be heard, and their meanings are modified by their being collocated in the same novel, in the same chapter, even in the same passage or paragraph. They bounce off each other with unexpected results.

By Chapter 23 of *Tess of the D'Urbervilles* it is clear to the reader that Tess and Angel Clare, the gentleman-turning-farmer who is learning his new skill at Talbothays Dairy, where Tess is a milkmaid, are falling in love. The other milkmaids there, set up as less considerable personages than Tess, are also in love with the handsome young harp-player (he is an *angel*). Summer brings this erotic mixture up to the boil, almost literally:

> The air of the sleeping-chamber seemed to palpitate with the hopeless passion of the girls. They writhed feverishly under the oppressiveness of an emotion thrust on them by cruel Nature's law – an emotion which they had neither expected nor desired. The incident of the day [Angel has *touched* them all for the first time, carrying them over a large puddle that blocked their path] had fanned the flame that was burning the inside of their hearts out, and the torture was almost more than they could endure.[7]

There is some brilliant play with lexical sets here: 'oppressiveness' belongs both in the climatic and the psychological sets; 'fever' connotes literal heat, psychological disturbance and disease (also dis-ease). Touches of scientific register here keep us on the outside, looking in, although we are also on the inside feeling the heat: 'Nature's law' is backed up by some scientific things in the immediately following sentence: 'The differences which distinguished them as individuals were abstracted by this passion, and each was but portion of one organism called sex' – the last word of which seems like a physical blow, being a synonym simultaneously of 'gender' (men-and-women), 'gender' (as a general scientific distinction) and the activity known to coy Victorian biologists as 'amphimixis'. Other registers are hinted at, too:

- 'Cruel Nature's law' is what linguists would call a 'marked' form – that is to say, it is an unexpected order. Instead of 'Nature's cruel law', which distances the cruelty slightly from Nature herself (in this more usual formulation she could have other less cruel laws; it might even be that *all* her other laws are benevolent) Hardy gives us an ineluctably cruel nature of whose cruelty this is but one typical example. The register involved here is produced partly by this inversion and partly by the capitalisation which makes 'Nature' participate both in Victorian scientific discourse and in the sort of religious discourse that capitalises words such as 'Man' (for 'humanity').

- There is an 'aside' quality to the words after the dash in the second sentence; 'an emotion' is picked up after the dash and repeated: 'an emotion which…'. This rhetorical (and therefore faintly spoken) phrasing implies the presence of commitment in the narrator, who is thus seen to be taking sides.

- The phrasal verb 'burn [something] out' is either the technical language of the iron foundry (or alchemist's laboratory) or it comes in as a colloquialism (as in 'eat your heart out'), in which case it is free indirect speech from one of the 'girls', who could have said: ''Tis burning my heart out.'

- Hardy returns again and again to a species of literary register, using different means to do so. Here it is alliteration that suggests what Roman Jakobson called a 'set towards the message', that is, a focus on the 'language itself':

      sleeping-chamber … seemed … hopeless
      palpitate … passion
      fanned the flame
      differences … distinguished … individuals

- 'but portion of' is a quasi-biblical version of 'only part of'.

This paragraph continues for another three sentences, the narrator musing on the strangely normal situation brought about by erotic infatuation, and is then followed by a one-sentence paragraph: 'They tossed and turned on their little beds, and the cheese-wring dripped monotonously downstairs.' The girls are being *wrung* by their feelings; the metaphor catches both the torture and its tedious endlessness rather well. But – *nota bene* – the vehicle of the metaphor is not, for instance, an eagle sent by Zeus to eat out Prometheus' liver, on a daily basis, while he is chained forever to a rock; it's just an ordinary old cheese-wring. It belongs, in other words, to a homely, not a tragic register. It brings another voice into text, one which we have hardly heard in the preceding paragraph. Then comes the dialect:

> 'B'you awake, Tess?' Whispered one [of the girls], half-an-hour later.
> It was Izz Huett's voice.
> Tess replied in the affirmative, whereupon also Retty and Marian suddenly flung the bedclothes off them, and sighed -
> 'So be we!'

Dialect is formally present here only in the two 'be's', the first of which is truncated to indicate its elision with the ensuing vocalic 'y'. A whole world of 'Wessex' speech is, however, imported by these deft touches. And this speech world, connoted by *dialect*, has exactly the same status as the other worlds we have been looking at, brought into being by *register* shifts, in the earlier section. An exact impression of class and social position is given – supported, of course, by the fact that the three girls share a bedroom, and feel free to cast off their bedclothes in front of each other and whisper like girls in a school dormitory. These are milkmaids of a humble order in whose speech some element in West Saxon dialect, from the days before the Norman Conquest, led to the non-adoption of the (northern) system of 'am – are – is', and so on, which became the standard conjugation of 'to be' in modern English. They will perhaps not expect much, not be pretentious, certainly not have the airs and graces that can go with education and wider horizons. They will also very probably be *good* people; true, Farmer Groby, in this same novel, is a harsh employer, and will shout at Tess in this very dialect, but even for him there are excuses aplenty and, on average, he is exceptional. Rural innocence is the order of the Wessex day, and Hardy's point here will certainly be that the natural passion of the girls for Angel is, precisely, innocent. All this is supported and suggested by those two 'be's'.

The voices of the text intermingle in a way that subtracts authority from any one of them and equalises all consciousnesses. This process includes registers and dialects, and treats them as belonging on the same plane. Thus the dialogue in the sleeping-chamber goes on:

> 'I wonder what she is like – the lady they say his family have looked out for him!'
>
> 'I wonder,' said Izz.
>
> 'Some lady looked out for him?' gasped Tess, starting. 'I have never heard o' that!'
>
> 'O yes – 'tis whispered; a young lady of his own rank, chosen by his family; a Doctor of Divinity's daughter near his father's parish of Emminster; he don't much care for her, they say. But he is sure to marry her.'

The non-standard dialect is obvious here: 'have looked out' for 'has looked out'; 'he don't much' for 'he doesn't much'. But that is not all; other dialects break in. Just as in the earlier section where the narrator *sounds like* a scientist or a poet or the Bible, so here the girls *sound like* the voices they have heard talking about Angel. This is heavily signalled by Hardy with his 'they say', ''tis whispered', and 'they say' again. And this 'they' whom the girls are quoting speak in a slightly different register from the normal one employed by Izz, Retty and Marian; 'they' refer to 'a young lady of his own rank', and can manage 'a Doctor of Divinity' (even if they rather let down the tone by employing the Saxon genitive after it – 'a Doctor of Divinity's daughter' – instead of keeping the tone formal by using 'the daughter of a Doctor...').

When we look back and see that the narrator has done the same thing ('B'you awake, Tess?' is answered not with 'I be' but with 'Tess replied in the affirmative'), we begin to realise that the voicing is ubiquitous, and that the shifts in register and dialect, whether they come in the diegesis (narrator talking) or in the mimesis ('dialogue'), form part of an intricate dance. Angel's supposed fiancée has been 'looked out for him' – a typical use of a Germanic phrasal verb for colloquial, even slang, purposes – according to the girls 'themselves', while when they are echoing what other people ('they') have said, this same idea becomes 'chosen by his family' – a typically Romance-based locution indicating that in the public world of 'they', the speech is a little more formal. 'Selected by his immediate relations' would be a quotation from a different source again.

Instead of a monologic romantic lament, Hardy offers us a dialogic dance in which the participants include the many voices of the narrator, largely using differing registers, and the voices of the characters, who use both dialects and registers. The result is that what is terrible in his work is made both better and worse. It is *better* because register shift, as we have often seen in this book, tends to be funny. At least it opens up some critical distance between reader and action, it foregrounds the written nature of the text, draws attention to the weave and thus temporarily away from the overall tendency of the garment (though in a literary text the notion of 'overall' interpretation is a chimera).

But it also makes Hardy's terrors *worse*, because it leaves no hiding place. A Byronic lamentation – Jeremiah himself, even – can be dismissed by the weary or unsympathetic reader. It is easy to sympathise with Matthew Arnold's dismissal of Byron's own agonies: 'He who through Europe bore/ The pageant of his bleeding heart'. But we are given few chances of escape in a novel such as *Tess*. Whether we look at life's tragedies tragically (as in the famous opening of *The Return of the Native*, for instance) or comically; whether we cast our analysis in scientific English or the simple words of country maidens, the pain remains. The pain remains and kills. Time will say nothing but 'I told you so.'

Multiplying: *Far from the Madding Crowd*

Hardy was given to double-voicing in a way that demonstrates very clearly the indistinguishability, in terms of semantic effect, of registers and dialects in fiction. The opening chapters of *Far from the Madding Crowd* repay close attention in this respect. The Dorset dialect becomes infected – at least for Joseph Poorgrass, with his 'Scripture manner' – by a species of what might be called Anglican register:

> 'Well, 'twas a most ungodly remedy,' murmured Joseph Poorgrass; 'but we ought to feel deep cheerfulness that a happy Providence kept it from being any worse. You see, he might have gone the bad road and

given his eyes to unlawfulness entirely – yes, gross unlawfulness, so to say it.'[8]

The 'so to say it' indicates a certain self-consciousness in Poorgrass's borrowing of the register of the parson in the middle of a dialect passage. And, conversely, the narrator's rather 'high' register can become infected by Dorsetisms:

A meditation on the obvious inference was indulged in by all, and during its continuance each directed his vision into the ashpit, which glowed like a desert in the tropics under a vertical sun, shaping their eyes long and liny, partly because of the light, partly from the depth of the subject discussed.[9]

Perhaps 'ashpit' need not be regarded as dialect, though I have not seen it used much in Standard English, but 'liny' is surely a Wessex expression – certainly not Standard, at any rate. It sits oddly, amusingly, among 'meditations' and 'obvious inferences' and 'vertical' suns. The result is something of an increase in the number of angles of vision the novelist can offer us – perhaps another version of what Joseph Poorgrass, inclined to drink strong liquors as well as read the Bible, calls 'the multiplying eye'.[10]

Workpoints

Social dialect and 'register' need not be differentiated. Which of the two do we need to describe the difference between the two following sentences used by someone opening a meeting?

'Good Morning, ladies and gentlemen. May we make a start?'
versus
'Hi everyone! Let's get going.'

What determines which one we use? The 'person we are' (Halliday's definition of 'social dialect') or the immediate situation (his definition of what determines register)?

Answer: Both. But unless we are proposing a view of human nature as entirely unchangeable, we had better stick to **register**, because in life, and *a fortiori* in literature, we can choose how to sound, what tone to adopt, and 'register' stresses this aspect rather than what we, seemingly unchangeably 'are'. (*See note 1 below for more on this.*)

Bakhtin sees dialect and register as indistinguishable in literature in *The Dialogic Imagination*. See, for instance, p. 294 of that astonishing volume.

> ah knew a linguist wance
> wanst ah knew a linguist
> shi used tay git oanty mi
> ah wish I could talk like you
> ahv lost my accent
> thi crux iz says ah
> shiftin ma register
> tay speak tay a linguist
> would you swear tay swerr
> an no abjure
> the extra-semantic kinetics
> uv thi fuckin poor
> ach
> mobile society
> mobile ma arse

This poem by Tom Leonard, from 'Ghostie Men' in *Intimate Voices* (1984), mixes the notions of dialect and register. It needs to be read extremely carefully, but it shows that a shift in register is *the same thing* here as a shift in dialect.

(Of course, the poem is only pretending to be about language. As ever, culture, society and power are what language is really talking abut; and talking.)

Is this poem in Scots or English?

Notes

1 There is a degree of confusion in Halliday's use of 'dialect' in his *Language as Social Semiotic* (1978). At first he makes a promising concession to our (literary) way of thinking about register and dialect by pointing out that at certain points 'dialects become entangled with registers'; but on closer inspection what he means here by 'dialect' is 'social dialect' which, in my view *is* register. Much later he defines

dialect as a language variety in which variation occurs 'according to the *user*', while in register the variation occurs 'according to the *use*' (p. 183). In other words, if I speak Scots English it is because I am Scots, but if I speak medicalese it is because I am working as a doctor. But then he must be using 'dialect' in two different ways: first as geographical dialect – the legitimate way in my view – whereby a Scots child who has not been exposed to any other dialect speaks Scots, without choice; and then as a 'social dialect' which, *by definition*, can work only where there are other social dialects present and is, thus, a choice. The confusion arises because of the original problem over the definition of 'dialect' (discussed in the following pages of this chapter): in fact a dialect is better thought of as having the same logical status as a *language*, rather than a *language variety*.

Further confusion is created by Halliday's definition of 'social dialects' to include 'urban' manners of speech in an increasingly non-homogeneous society. These, however, must either be tantamount to the old geographical dialects (just a bit more complicated because of the tightknit geography of the town as opposed to the country) or be what we would call registers.

In any event, even if 'social dialect' is a useful or clear term in linguistics, it falls under the same heading as all other forms of dialect as discussed below in this chapter: for the purposes of literary analysis, dialects perform exactly the same functions as registers. Thus if Mr Pickwick is constructed as a naive, benevolent, Christian bourgeois by his *register* ('Let me make a memorandum of that!', 'My good man!', and so on), Sam Weller is made, in exactly the same way, into an urban, streetwise, humorous, kind-hearted Cockney Sparrer by what Halliday would call his 'social *dialect*'. Here is a distinction without a difference. What difference, anyway, would you be making if you tried to say that the lexis of an eighteenth-century parson was part of his social dialect (upper-middle-class professional) *and* that he employed the registers (involving formality, admonition, biblical phrasing, authority, and so on) of his class and profession? We don't need both terms here, surely?

Halliday comes pretty close, in the end, to marrying these two terms which he has (for these purposes) unnecessarily separated. He admits, for instance, that dialect and register overlap – that bureaucratic register, for instance, demands standard dialect and farming register rural dialect. He solves the problem this overlap poses by adding: 'Hence the dialect comes to symbolise the register; when we hear a local dialect, we unconsciously switch off part of our register range' (p. 186). Precisely; but this implies that for analytical purposes (literary-analytical purposes at least) they may as well be considered as the same thing.

2 See T. Hill ('Problèmes linguistiques', *Orbis*, viii, 2 [Louvain, 1958], pp. 441ff.), who stresses the arbitrary nature of what becomes a language from among the 'dialect continuum' of any 'tongue' (his neutral term). All things seem possible. A *koine* (demotic speech) may become a 'language' *within* a dialect continuum (e.g. Standard English) or come from outside (English among Gaelic-speaking Highlanders; Swahili; Latin). One point on the continuum comes to dominate, and status and prestige follow for political reasons

3 Anthony Powell, *The Valley of Bones* (1964) (Fontana, 1973), p. 5.

4 *Ibid.*, p. 9.

5 Thomas Hardy, *Jude the Obscure*, 1896, chapter 1.

6 Florence Emily Hardy, *The Life of Thomas Hardy 1870–1928* (Macmillan, 1962).

7 Thomas Hardy, *Tess of the D'Urbervilles* (1891), chapters 24, 25.

8 Thomas Hardy, *Far from the Madding Crowd,* 1874, chapter 8.

9 *Ibid.*

10 All modern students of Hardy's language are indebted to three monographs in particular: Ralph Elliott, *Thomas Hardy's English* (1984); Raymond Chapman, *The Language of Thomas Hardy* (1990); and Dennis Taylor, *Hardy's Literary Language and Victorian Philology* (1993).

10

'Singing, each to each': sounding like poetry

Poetry is poetic

The first thing to be said about most poems is that they are *like other poems*. This is because until modernism – but in some measure even during and since modernism – poetry tended to be written in a recognisably poetic register, and also because 'poetry' is a genre such that for the most part a text either definitely participates in it or does not. Normally the poet writes in the same 'language' as other poets or, in some recognisable sense, works with the same structures. The most superficial but ineluctable demonstration of this fact is that all poetry is signalled to be such either by the familiar special printing conventions or by a subtitle such as 'prose poem'. Poetic register or registers are, of course, available to writers in all genres, but just because George Eliot (as novelist) or your computer manual or the Home Secretary happens to indulge in some poetic flourishes (markers of poetic register), we do not assume that their novels, chapters or speeches 'are poetry'; we are entirely clear that they are not. Poetry is a very strong genre indeed.

Some poems participate less obviously in poetic registers than others, it is true, but I believe that all readers who are conscious that they are reading poetry (and it would be hard *not to notice*) read with a special attention to rhythm and in a special internal voice that is different from the voice in which they read non-poetry. This is very clear in the case of a topic that lies outside the scope of this book – phonetics. It is virtually impossible to read a poem aloud (and therefore virtually impossible to read it privately) without a special intonation, a special pattern of emphasis, breathing and pausing. This is merely the oral–auditory equivalent of the special tone, the special register in which poetry is *written* and in which it is certainly *received*. The reader is not fooled: if you signal that he or she is reading a poem certain consequences inevitably follow. Ask anyone to read any piece of text 'as though it were a poem', and you will get a result different from any reading of the same text based on any other premiss.

Generically any piece of text can be chopped up, chopped off, rearranged, so that it signals the genre 'poetry' to the reader, and the result will be quite predictable. The 'E. Jarvis Thribb' column in *Private Eye* is based on the notion that any old scraps of prose, printed in the lineation of verse, can achieve something of the quality of poetry, and can become compulsorily read in a special way. From a *register* point of view, and most interestingly, these ludicrous bits and pieces of submodernist doggerel retain, besides the lineation, something of the essential rhythm of English verse; 'So farewell then…' runs the first line of most of the 'Thribb' pieces (they are usually obituary verse), which is an iambic dimeter ('So fárewell thén'). The iambic rhythm in itself pulls any line of English towards the poetic – it is the bedrock of the business of 'sounding like poetry' in this language. From a million examples, I shall cite just this from Tennyson's *Morte d'Arthur*: 'So all day long the noise of battle rolled/ Among the mountains by the winter sea', where the first four syllables could be replaced, metrically speaking, by the first four syllables of Thribb's characteristic opening.

I am stressing the blindingly obvious: poetry, once the genre has been signalled, is read *as* poetry – it is, so to say, 'poetic'; and this may be the single most important register fact about it, as well as an unavoidable genre fact. There is no question here of proposing anything essentialist; there is nothing that can be excluded *a priori* from the category 'poetry' and I have no desire to establish any norms whatsoever for the genre. As Jonathan Culler, among others, has demonstrated: 'There is nothing so definitively unliterary that it may not turn up in a book of poems' – an observation he expands into an anti-definition: 'The essence of literature is to have no essence, to be protean, undefinable, to encompass whatever might be situated outside it.'[1] But it remains the case, *de facto*, that poetry is the sort of thing of which one can say: You Know It When You Meet It.

Here is a text:

> One bed, with sheets and duvet.
> One desk.
> One small Anglepoise lamp.
> One armchair.
> Six posters.
> One typewriter, with ribbon and piece of paper inserted.
> Two coffee mugs.
> One suitcase.
> One glass with a toothbrush in it.

This text could be extended to considerable length being, clearly enough, a list of objects in a university student's study-bedroom *circa* 1980. In one sense I could call it a 'naturally occurring' text in that I encountered it in the real world rather than in my example-seeking imagination. It went on for several dozen more lines, all in the same mode. And I might have encountered this text in various contexts: I might have been an employee working in an Accommodation Office that demanded inventories from student tenants of a hall of residence, or possibly an anxious parent who had demanded reassurance that my darling offspring had 'enough to make life tolerable' at university. The imagination can supply plenty of contexts for any text. But as a matter of fact, this text came to me, through the air, at a poetry reading. And spellbinding stuff it was. The poet declaimed his lines as 'neutrally' as possible, but neither at dictation speed (inventory) nor at breakneck speed (sarcastic listing of the excessive amount of gear possessed in response to an overanxious enquiry.) Instead, he spoke the lines *as poetry*. There was a special intonation involved, pauses at the ends of lines, slight shades of contrast between the different elements listed, self-conscious humour at one point. The audience did not shuffle its feet or talk among itself; nobody interrupted; there were no demands for clarification ('Sheet of *what* inserted?'). The reading was followed by applause.

This was the auditory equivalent of finding the same text in a book entitled *Poems*. In that (printed) case, one would have to say that it would be the generic frame, implying or stating 'Here be poetry', that would constitute the register marker. The first and most important feature of poetic register is the announcement that the text is being presented as poetry. This is not altogether compulsory, of course; it is just conceivable that the Accommodation Office would accept the poem in lieu of a proper inventory, and thus read it just as a list and without any 'set towards the message'. But if we are offered something as a poem, and if we accept that offer, then we have already entered into the register game of poetry willy-nilly. Thus far there need be nothing metrical or lexico-grammatical or figurative or interestingly cohesive about the text to signal that it is poetry (most of these features are absent in the example under discussion), but we will read it as poetry all the same.

By way of introducing his volume *New Numbers* (1969) Christopher Logue wrote a foreword which was itself in verse. It's called 'Foreword', all right, which signals a prose genre, and its register doesn't immediately strike one as poetic:

> This book was written in order to change the world
> and published at 12/- (softback), 25/- (hardback) by Cape
> of 30 Bedford Square, London, WC1
> (a building formerly occupied by the Czarist Embassy)
> in 1969.
> It is generously scattered with dirty words
> particularly on pages 9, 31, 37 and 45,
> and was written by C. Logue
> a sexy young girl living among corrupted villagers
> who keeps her innocence through love;
> its weight is 7.926 oz,
> its burning temperature is Fahrenheit 451,
> and it was printed in Great Britain by
> Butler and Tanner of London and Frome.

Except for one or two small signals, these two sentences have nothing of poetry about them – that is presumably the 'point' of the poem. There is no rhyme, no detectable regularities in the scansion, no elevated or even surprising lexis, no grammatical or syntactic fireworks, no initial capitalisation besides the first words of sentences, only restricted metaphor. It is very nearly just a string of sentences from non-poetic registers, and its independent or 'internal' claim to be poetry, to be read as poetry (independent of the fact that, being 'externally' presented as poetry – by special lineation – it *has* to be read as poetry), is based largely on the fact that so many registers are herded together for no discernible purpose other than the poetic one. Thus the proclamation of the first line is immediately involved in a register clash with the lines that follow; a phrase such as 'written over the last five years' might go with the price and publisher, but 'written to change the world' belongs somewhere a good deal more romantic than a publisher's catalogue. Similarly, the lines about the 'sexy young girl' belong to the 'blurb' genre – those summarising and would-be tantalising descriptions of the 'contents' of books that appear on their back covers. Nothing else in the poem, so far, connects with or justifies this register provenance of these lines, unless it be the faint lexically cohesive tie between 'sexy' and 'dirty words' three lines before. Then the weight of the book is not relevant to any of the previous registers, nor is its burning temperature, though that seems to be intertextually related to a novel called *Fahrenheit 451*. Even 'printed in Great Britain…' goes wrong, because although it is a highly familiar collocation of terms, it is not normally preceded by the words 'and it was', which strike a more colloquial register than one usually finds behind the title page of a book.

So the Logue poem – even if it were not presented as such, and even if it appeared under the disguise of prose (which wouldn't be very difficult to bring about) – would still have something residually 'poetic' about it. Perhaps this is difficult to avoid, but the overall impression given by 'Foreword' is of a collection of non-poetic registers cleverly woven together into a poem. This, and 'One Bed', are at one extreme of the range that goes from poetry written in the most highly poetic language to poetry written in entirely unpoetic language. But all we do with them, as soon as we meet them in a context which claims them as poetry (the Logue poem was reprinted by Philip Larkin in his *Oxford Book of Twentieth-Century English Verse* [1973]), is to set their non-poetic linguistic features against the linguistic features that we have come to expect from poetry. The inference from such poems is that they are in some sense deliberately flouting convention and gaining an extra semantic charge out of doing so, in just the same way as any register clash does. Those who would maintain that there is no such thing as poetic register need to answer the question: what is it that such poems as these are reacting against?

Poetic prose

The second point about the poetic register is a more purely prag-
matic one: poetry – that is, the texts offered for the kind of reading we have been discussing – has, *as a matter of contingent fact*, very
frequently been written with certain linguistic patterns to the fore,
certain grammatical structures, a particular lexis and special features of expression. It has been pointed out that among Hardy's
many lyrics, no two employ the same metre, rhyme and stanzaic
structure. But none of them could convince us for a moment that
it was not verse; they all seem extremely formally familiar, well-
known kinds of shorter poem. Equally, at the level of lexical
patterning, syntax and metaphor they participate fully in the expected range of styles for English poetry in the three hundred
years before they were written. Opening the *Complete Poems* at
random, one finds this sort of first stanza (the poem is called
'Unknowing'):

> When, soul in soul reflected,
> We breathed in aethered air,
> When we neglected
> All things elsewhere,
> And left the friendly friendless
> To keep our love aglow,
> We deemed it endless...
> – We did not know!

Here one can perform the opposite and complementary opera-
tion from the one we performed on the inventory poem 'One
bed...'. For here there are conventional signals of the poetic in
abundance, and even if we did not know that this was 'a poem by
Thomas Hardy', and even if the lineation were somehow sup-
pressed, and even if the scansion were by some cunning reduced
to the unnoticeable, and even if the rhyme, assonance and alliteration were eliminated, it would remain the case that we would
construe this as 'poetic' because, by convention, the lexis and
grammar and several other features are those of poetry as it has
been written in English since the Renaissance. Two examples: the
sentence that constitutes this stanza is very 'left-branching' indeed; there are four (or five) subordinate clauses, mostly of time,
before we get to the main clause ('We deemed it endless...'); this

has been characteristic of certain kinds of verse, and very few kinds of prose outside religious discourse, certainly since Shake- speare's sonnets, which often hold up the main clause for some considerable time:

> When lofty trees I see barren of leaves
> Which erst from heat did canopy the herd...

or:

> When forty winters shall besiege thy brow
> And dig deep trenches in thy beauty's field...

or:

> When in disgrace with fortune and men's eyes
> I all alone beweep my outcast state...

In the same way the vocabulary choice of 'aethered', 'deemed' and, perhaps, 'aglow' belongs to a general register which it would be difficult not to call poetic; such locutions as 'All things elsewhere' seem to belong either to the devotional or to the poetic.

Poetry has so often been written in certain ways that the presence of any hint of those ways suggests a poetic register. A touch of the iambic, an extended metaphor, a left-branching sen- tence, personification and a host of other things at all levels of the discourse make the term 'poetic register' not merely meaningful but unavoidable. Here is Lowes Dickinson, writing in an imaginary Chinese persona; the 'poetic' Chinese is pointing out to a modern industrialised Englishman what he, the Englishman, has lost with his factories and his 'progress':

A rose in a moonlit garden, the shadow of trees on the turf, almond bloom, scent of pine, the wine-cup and the guitar; these and the pathos of life and death, the long embrace, the hand stretched out in vain, the moment that glides forever away, with its freight of music and light, into the shadow and hush of the haunted past, all that we have, all that eludes us, a bird on the wing, a perfume escaped on the gale – to all these things we are trained to respond, and the response is what we call literature. This we have; this you cannot give us; but this you may so easily take away. Amid the roar of looms it cannot be heard; it cannot be seen in the smoke of factories: it is killed by the wear and the whirl of Western life.[2]

Reading the opening of this brief passage, one is bound to think of poetry. First and most obviously, there is the scansion: 'A róse in a móonlit gárden, the shádow of trées on the túrf'. An iambic foot, a dactyl, an iambic foot, three dactyls; a mixture of the two most conventional feet in English poetry adding up to a familiar kind of hexameter – for instance, in Swinburne. This is an exact metrical match from the *Hymn of Man* – 'But God, if a God there be, is the substance of men which is man' – where the pattern of iambics and dactyls is the same as in Lowes Dickinson and the caesura, though displaced by one syllable, falls so that there are three stresses in each half of the line.

Besides meter there are several other things in this prose passage that suggest a 'poetic' register. The first sentence is wildly 'left-branching'; what looks like a string of subjects turns out, by a grammatical trick, to be a string of indirect objects:[3]

> A rose in a moonlit garden,
> the shadow of trees on the turf,
> almond bloom,
> scent of pine,
> the wine-cup and the guitar;
> these
> and the pathos of life and death,
> the long embrace,
> the hand stretched out in vain,
> the moment that glides forever away, with its freight...
> all that we have,
> all that eludes us,
> a bird on the wing,
> a perfume escaped on the gale
> all these things
> *we are trained to respond to.*

Now this structure, which is peculiar in that it is palindromic – that is, the clauses of which it is made up could be written in reverse order without loss of meaning (except at the discursive level, perhaps) – is rare in most registers: one could imagine a sermon or a highly rhetorical speech catching something of this tone, as in Donne on death:

> In the Bull of Phalaris, in the bulls of Basan, in the bulls of Babylon, the shrewdest bulls of all, in temporall, in spirituall persecutions, ever

since God put an enmity between Man, and the Serpent, from the time
of *Cain* who began in a murther, to the time of Antichrist, who pro-
ceeds in Massacres, *Death hath adhered to the enemy*, and so is an enemy.

This is a string of adjuncts preceding the main clause, a long
suspension of meaning for the usual rhetorical purposes of the
preacher preaching in prose. But for the most part this left-branching is found in poetry, as in this well-known opening of Donne's,
where it is a multiple subject that delays the semantic payoff:

> All Kings, and all their favourites,
> All glory of honors, beauties, wits,
> The Sun it selfe, which makes times, as they passe,
> *Is elder by a yeare, now*, than it was...

Other features of the Lowes Dickinson passage that make us reach
for the term 'poetic register' would include the alliteration at the
end ('the wear and the whirl of Western life'); the 'poetic inversion' in 'Amid the roar of looms it cannot be heard'; and the
balancing and repetition involved in such sentences as the one
beginning 'This we have'.

But of course, there is already something 'poetic', of a very
identifiably nineteenth-century kind, in the lexis. Even without
regular rhythms and rhetorical strategies such as left-branching,
certain expectations are engendered by moonlit gardens, wine-cups
and the gliding away of the moment. Such elements are the staple
of a certain kind of Romantic lyric, notably that of the whole
tradition that stretches from Keats through Tennyson to Fitzgerald,
Arnold, Swinburne and the minor poets of the end of the century.
There is no compulsion for poetry to include these elements, but
intertextuality is a firm-handed master, and once a topos has been
established it is hard to shake off its claims. One way of identifying
it in prose is to call it poetic.

Intertextuality: the power of the topos

I suppose it is possible that in nature the evening is less meteoro-
logically dramatic than other parts of the day. Perhaps sunset, or
the moment when onshore breezes and offshore breezes change
place, involves some lessening of the wind; perhaps storms are

commonest in full daylight or after full dark. Frankly, I should be surprised to discover that this was the case; after all, wouldn't sunrise be liable to share the weather phenomena of sunset? But whether it is true or not, there is no doubt that there is a poetic topos connected with evening being 'quiet'. The game is given away (the game in question is to pretend that this is nature when we know that it is culture) when we look more closely at the words used for this quiet quality of evening:

Meteorological possibility (unlikely but possible: 'Nature')

- Average low readings on the Beaufort Scale of wind speed between one hour before sunset and one hour after it;
- especially, low frequency of the *gale* and *storm* levels of wind at those times.

Poetic topos certainly established ('Culture')

- Evening exists, apart from afternoon and night, as a recognisable and separate 'time of the day';
- evening is 'quiet', 'peaceful', a time more suitable for thought than any other period of the 'twenty-four hours';
- evening is thus anthropomorphised by *not* being 'fierce', 'wild', 'rough', 'angry', full of labour or intrusive.

In the eighteenth century, William Collins encapsulated the full range of material connected with this topos in his 'Ode to Evening':

> If aught of oaten stop or pastoral song
> May hope, O pensive Eve, to soothe thine ear
>   Like thy own solemn springs,
>   Thy springs and dying gales...

Evening is 'Eve', both a time and a woman; later in the poem she will be 'nymph' and 'maid composed'. She is thoughtful, soothing, solemn, *diminishing* ('dying', later 'hush'd' and 'soften'd') and populated by small and unobtrusive fauna (bats and beetles). Her 'gleams' are 'religious', her 'rule' is 'quiet', and if perchance Winter is also present, then the spirit of evening is clearly put out:

> While sallow Autumn fills thy lap with leaves;
> Or Winter, yelling through the troublous air,
>   Affrights thy shrinking train
>   And rudely rends thy robes...

So here the game is played with an extra finesse: there can be meteorological dramatics at evening, but they are alien to the true nature of the mild maiden that is Eve, a violation of her chaste religious calm.

As all this implies, evening is a good time for God, as Wordsworth knew:

> It is a beauteous evening, calm and free;
> The holy time is quiet as a Nun
> Breathless with adoration; the broad sun
> Is sinking down in its tranquillity;
>
> The gentleness of heaven is on the Sea:
> Listen! The mighty Being is awake...

The god is a god of Nature, but the quasi-Christian metaphor is clear: evening is female, quiet, adoring ('breathless' is good – this means she's rapt in prayer, *excited* yet passive, and that the wind isn't blowing). The capitalisation gives us the Nun, the Being and the Sea; God is on the sea and evening is worshipping Him like a nun in a cathedral. Female worships male; in the quietness Nature can hear the Divine and bow down.

Thomas Campbell joins the chorus in his 'Song to the Evening Star':

> Star that bringest home the bee,
> And sett'st the weary labourer free!
> If any star shed peace 'tis Thou
>   That sends't it from above,
> Appearing when Heaven's breath and brow
>   Are sweet as her's we love.

Of course; *that's* what it is: we feel peace at the end of the day because we can stop working and go home. So evening brings small animals (the 'bee') and quietness, religious thoughts and – accurately enough in those days – sight of the female we love. The peace is pathetically fallacious enough (in the next stanza the cottage smoke is 'unstirr'd' because there is no wind – within is echoed by without) and the deconstructibility comes built in: for the evening star is, of course, Venus, and to say that that goddess normally presides over peaceful scenes and tranquil emotions would be stretching optimism to breaking point.

Walter Scott takes up the topos in 'Datur Hora Quieti':

> The sun upon the lake is low,
>   The wild birds hush their song,
> The hills have evening's deepest glow,
>   Yet Leonard tarries long.
> Now all whom varied toil and care
>   From home and love divide,
> In the calm sunset may repair
>   Each to the loved one's side.

The birds are conveniently quiet; the female (presumably) awaits her mate ('Leonard') and the time of 'calm' has come. Evening is a time of 'home and love' from which we have been 'divided' during the day, a time when we seem free to be ourselves.

Once you notice it, the topos begins to appear everywhere:

Cowper: 'So let us welcome peaceful evening in';

Blake: 'Evening mild';

Lamb: 'The not unpeaceful evening of a day/ Made black by morning storms';

Browning: 'The quiet-coloured end of evening…'

Working backwards, we find this in Milton, who talks of 'still evening', and then:

> Sweet the coming on
> Of grateful evening mild, then silent night
> With this her solemn bird, and this fair moon,
> And these gems of heaven, her starry train.

Here I have quoted on from evening into night to give a flavour of another topos, the complex collocations and expectations aroused by 'night'. Milton's use of 'with' indicates the conventional nature of this lexically cohesive set: owls, moons, stars as jewels and as ornaments on the garments of the Queen of Night. But back at evening, here is Marlowe's Faustus, asking first whether Helen's was the face that launched a thousand ships and carrying on:

> Oh thou art fairer than the evening air
> Clad in the beauty of a thousand stars.

Two topoi come together: the 'fairness' of evening (Helen's face is gentle, mild) and the beauty of the starriness of the post-sunset sky; so she is Queen of Night as well as holy peace, thus bringing together the two things that the best side of Faustus has shown a taste for: physical and spiritual perfection.

One could go on, tracing the history of the terms and expressions connected with evening (or night) and related topics; they seem to circle around a small number of semantic points, and our expectations are triggered as soon as any mention of evening is made. So the semantic charge of Prufrock's love song is in part at the discursive level, the level where intertextuality becomes a species of dialogue; his first two lines invite us to activate the expected topos:

> Let us go then, you and I,
> When the evening is spread out against the sky...

We know that evening is a good quiet time for 'you and I' to get together, a moment of holy peace for the less strenuous side of love to flourish in. But then the damaging simile 'Like a patient etherised upon a table'. The patient is *quiet* all right, and indeed possessed of patience, but there is little spiritual tranquillity, little breathless adoration, few wider horizons, in the notion of the operating theatre. The dialogue is between what we expect and what we get – it is a dialogue of registers. For the established topos concerning evening is a part of poetic register, while the simile belongs to the medical register of a particular time and place (London 1917). The fact of the simile being so prominent is poetic, but the vehicle of the simile is clearly not.

Collocation and topoi

Collocations are the essence of poetic topoi. When Yeats thinks of lovers embracing in 'Sailing to Byzantium', he has 'The young in one another's arms', exactly as Milton has Adam and Eve 'imparadis'd in one another's arms'. The crucial collocation is of *lovers* and *mutual embraces* – so much so that the phrase *in one another's arms* automatically connotes young lovers. The iambic rhythm of the phrase makes it attractive to poets and marks it as a possible component of a poetic register; but the clinching point is that young people and this phrase are found together sufficiently often for it to have become a conventional marker of that register.

One might not at first see the connection between night, Ethiopians and jewellery as very obvious. All extended metaphors are inclined to signal the poetic voice, of course, and certain archaisms have the same effect ('Ethiopians', unless it is a mistake, is archaic), but there is something more absolutely definitive when we find the intertextual repetition of the vehicular elements of an extended metaphor. Shakespeare's representation of the thoughts of Romeo on first seeing Juliet has been much admired:

> It seems she hangs upon the cheek of night
> Like a rich jewel in an Ethiop's ear;
> Beauty too rich for use, for earth too dear.

The conceit (black skin setting off a jewel = night setting off a woman's beauty) is confirmed by certain Renaissance and later paintings in which black skin forms part of the system of colour balances in a *rich* setting of clothes and jewellery. Here is a slightly later version of the same topos in a poem, 'Nox Nocti Indicat Scientiam', by one William Habington, who was born ten years after *Romeo and Juliet* was probably written:

> When I survey the bright
>   Celestial sphere:
> So rich with jewels hung, that night
> Doth like an Ethiop bride appear...

This contains some of the elements of the image in Shakespeare, but we have to wait ten stanzas before we get to the clinching point. Just as Juliet's beauty is 'for *earth* too dear', so the jewels of the night sky, the stars, have looked on while Habington, at the end of his poem, has been disappointed:

> they have watched since first
>   The World itself had birth:
> And found in sin itself accursed,
> And nothing permanent on *earth*.

The idea is repeated by the second poet: only things that can be compared with the everlasting stars have permanence; other, sublunary things, the ordinary things of earth, cannot be compared with them.

Such metaphorical writing becomes, as it were, overdetermined in its adherence to the register of poetry. As writing it is simultaneously: presented in the lineation, rhyme and rhythm that characterises much verse; working according to a convention of extended and elaborate metaphor which is rarely used outside poetry and, finally, *topical* in the special sense of *belonging to an identifiable topos in poetry*. So firmly do collocated expressions cling to one another that where some of them are present the others will very probably appear; night, Ethiopians and jewellery predict a mention of earth, and earth duly appears in the text.

Similarly, roses and lilies seem to have a long association together which, when activated, promotes them to higher levels of meaning. The implicature of the *collocation* of these two flower names can be considered over and above the symbolic meanings of the names themselves. We can put together two examples, the first being from Marvell's 'The Girl Describes her Fawn'. The fawn lives in a garden overgrown with roses and lilies; it sleeps among the latter and eats the former:

> Upon the roses it would feed,
> Until its lips e'en seemed to bleed:
> And then to me 'twould boldly trip,
> And print those roses on my lip.
> But all its chief delight was still
> On roses thus itself to fill,
> And its pure virgin limbs to fold
> In whitest sheets of lilies cold:–
> Had it lived long it would have been
> Lilies without – roses within.

There are almost endless possibilities of interpretation here, but the collocation carries the implication that roses are life and lilies are death, and that there is a balance to be struck between the *carpe diem* topos ('Gather ye *rose*buds…', we shan't 'live long') and the demands of the Christian virtue of purity. Purity (lilies) is beautiful, too, but cool and bloodless, while life (roses) is tasty, delightful and bleeding. This collocation subtly alters the usual meanings available in these two much-used specimens of flora, a fact brought out rather starkly by a comparison between this poem and the danger-ous lines of Swinburne's 'Dolores', where the poet asks:

> Who would not change in a trice
> The lilies and languors of virtue
> For the roses and raptures of vice?

In many senses this is different territory, but the symbolism de-pends on the deployment of the topos of roses-and-lilies collo-cated. Life, it is implied, is impure (bleeding lips; vice) but the purity of its opposite is insufficient to determine the actions of, shall we say, a red-blooded person.

The poetic register, like most others, can be called up by the slightest hint. High lexical choices are not necessary, even rhythm is inessential to strike the chord. I have tried to find what might count as a sort of minimum example, the least amount of poetical language that might signal entry into the register of the poetic. Keats and T. S. Eliot supply this:

> The carved angels, ever eager-eyed,
> Star'd, where upon their heads the cornice rests,
> *With hair blown back*, and wings put cross-wise on their breasts.
> ('St Agnes Eve', stanza iv)

> Combing the white *hair* of the waves *blown back*.
> ('The Love Song of J. Alfred Prufrock')

This may not seem the most exciting intertext, but the slightly special use of the noun–past-participle–preposition construction, effectively putting the adjective after the noun in both cases ('hair blown back'), though not uncommon in English (compare, as an alternative perhaps to Keats's formulation above, 'with wings folded up'), indicates a possible 'poetic inversion', while the Romanticism of the topos (youth, nature, dynamism) points in the same direc-tion. Were one to come across this expression elsewhere, I submit, one would feel oneself to be faintly in the presence of the poetic.

Nonsense poetry

Is nonsense poetry possible? It would appear from what has been said so far in this chapter that it is not. After all, at the level of genre, *any* words arranged in a recognisable poetic form must presumably be 'allowed to be' poetry if even an inventory can achieve that status. And, at the level of discourse, any words will belong, in however bizarre and tangential a way, to a register within the language. This is notoriously the case with 'Jabberwocky' and other much-analysed specimens of Victorian 'nonsense'.[4] We make sense of poems by *making* them make sense at some level; one such level is the level of register.

This poem is by Charles Bernstein and is called 'Live Acts'. I have chosen it because it has already been considered in some detail by a good stylistician,[5] and exhibits the need for register analysis. I have added line numbers.

Impossible outside you want always the other. A continual	1
recapitulation, & capture all that, against which our redaction	2
of sundry, promise, another person, fills all the	3
conversion of that into, which intersects a continual	4
revulsion of, against, concepts, encounter,	5
in which I hold you, a passion made of cups, amidst	6
frowns. Crayons of immaculate warmth ensnare our	7
somnambulance to this purpose alone.	8
The closer we look, the greater the distance from which	9
we look back. Essentially a hypnotic referral, like	10
I can't get with you on that, buzzes by real fast, shoots	11
up from some one or other aquafloral hideaway,	12
emerging into air. Or what we can't, the gentleman who	13
prefers a Soviet flag, floats, pigeoning the	14
answer which never owns what it's really about.	15
Gum sole shoes. The one that's there all the	16
time. An arbitrary policy, filled with noise, & yet	17
believable all the same. These projects alone contain	18
the person, binding up in an unlimited way what	19
otherwise goes unexpressed.	20

Both themes of this chapter seem to apply to this poem. First it becomes a poem by being so presented: the lineation conventions are adhered to, and Bernstein is known as a member of a *school* of poetry – one of the American 'language poets', no less. For these reasons it is primarily readable only *as* poetry, however 'unpoetic' any of its register or other features might be. But, second, this reading-as-poetry, with its special semantic charge, tends to receive confirmation at various levels of analysis because the register of poetry in English is so strong and so well-established that once we know we are reading a text 'as poetry' we automatically discover poetic features in it. The first point hardly needs demonstration; only a perverse reader would try to do anything with this text other than read it as poetry. The second point leads to the following observations concerning 'Live Acts' as a poetic text.

(a)   This poem is metrically 'sounder' than might at first appear; it is made up of five-stress sections, often in iambic patterns, and it works, being unrhymed, much like the Blank Verse in which so much of English poetry has been written. It thus participates, however faintly and only in its aural 'tone' of course, in the dense and meditative semantics of Shakespeare, Milton, Wordsworth and T. S. Eliot:

> Line 1 includes a sentence which has twelve syllables but only four stresses and thus, splitting the difference, has the metrical value of pentameter;
>
> Lines 1 and 2 include the ten-syllable phrase 'A continual recapitulation';
>
> Line 2 then continues with a pretty good near-iambic pentameter.

[So in two graphic lines we have actually *heard* three lines of poetry which would not have disgraced, as far as their metrics go, the later plays of Shakespeare.]

> Lines 3, 4, 5, 9, 10, 15 and perhaps 19 seem to me to have five stresses each;
>
> Line 6 is an almost perfect iambic pentameter up to 'cups';
>
> Lines 6 and 7 from 'amidst' to 'our' form a five-stress line;
>
> Line 8 has ten syllables...;
>
> Line 20 has four stresses, a familiar pattern, as in 'Névermóre to sée her thére.'

And so on. In other words, concealed behind the lines as printed there is a fairly regular pattern of scansion – so we cannot say that this is *metrically* nonsense; it sounds like poetry.

(b) The normal poetic assumption that the metaphorical will predominate and even be aware of itself is certainly not contradicted here. There would appear to be no reason to take any of the earlier part of the poem literally except, possibly, the pronouns 'you', 'our' and 'I' (and these are shifters). For the rest we could say – following Riffaterre's division of poetic semantics into 'meaning' and 'significance'[6] – that just because there is no immediately obvious *meaning* here, on the level of theme or coherence, that does not mean that the lines lack *significance*. 'Impossible outside you want always the other' is multiply ambiguous, but it has a significance as a protest, of the sort familiar in European poetry since the *planh* of the troubadours (which became the 'complaint'), in which the lover protests at the difficulty and danger of his position; 'the other' need not literally mean one specific other person and must be susceptible of more general application, and thus *stand in for* various possible 'others'. The 'recapitulation' and 'capture' are thus determined as the start of a chain of metaphors concerning personal interaction, including terms such as 'revulsion', 'encounter', 'hold', 'look', 'get with you', and stretching down to 'the person' of the penultimate line.

(c) Extravagant or unusual metaphors predominate in poetry – or, at least, are rare elsewhere. Thus we are not surprised that 'warmth' here can be 'immaculate' and be made up by 'crayons'.

(d) There is a lexically cohesive chain running through the poem which directs the reader towards meaning:

> you – the other – capture – promise – another person – encounter – I hold you – passion – warmth – looking closely – hypnosis – we can't – what it's really about – the one that's there all the time –

This string holds the poem together in the conventional way, setting up a descriptive system that will help us to make sense where otherwise we can see none. This 'sense' cannot be *definitive* in any monological sense, but then where is the definitive reading of even the most apparently transparent text?

Charles Bernstein himself points us towards a register reading of his poems. His aim, he says, is to write a 'multidiscourse text'; this he defines as 'a work that would involve many different types and styles and modes of language in the same "hyperspace". Such a textual practice would have a dialogic or polylogic rather than monologic method.'[7] This highly Bakhtinian aspiration perhaps explains why 'Live Acts' appears to be without direction or centre, and hints at a register analysis that will show what it is made up of if it is *not* centred, teleological, a monologue from poet to reader. Toolan describes the poem as 'a patchwork or mosaic of discourses, some of them traceable to specific discourse practices in the everyday world, others elusive or untraceable'.[8] Clearly, reading such poetry will not generate the same sense of arrival at meaning as the conventional reading of what I suppose should be called 'sense' poetry, but the semantic charge is not absent for all that. There are *meanings* in 'Live Acts' as clearly indicated as those in Matthew Arnold or Shelley; indeed, the absence of centre or telos may be taken to be an advantage that Bernstein has over, for instance, Shelley in that the ultimate signified of many of the great Romantic's poems is obscure to the point of a bafflement more profound than that produced by this sort of 'language poetry'. At least, one might say, with the likes of Bernstein there is no pretension towards a meaning that crumbles in your hands. From the beginning, what you get in Bernstein is what you see: crumbs of discourse.

These crumbs are first and foremost snippets of registers. Apart from the lexically cohesive chain 'traceable' to love literature that we have already identified, we can find:

bureaucratese 'our redaction of sundry' – 'an arbitrary policy' – 'These projects'

academic English 'recapitulation' – 'intersects a continual' – 'Essentially a' – 'concepts'

'poetic' figures 'a passion made of cups, amidst' – 'aquafloral hideaway' – 'crayons of immaculate warmth' – 'pigeoning the answer' – 'emerging into air' – 'filled with noise' – 'binding up' – 'floats'

something scientific 'the conversion of that into' – 'hypnotic referral'

sententiousness 'The closer we look, the greater the distance from which we look back'

> *colloquialism* 'all that' – 'like / I can't get with you on that' –
> 'buzzes by real fast' – 'what we can't' – 'what it's really about'
>
> *medicalese or harvester-speak* 'binding up'
>
> *detective jargon* 'Gum sole shoes'
>
> *ironic speech-maker* 'the gentleman who prefers a Soviet flag'

These are some of the 'languages' – that is, the registers – of which the poem is made. These are the voices we hear jostling one another in the twenty lines that are, perhaps, 'going nowhere', but which don't 'mean nothing'. At the level of Riffaterre's significance – that is to say, at the level of *text* or *discourse* – these registers, without amounting to something that would be greater than the sum of their parts, cast a definite semantic shadow. The poetic persona, the 'voice' that holds all these voices, may be indistinguishable behind all the camouflage, but the voices are those of modern America (indeed, of the USA between 1950 and 1990 – see 'Soviet') in which an anxiety has been felt about 'Life' and among which too many options obscure the conceptual horizon for peace or comfort, a fact that is echoed in some elements of the poem's 'meanings' such as the chain:

> Impossible – continual – continual – revulsion – this purpose alone –
> distance – I can't get with you – real fast – shoots – hideaway – Or –
> what we can't – the answer which never owns what it's really about –
> arbitrary – filled with noise – these projects alone – unexpressed.

This chain could serve as an anthem in the cacophonic hymn that is postmodernism and is thus of considerable significance in a postmodernist poem.

Workpoints

It is worth working on any poem with register in mind. The exercise would be to identify and list all the registers present in the poem that come from the non-literary world and then to identify such elements as are clearly 'literary'. Intertextuality will ground the second of these lists; reference to those other texts that make up the language of 'real life' would ground the first.

In Shelley's poem 'To the Moon' there seems to be almost no trace of non-literary register:

> Art thou pale for weariness
> Of climbing heaven and gazing on the earth,
> Wandering companionless
> Among the stars that have a different birth, –
> And ever-changing, like a joyless eye
> That finds no object worth its constancy?

Is that true? Can any text really be said to be divorced from 'reality' in the way I am claiming this is?

Notes

1 Jonathan Culler, *On Deconstruction* (Routledge & Kegan Paul, 1983), p. 182. Culler is quoting P. Lacoue-Labarthe and Jean-Luc Nancy, *L'Absolue littéraire* (Seuil, 1978).

2 From J. Lowes Dickinson, *Letters to John Chinaman*, quoted in R. A. Howard, *The Proper Study of Mankind* (Ginn and Co., n.d. [1940s]).

3 If 'respond to' is taken to be a phrasal verb, which would be rational enough, then the string is a string of direct objects.

4 See, for instance, the brilliant discussions of Lewis Carroll in Jean-Jacques Lecercle's *Philosophy through the Looking-Glass* (Hutchinson, 1985); and his *Philosophy of Nonsense* (Routledge, 1994).

5 Brian McHale, 'Making (non)sense of postmodernist poetry', in Michael Toolan (ed.), *Language, Text and Context: Essays in Stylistics* (Routledge, 1992).

6 Michael Riffaterre, *Semiotics of Poetry* (Methuen, 1978), pp. 2–3.

7 Quoted in Toolan, *Language, Text and Context*, p. 19.

8 *Ibid.*

Select bibliography

Bakhtin, Mikhail, *The Dialogic Imagination* (University of Texas Press, 1981).

Carter, Ronald, *Language and Literature: An Introductory Reader in Stylistics* (Unwin Hyman, 1982).

Carter, Ronald and Paul Simpson (eds), *Language, Discourse and Literature* (Unwin Hyman, 1989).

Christie, Frances, and J. R. Martin (eds), *Genre and Institutions: Social Processes in the Workplace and School* (Cassell, 1997).

Crystal, David and Derek Davy, *Investigating English Style* (Longman, 1969).

Eagleton, Terry, *Literary Theory: An Introduction* (Blackwell, 1983).

Freeborn, Dennis, *Style* (Macmillan, 1996).

Ghadessy, Mohsen, *Registers of Written English* (Pinter, 1988).

Ghadessy, Mohsen, *Register Analysis: Theory and Practice* (Pinter, 1993).

Graddol, D. and O. Boyd-Barrett, *Multilingual Matters* (Open University, 1994).

Halliday, M. A. K., *Language as Social Semiotic: The Social Interpretation of Language and Meaning* (Edward Arnold, 1978).

Halliday, M. A. K., *Spoken and Written Language* (Deakin University Press, 1985).

Halliday, M. A. K., and Ruqaiya Hasan, *Language, Context and Text: Aspects of Language in a Social-Semiotic Perspective* (Deakin University Press, 1985).

Halliday, M. A. K., A. MacIntosh and P. Strevens, *The Linguistic Sciences and Language Teaching* (Longman, 1964).

Hasan, Ruqaiya, *Linguistics, Language and Verbal Art* (Deakin University Press, 1985).

Leckie-Tarry, Helen, *Language and Context: A Functional Linguistic Theory of Register* (Pinter, 1995).

Leech, Geoffrey and Michael Short, *Style in Fiction: A Linguistic Introduction to English Fictional Prose* (Longman, 1981).

Quirk, Randolph, *Style and Communication in the English Language* (Edward Arnold, 1982).

Riffaterre, Michael, *Semiotics of Poetry* (Methuen, 1978).

Riffaterre, Michael, *Text Production* (Columbia University Press, 1983).

Shepherd, Valerie, *Language Variety and the Art of the Everyday* (Pinter, 1990).

Simpson, Paul, *Language through Literature: An Introduction* (Routledge, 1997).

Toolan, Michael (ed.), *Language, Text and Context: Essays in Stylistics* (Routledge, 1992).

Uribe-Villegas, Oscar, *Issues in Sociolinguistics* (The Hague, Mouton, 1977).

Van Peer, Willie, *The Taming of the Text: Explorations in Language, Literature and Culture* (Routledge, 1989).

Vinay, J.-P. and J. Darbelnet, *Stylistique comparée du français et de l'anglais* (Didier, 1958 [2nd edn 1969]).

Wales, Katie, *A Dictionary of Stylistics* (Longman, 1989).

Index

Note: 'n' after a page reference indicates a note number on that page.

Aristophanes 26
Aristotle 26, 118 (workpoint)
Ashberry, John 44

Bair, Deirdre 169 n7
Bakhtin, Mikhail 14, 17, 27, 45, 76,
    79–84, 86, 93 n3, 107–10,
    115–16
Banks, Iain 42
Barthes, Roland 30–1, 76–8, 115,
    131 n5
Beckett, Samuel 126, 133–5, 140,
    chapter 8 *passim*
Benson and Greaves 50
Bernstein, Charles 44
Brecht, Bertolt 113
Bridges, Robert 27
Bronte, Anne 158
Bronte, Charlotte 158
Bronte, Emily 174
Burton, Robert 27

Campbell, Thomas 200
Carlyle, Thomas 117
Carter, Ronald 80
Catford, J. C. 38
Caxton, William 27
Cicero 26
Collins, William 199
Crystal, David 39–40, 44
Culler, Jonathan 191

Derrida, Jacques 2, 15, 30
Dickens, Charles 22, 34, 109, 174

Donne, John 197–8

Eagleton, Terry 30
Eliot, T. S. 42, 127, 202, 205
Ellis, Jeffrey *see* Ure
Ellis, John 97

Firth, J. R. 28
Fitch, Brian 134–5, 145 n2
Foucault, Michel 15, 30, 83–4
Fowler, Roger 79–80
Fowles, John 101–7

Geyer-Ryan, Helga 113
Ghadessy, Mohsen 44
Gibbon, Edward 63–4, 126
Gray, Thomas 33
Gregory, Michael 38, 40

Halliday, M. A. K. 6, 24, 29–30, 32,
    41–2, 43–4, 47 nn18 and 19,
    50, 79–84 *passim*, 170, 187 n1
Hardy, Thomas 14, 117, chapter 9
    passim, 195–6
Harrison, Tony 113
Hasan, Ruqaiya 41–2, 114–15
Hegel, G. W. F. 42
Hemingway, Ernest 53–4
Hill, T. 189 n2
Hopkins, G. M. 27
Horace 26

Jakobson, Roman 126
James, Henry 16

Johnson, Dr Samuel 26, 53–6
Jonson, Ben 27
Joyce, James 127, 153

Kristeva, Julia 94 n16, 115

Lacan, Jacques 30
Lawrence, T. E. 64–6
Leckie-Tarry, Helen 44, 123–4
Lemke, Jay 110–11
Leonard, Tom 187 (workpoint)
Logue, Christopher 193–4
Lowes Dickinson, G. 196–8

Marlowe, Christopher 201–2
Martin, J. R. 122–3
McHale, Brian 44
Milton, John 201–2
Mourão-Ferreira, David 141–4
Murdoch, Iris 15–22, 23 n6
Murray, Sir John 61–2

Ockham, William of 32

Parker, Dorothy 140–1
Pinter, Harold 51–2
Pope, Alexander 127–9
Powell, Anthony 20, 174–6
Powys, J. C. 109
Private Eye 10–11, 191
Prynne, J. H. 44
Puttenham, George 28

Quirk, Randolph 112

Reid, T. B. W. 24–6, 29
Rhys, Jean 124–6
Rothery, Joan 44

Scott, Paul 84–8
Scott, Sir Walter 129–31, 201
Segal, Erich 52–3
Shakespeare, William
    Hamlet 33
    Julius Caesar 20
    Love's Labour Lost 27
    Romeo and Juliet 203
    The Tempest 112
Sidney, Sir Philip 26
Simpson, Paul 45, 118 n1
Spenser, Edmund 27
Stenglin, Maree 44
Stevenson, Robert Louis 58–61,
    69
Swift, Jonathan 26–7, 61

Tennyson, Lord Alfred 191
Thackeray, William 88–92, 116
Tolkien, J. R. R. 111–12
Toolan, Michael 44

Urbe-Villegas, Oscar 23 n2
Ure, Jean and Ellis, Jeffrey 8, 13,
    23 nn2 and 5

Valéry, Paul 175
Van Peer, Willie 113
Vinay and Darbelnet 136–41, 152

Waugh, Evelyn 56–8, 72 n11
Wilde, Oscar 6
Wodehouse, P. G. 35–8, 41, 135
Wordsworth, William 27, 42, 109,
    116, 117, 200

Yeats, W. B. 202